Ethnographies of Uncertainty in Africa

Anthropology, Change and Development

Series Editors:

Laura Camfield, Senior Lecturer, School of International Development, University of East Anglia, UK
Catherine Locke, Reader in Gender and Social Development at the School of International Development the University of East Anglia, UK
Lan Anh Hoang, Lecturer in Development Studies at The University of Melbourne, Australia.

Mainstream development studies have tended to neglect important aspects of experience in developing countries that fall outside the conventional preserve of development intervention. These neglected phenomena include consumption, modernity, and mobility and ambivalent experiences such as uncertainty, mistrust, jealousy, envy, love, emotion, hope, religious and spiritual belief, personhood and other experiences throughout the lifecourse. They have most closely been addressed through critical ethnography in the context of contemporary developing societies. We invite volumes that focus on the value of ethnography of these contemporary experiences of development (as change), not only to address these neglected phenomena, but also to enrich social science thinking about development.

Ethnographies of Uncertainty in Africa

Edited by

Elizabeth Cooper
Simon Fraser University, Canada

David Pratten
Oxford University, UK

palgrave
macmillan

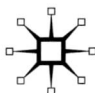

First published 2015 by
PALGRAVE MACMILLAN

Palgrave Macmillan in the UK is an imprint of Macmillan Publishers Limited,
registered in England, company number 785998, of Houndmills, Basingstoke,
Hampshire RG21 6XS.

Palgrave Macmillan in the US is a division of St Martin's Press LLC,
175 Fifth Avenue, New York, NY 10010.

Palgrave Macmillan is the global academic imprint of the above companies
and has companies and representatives throughout the world.

Palgrave® and Macmillan® are registered trademarks in the United States,
the United Kingdom, Europe and other countries

ISBN: 978-1-137-35082-4

Library of Congress Cataloging-in-Publication Data

Ethnographies of uncertainty in Africa / [edited by] Elizabeth Cooper (assistant professor, Simon
Fraser University, Canada), David Pratten (associate professor, Oxford University, UK).
     pages cm
     Summary: "This collection explores the productive potential of uncertainty for people living
in Africa as well as for scholars of Africa. The relevance of the focus on uncertainty in Africa is not
only that contemporary life is objectively risky and unpredictable (since it is so everywhere and
in every period), but that uncertainty has become a dominant trope in the subjective experience
of life in contemporary African societies. The contributors investigate how uncertainty animates
people's ways of knowing and being across the continent. An introduction and eight ethnographic studies examine uncertainty as a social resource that can be used to negotiate insecurity,
conduct and create relationships, and act as a source for imagining the future. These in-depth
accounts demonstrate that uncertainty does not exist as an autonomous, external condition.
Rather, uncertainty is entwined with social relations and shapes people's relationship between
the present and the future. By foregrounding uncertainty, this volume advances our understandings of the contingency of practice, both socially and temporally"— Provided by publisher.
     ISBN 978-1-137-35082-4 (hardback)
     1. Africa—Social conditions—1960- 2. Uncertainty—Social aspects—Africa. 3. Pragmatism—
Social aspects—Africa. 4. Forecasting—Social aspects—Africa. 5. Social problems—Africa.
6. Ethnology—Africa. I. Cooper, Elizabeth, 1976- II. Pratten, David.
     HN773.5.E88 2014
     306.096—dc23
                                                                                      2014028136

This book is printed on paper suitable for recycling and made from fully
managed and sustained forest sources. Logging, pulping and manufacturing
processes are expected to conform to the environmental regulations of the
country of origin.

A catalogue record for this book is available from the British Library.

A catalog record for this book is available from the Library of Congress.

Table of Contents

Series Preface

This book series, 'Anthropology, Change and Development', fosters engagement between critical anthropology and development studies through the notion of thinking about development *as* change. Both applied anthropology and the anthropology of development have made significant strides in building a more critical engagement between anthropology and development and both are widely acknowledged as pertinent in various ways for students, researchers and, to a lesser degree, practitioners of international development. This recognition inadvertently sustains, on the part of development studies, a somewhat selective engagement with critical historical ethnography, often limited to that which is easily 'legible', as well as a clear disconnect with a wider swathe of critical ethnography about modernity in developing countries (for example, Burawoy, 2009, Murray Li, 2007, Ong, 2011). Whilst both can contribute substantially to understanding and valuing change, such ethnographies are mistakenly seen as being less relevant to the concerns of contemporary development. Non-anthropologists and those working from a more pragmatic development orientation may find that they make 'difficult' and 'uncomfortable' reading. However it is precisely this theoretical rigor and the determination to unsettle conventional perceptions about development that lies at the centre of the value of critical anthropology for development.

This series goes beyond the remit of an 'applied anthropology' framework to include phenomena that have been overlooked by development studies. It focuses precisely on the important aspects of experience in developing countries that fall outside the conventional preserve of development intervention. These neglected phenomena include uncertainty, mistrust, jealousy, envy, witchcraft, and ambivalent experiences such as love, emotion, hope, consumption, modernity, aspiration, social mobility, religious and spiritual belief, personhood and other experiences throughout the life course. They might also include the sensory dimensions of life, for example, the pleasures of consumption in festivals and malls, the experience of love, and other less celebrated emotions. Other marginal phenomena include the subjective and relational aspects of life in developing countries that contribute to anthropological and sociological critiques of development and modernity. Rich applications of life course analysis to developing country experiences, as well as deeper approaches to experiences of time, and related emotions of hope and aspiration, are offering more meaningful ways of understanding how different individual's experience, influence and are shaped by complex, and often rapid, processes of wider societal change.

The purpose of this series is to bring ethnographic research on these phenomena into conversation with contemporary development discourses and debates and enrich social science thinking about change and development. The contributions to this series show that these phenomena *matter* in contemporary developing societies and in doing so offer new theoretical insights for anthropological engagement with contemporary change and development. Whilst development debate over time has substantially opened up discussion about phenomena previously considered as being beyond its preserve, such as rape, taking a step back from the 'development lens' (Jackson, 2011) makes visible core elements of everyday experience that are still not spoken about within development. Factors like envy that, as any practitioner can confirm, are a well-recognized reality in poor communities, are rarely seen as a fit subject for theoretical analysis within development studies. Placing these phenomena outside the frame of investigation, rather than as analyzing them as central dynamics of situated developing contexts, severely undermines the capacity of development studies to develop rigorous theoretical explanations about change. This series makes a contribution towards focusing more direct empirical and theoretical attention on these various kinds of social phenomena.

In doing so, the series deliberately aims at extending the conversation between anthropology and development in ways that will deepen theoretical frameworks and raise questions about development. This is an intrinsically critical endeavor that involves close attention to multisited power relations, including those of gender, and reflexivity. Readers will need to look elsewhere for development 'solutions', policy 'recommendations' or visionary 'agendas': Instead, the series offers a serious ethnographic treatment of hitherto neglected phenomena that are central to contemporary experience in developing contexts. The series encompasses contributions from anthropologists, other social science researchers and development practitioners using anthropological and ethnographic methodologies to engage with processes of change and raising questions about what they mean for development.

Cooper and Pratten's edited volume addresses the neglected phenomenon of uncertainty, and uses this as a problematique for analysing contemporary life in Africa. The ethnographies included in the volume examine people's everyday experiences of conflict in Guinea-Bissau, economic livelihoods in Ethiopia and Mozambique, development and power in Kenya, and health regimes and outcomes in Uganda, Tanzania and Cameroon. In doing so it shows how people engage with and understand global processes such as risk and vulnerability, and how they manage different forms of uncertainty in their daily lives. The volume draws on literature from anthropology, African studies, and development studies, and sets the perspectives and actions of individuals against the collective implications of uncertainty for societies. It shows how situated ethnographies of contemporary experiences of development (as change) can enrich development studies and make a conceptual as well as an empirical contribution.

Acknowledgements

This volume is the product of a series of workshops held in Oxford between 2011 and 2012. We gratefully acknowledge the contribution of the Institute of Social and Cultural Anthropology towards these workshops, along with the contributions of Achille Mbembe, Sarah Nuttall, and AbdouMaliq Simone in leading our discussions.

Contributors

Julie Soleil Archambault: African Studies Centre and the Institute of Social and Cultural Anthropology, Oxford University

Nadine Beckmann: Department of Life Sciences, University of Roehampton

Elizabeth Cooper: School for International Studies, Simon Fraser University

Godfrey Etyang Siu: Child Health and Development Centre, Makerere University

Adam Gilbertson: Institute of Social and Cultural Anthropology, Oxford University

Marco Di Nunzio: Laboratoire d'anthropologie des mondes contemporains, Université Libre de Bruxelles

David Pratten: African Studies Centre and the Institute of Social and Cultural Anthropology, Oxford University

Susan Reynolds Whyte: Department of Anthropology, Copenhagen University

Simon Turner: Centre for Advanced Migration Studies, Copenhagen University

Henrik Vigh: Department of Anthropology, Copenhagen University

Ethnographies of Uncertainty in Africa: An Introduction

Elizabeth Cooper and David Pratten

Uncertain Definitions

The starting point of this collection is to understand the positive and productive potential of uncertainty in Africa. The relevance of the focus on uncertainty in Africa is not only that contemporary life is objectively risky and unpredictable (since it is so everywhere and in every period), but that uncertainty has become a dominant trope, an 'inevitable force' (Johnson-Hanks 2005: 366), in the subjective experience of life in contemporary African societies. This routinized perception of uncertainty is sometimes coined as 'the crisis' – the conjunction of economic depression, instabilities, fluctuations, and ruptures – giving rise to experiences lived by people at all levels of society defined by physical and mental violence (Mbembe & Roitman 1995: 324). It is against this context of 'incoherence, uncertainty, and instability' that we may better account for the ways in which people weave their existence. Indeed, by foregrounding 'crisis as context' (Vigh 2006) we begin to see how uncertainty critically shapes ways of knowing and being on the continent. Hence, the analysis of radical, routinized uncertainty offers a productive conceptual apparatus to describe Africa's complexity and to account for 'the power of the unforeseen and of the *unfolding*...[and] people's relentless determination to negotiate conditions of turbulence to introduce order and predictability into their lives' (Mbembe & Nuttall 2004: 349).

Our focus is on uncertainty as a structure of feeling – the lived experience of a pervasive sense of vulnerability, anxiety, hope, and possibility mediated through the material assemblages that underpin, saturate, and sustain everyday life. Uncertainty is implicated in a complex semantic field. Uncertainty belongs to a family of concepts that also includes insecurity, indeterminacy, risk, ambiguity, ambivalence, obscurity, opaqueness, invisibility, mystery, confusion, doubtfulness, scepticism, chance, possibility, subjunctivity, and hope (Whyte & Siu this volume). Such fecundity offers ample opportunity for analysis, as well as many

1

challenges to conceptual clarity. As a conceptual lens, uncertainty is often used in its negative and constraining sense in referring to a lack of absolute knowledge, the inability to predict the outcome of events or to establish facts about phenomena and connections with assurance. Yet, we also see uncertainty in a positive, fruitful, and productive framing. Uncertainty is not always and exclusively a problem to be faced and solved (Berthomé et al. 2012). Uncertainty is a social resource and can be used to negotiate insecurity, conduct and create relationships, and act as a source for imagining the future with the hopes and fears this entails. As such, uncertainty becomes 'the basis of curiosity and exploration; it can call forth considered action to change both the situation and the self' (Whyte 2009: 213–14). In short, uncertainty is productive. The ethnographic cases in this volume therefore highlight how uncertainty produces new social landscapes and social horizons. They show how patterns of interrelatedness and projections of the future are shaped by uncertain material and temporal contexts.

The papers in this collection therefore draw out two related axes in the study of uncertainty in Africa – the relational and the temporal – and we have ordered the papers in two corresponding parts (Social Contingencies and Future Visions). The first theme is an appreciation of the way in which uncertainty is fundamentally a product of social contingencies. This is to extend the idea that uncertainty is perceived through society's lens and to examine changing forms of social dependence in shifting institutional contexts and political economies. It is to embrace Bledsoe's notion of the use of the term 'contingency' to connote 'a sense of social ties that underlie all aspects of life' (Bledsoe 2002: 25). Studies of how people live in and through uncertainty demonstrate that uncertainty does not exist as an autonomous, external condition. Rather, uncertainty is entwined with social relations; in some situations social relations create uncertainty, while at other times social relations alleviate uncertainty, and often the equilibrium is held in suspense.

The second theme is temporal and points to the ways in which uncertainties shape people's relationship between the present and the future. Our aim is not to collapse this moment into an ahistorical sense of 'life in uncertain times' but rather, as Guyer (2007: 418) argues, to acknowledge the 'historical specificity to uncertainty now'. By attending to people's conceptions and experiences of short- and long-term temporal horizons, we begin to see the significance of present contingencies or 'vital conjunctures' (Johnson-Hanks 2005: 377). This future-orientation embraces a range of anticipated projections – vigilance, planning, aspiration, despair, and hope. Others have captured this range of responses to uncertain futures in the anthropologies of hope (Crapanzano 2003; Miyazaki 2004; Zigon 2009), despair (Ferguson 1999), doubt (Pelkmans 2013), and fortune (da Col 2012; da Col & Humphrey 2012). While it may be argued that uncertainty itself is circumstantial and contextual and that hope or doubt are uncertainty writ large, or 'activated uncertainty' (Pelkmans 2013: 17), our approach is not to see uncertainty as an inert background given. The lived experience of uncertainty itself, as the chapters below illustrate, becomes a productive resource – by understanding chance, contingency, and precariousness as fundamental properties of experience in the world, we are better able to understand people's pragmatic quests for certainty (Dewey 1929). Dewey's legacy to this study is precisely the understanding that action and uncertainty are so mutually entwined that they need to be perceived within the same frame: 'The distinctive characteristic of practical activity, one which is so inherent that it cannot be eliminated, is the uncertainty which attends it' (Dewey 1929: 6).

Our approach, then, is to take uncertainty as a productive and investigative cue, or the 'grounds for action' (Di Nunzio this volume). It is about acknowledging the probabilistic uncertainty of events in the world and focusing on the subject's 'experience or posture of uncertainty' (Johnson-Hanks 2005: 364). Our aim is to show how uncertainty about issues that matter (diagnoses, investments, plans) spur both imaginations and practices. We must simultaneously appreciate uncertainty for its existential and social significance, its production of action and imagination. This combination amounts to a mode of 'reflexive action', or what others have referred to as 'pragmatic skepticism' (Gable 1995: 255) and 'subjunctive habitus' (Johnson-Hanks 2005: 367). Indeed, we may conclude, with Wagner-Pacifici (2000), that a theory of contingency or uncertainty is best approached as a theory of action in the 'subjunctive mood' – action that attends to that yet to happen. The subjunctive mood, Whyte explains, 'is the mood of doubt, hope, will, and potential...it is not a quality of life, or of particular persons, but a mood of action: a doubting, hoping, provisional, cautious, and testing disposition to action' (Whyte 2005: 250–51). To foreground uncertainty is to search for an understanding of the contingency of practice, both socially and temporally.

Social Contingency and 'Subjunctive' Subjects

Each of the chapters in the first section shows how living is perceived to be dependent on creative collaborations and a broad and deep investment in social relations. This focus on how people negotiate and create relationships highlights 'the productivity of uncertainty at the heart of human sociality' (Berthomé et al. 2012: 130). The analysis of sociality in African cities, for instance, is highly suggestive in this context. Survival in precarious conditions is conventionally conceptualized as a process of 'narrowing one's universe to a manageable domain of safety or efficacy' (Simone 2005: 517). And yet, as Simone argues, these conditions of vulnerability are also possibilities for the creation of new urban sensibilities and collaborations. Rather than 'narrowing down' to more proximate forms of relatedness, people also 'open up' their social capital to broader and more diverse configurations of solidarity.

This insight from the focus on uncertainty revisits an earlier Africanist argument that highlighted the postcolonial strategy to limit reinvestment in productive enterprise in favour of investing in social institutions to enhance social identity and status in networks that would enable access to state-controlled resources (Berry 1989). As Berry highlighted, investment in migration, marriage, and ethnic associations may all be seen in the context of competition for access to local resources and as forms of social insurance and social capital. By looking through the lens of uncertainty, however, we can recognize that such capital is double-edged. Institutions and impersonal factors need to be navigated through social networks to access resources of positive benefit; yet the negative impact of institutional and distant political factors on people's lives is interpreted as the actions of the self-same network of individuals. This is one of the dangers of intimacy – as Geschiere says, 'The very ambiguity of intimacy – comforting yet at the same time inherently dangerous – means that trust can never be an ontological certainty' (Geschiere 2013: ix).

Indeed, it is the profoundly provisional and revisable character of social relations which means that in a Cameroonian case 'every contract or negotiation constitutes in itself a vast field of ambiguity which, as such, leaves enormous potential for dispute, argument, and discord' (Mbembe & Roitman 1995: 342). This is why, as Johnson-Hanks writes, there exists a '…widespread sense that disadvantage and unpredictability permeate not only the economy but also social and personal relationships' (2005: 366). To explore this further, these chapters illustrate that while certainty and security are sought by investment in social relations, so those proximate, intimate social relations provide no guarantee and may produce further uncertainties. In her classic analysis of West African women's life-courses being determined by chains of social contingency, Bledsoe states that '[a] sense of vulnerability applies even to intimate social relations despite the security these relations appear to offer' (2002: 21).

By taking open-ended approaches to tracing people's experiences of uncertainty, the case studies here avoid pre-emptively casting the impact of vulnerability to others and events as inevitably negative. Of course, studying the contingencies of people's lives is far from straightforward. There are multiple contingencies, some of which are known, and others of which we may poorly understand or not acknowledge at all. Moreover, as Bledsoe has described, there is often 'a dynamic of accumulation, in which the effects of events build upon each other' and 'the effects of contingent events may be not simply additive (or decremental) but spiraling' (2002: 22). Nevertheless, in tracing particular contingencies in people's lives as sources of uncertainty, the cases seek to address 'how beneficial and deleterious possibilities follow on from relationships', and to account for the fact that it is importantly through social contingencies that cause-and-effect attributions are perceived.

'To be contingent', Susan Reynolds Whyte and Godfrey Etyang Siu argue, 'is to be related: to people, institutions happenings, circumstances'. In learning from Ugandan people's personal histories of living with the uncertainties of HIV and treatment, especially through variable access to antiretroviral therapy (ART), Whyte and Siu discern what they call 'an ethos of contingency'. Their research shows how for those given a 'second chance', life with HIV is perceived as a series of steps facilitated or impeded by other people. Life here is perceived as depending not on an individual's agency, not on the vagaries of unseen macro forces, but on specific, personal dependencies on others. Hence the research focuses on people's preoccupation with social connections, especially connections who can provide access to health care. This understanding of how their well-being may be contingent on the actions of others encourages an attentiveness tinged with 'a sense of possibility' which is not limited to apprehension about negative potentiality, but can also take the form of 'a kind of watchfulness for positive possibility'. This combined sense of dependence and possibility, Whyte and Siu find, underpins a disposition of civility: people avoid open confrontations to maintain relationships – they 'just keep quiet' to hold the peace. This is not trust, but tentativeness in how particular relations, both interpersonal and institutional, might affect one's chances.

Trust and mistrust are also central to Elizabeth Cooper's genealogy of suspicion in the workings of transnational child sponsorship charities in Kenya. Not all contingencies are obvious, and this analysis shows how 'differentiated access to knowledge makes possible different types of causative analysis of what is behind uncertainty'. Cooper traces experience-near and experience-distant attributions in an institutional ethnography to account for not only what people are uncertain about and why, but also how particular inequalities are structured and maintained. In her study in a village in western Kenya with a long history of changing charitable interventions, Cooper finds that people hold ambivalent and sceptical attitudes towards external charitable and developmental interventions. A low estimation of the chances that charity might bring, in terms of who might benefit and how, is compounded by a lack of trust in the integrity of the relationships that such charity rests on. This distrust plays out between Kenyan children and their families and the Kenyan employees of the international charities with what Cooper argues can be damaging consequences for local ideas of collective purpose and efficacy. The brokerage of institutional policies through local people's interpersonal relations generates blurred distinctions between the accountable and unaccountable, which in turn encourage a pervasive uncertainty about what, and who, can be trusted to affect life's chances. This 'political economy of chance' gives rise to hope and apathy and a practical orientation towards the aid industry and the good fortune it promises that may be seen as 'learned ambivalence'.

Tentativeness, testing, and mistrust are central to the social contingencies Nadine Beckmann highlights in her analysis of the perilous risk of childbirth within a Zanzibari maternal health-care system subject to rapid recent privatization and a complex of new business and political interests. As others have shown (Bledsoe 2002; Johnson-Hanks 2005), maternal health care is an uncertain terrain, even for the middle class with the resources to contemplate options. The paradox that Parkin identifies, that 'trust rests on, but also tries to surmount uncertainty' (2011: 9), is conspicuous in Zanzibari women's deep anxieties. Their uncertainty gives rise to embodied tactics. Women are active in seeking security during this perilous time by eating correctly, following Islamic rules, avoiding anger or envy, and engaging in exercise. But most significant is their testing of experts in their search for diagnosis and prescription in the event of pregnancy complications and childbirth emergencies. Therapeutic trajectories are navigated on the basis of trusting personal contacts within state institutions (of putting a 'face' to abstract forces), and mistrusting ('trying out') alternative health-care providers in their attempts to gain more confidence and security about their condition. Thus women test health practitioners' quality of care through various means, including consulting care providers, friends, and relatives about a variety of symptoms, comparing different sources of advice, and hiding previous diagnoses from practitioners to judge their own diagnostic acuity. The state and the market – socially distant forces – are perceived as unreliable, and ultimately trust is invested in those socially and spiritually close.

Adam Gilbertson's study shows how uncertainty and tension underpin the everyday relations of husbands and wives seeking food security for their households in the Bangladesh settlement in Mombasa, Kenya. In this context, where many households are chronically food insecure, daily efforts to secure food are prominent in couples' negotiations of power and estimations of the security of their conjugal relations. The uncertainties of food provision, preparation, and consumption cause instability and anxiety that is experienced differentially through a heavily gendered matrix of domestic power, identity, and authority. Failures of obligations – of men to procure ingredients and of women to prepare well-cooked meals – give rise to anxieties not only about nutrition and health, but of the viability of the conjugal units themselves. This conflict in the household is manifest in mistrust and fears of infidelity and can lead to domestic violence. This evidence challenges the assumption that households simply exist as safe and certain havens: 'households cannot be conceived of as bastions of safety and security within the greater risk environment of the informal settlement without simultaneously considering their potential contributions to risk in terms of conflict, abuse, and food insecurity'. Even the most proximate kin relations cannot, therefore, be assumed to provide a security net. Another aspect of the 'dark side of kinship' (Geschiere 2003), not only does food insecurity call into question the viability of households, but the vulnerability of these conjugal relations can create further food insecurity.

The stakes are high for the people discussed in this section – food security, childbirth, and antiretroviral treatment. And what they indicate is how uncertainty can encourage an ethos of 'thick sociality'; that is, uncertainty and insecurity may prompt people to extend and deepen their social relations and engagements. This does not mean that people are naive or disinterested in the further removed forces that affect their lives. Women in Zanzibar critically appraise the Tanzanian government's and various NGOs' changing policies and practices for antenatal care; Kenyan children and their relatives are wary of outsiders' capacities to improve local livelihood conditions in meaningful and sustainable ways; and HIV-positive Ugandans follow the changing policies of their government, employers, and international programmes. Focusing energies on the potential of proximal social relations should thus not be read as a denial that power is more widely dispersed. But, as Whyte and Siu note, recognizing the power of distant forces on present life does not necessarily help people to resolve the immediate uncertainties and insecurities that they experience.

Combined, these ethnographies show how people have learned from experience that socially distant forces are unreliable and largely beyond individuals' control, and that access to resources is dependent upon the contingencies of social networks – 'technical know who' in Ugandan English. But these forms of 'social capital' also provide the impetus for ways of knowing and being. In his conception of 'people as infrastructure', Simone (2004) shows how people's interpersonal collaborations come to constitute infrastructure in its own right. As social infrastructure, interpersonal collaborations become 'a platform providing for and reproducing life' (408) in the context of inadequate and unreliable official policies and economies. The productivity and cumulative potential of social relations produces a 'specific economy of perception and collaborative practice' that structures how people engage in and anticipate the possibilities of their collaborations with others.

In these case studies, collaboration structures modes of comportment and practical strategies that we may frame as 'subjunctive subjectivities'. These micro-sociologies of uncertainty highlight the generative potential of uncertainty in open-ended relationships (Berthomé et al. 2012: 133). For Ugandan railway workers, maintaining cordial social relations requires a facade of civility, geniality, politeness, and discretion. For families in Kenya, presenting the moral rectitude of the 'deserving poor' can help to make one's 'need' for child sponsorship recognizable. For pregnant women in Zanzibar, the efficacy of dietary and spiritual prescriptions depends on the avoidance of anger or envy. And for households in Mombasa's informal settlements, certainty and trust is achieved through eating as a family and undone when individuals eat alone. Each case resonates with a set of tactics that are highly provisional and that, as a 'subjunctive mood', hold analytic potential. As Whyte (2005) argues, this is not a personal characteristic, but a mood of action that recognizes the radical uncertainty of its effects: a doubting, hoping, provisional, cautious, and testing disposition.

Future Visions: The Future as a Cultural Fact?

Appadurai (2013) argues that the anthropological lens has been dominated by a focus on 'pastness', and that to recalibrate attention on future-making the discipline needs to focus instead on aspiration, anticipation, and imagination. At intervals this has been a familiar complaint within the discipline (cf. James 1995; Wallman 1992) notwithstanding the observation that '[c]onjectures about the future [are] an implicit part of the understanding of the present' that has been the ethnographers' familiar habitat (Moore 1987: 727). In contrast to the retrospective and introspective perspectives within Africanist anthropology (Pratten 2012), recent ethnographies have indeed sought to reframe the ethnographic lens towards the future. For example, Cole's (2010) *Sex and Salvation*, Piot's (2010) *Nostalgia for the Future*, and Weiss's (2009) *Street Dreams and Hip-Hop Barbershops* all attend to the ways in which the future comes into the present of anthropological research.

The barbers of Arusha, Tanzania, discussed in Weiss's study navigate the inequities of the neo-liberal economy through a subjectivity of tough 'invincibility' and employ hip-hop sensibilities and consumer symbols to generate a sense of power. This 'thug realism' is a fantasy of mobility and modernity generated by the very same global forces that undermine their capacity to secure their futures (2009: 238). Cole argues that a generation of Madagascan young women have become 'disembedded', dislocated from older networks of social relations. Inspired by film and fashion, they navigate a sexual economy in which they risk shame for the prospect of transnational marriages and migration (Cole 2010). And in Togo, Piot observes that forward-looking nostalgia is a longing represented in Christian 'end times' narratives in which the unexpected interventions of the Holy Spirit condition congregants to embrace a radical orientation towards time and the everyday: 'Immersed in a time and rhetoric of crisis everyone, it seems is hedging their bets on the afterlife, on the lottery, on the miraculous appearance and capture of an NGO – hoping for an intercession that might be life-transforming' (Piot 2010: 66).

Each of these ethnographies concerns the everyday quests for certainty of a cohort of young people who are grappling with social exclusion, economic disempowerment, and political disenfranchisement (Cole & Durham 2007). These are portraits of a generation growing up in uncertain times (Amit & Dyck 2012; Cole & Durham 2008), and who occupy a state of 'waithood' as access to the attributes of adulthood recede (Honwana 2012). Common to these ethnographic portraits are the tactics this generation deploy to confront the inequities of these uncertain futures: international marriage and migration, patterns of consumption (of films, fashion, and music) and modes of congregation. In addressing the future, these ethnographies show that uncertainty produces a stress on shifting forms of sociality (networks, marriage, and congregation) and on radical orientations towards time that are hyper-vigilant to an indeterminate present and its unfolding future prospects.

The chapters in this volume's second section take their cue from these approaches and similarly argue that present and future are not disconnected horizons of social practice. A 'forward reading' that is attentive to productive processes (Ingold & Harram 2007: 3) enables us to see the way in which our actions are constantly shaped and reshaped in relation to the immediate and imagined movement of the social environment. This view of praxis, or 'social navigation', takes into consideration the fact that we plot and live our lives in changing sociopolitical environments and thus enables us to focus on the relationship between what is happening with and *within* structures (Vigh 2010). This approach to the provisional mode by which people are able to navigate post-conflict societies, urban underemployment, and forced displacement characterize the ethnographies in this section of the book.

In the context of Guinea-Bissau's recent history of ongoing insecurity and strife, Henrik Vigh's chapter points to the ways in which people make sense of profound uncertainty in suspicions of covert and concealed figures and forces. Vigh's analysis links rumours about the tenacity of politicians' careers to those getting by on the street, and stresses the significance of foresight, apprehension, or 'having eyes' as a key attribute in tackling uncertainty. At once an embodied feature of the calculus of the 'big man' (Apter 2000; Bayart 1993), seeing beyond the surface and into the future tends to be interpreted in supernatural terms. Hence, the revelation of concealment and conspiracy intersects with 'occult cosmologies' which 'claim that power operates in two separate yet related realms, one visible, the other invisible' (Sanders & West 2003: 6–7). Like Azande witchcraft accusations, 'having eyes' is a way of perceiving and negotiating the impact of unseen external forces on visible social interaction (Evans-Pritchard 1976). Apprehension, therefore, serves as an apt term since it combines both the reflexive fear of invisible forces with action and engagement as people try to avoid and pre-empt their touch in the future.

Uncertainty can produce hyper-vigilance – looking ahead and scanning for future possibilities that would offer interludes of respite. Indeed, as Julie Soliel Archambault illustrates in her analysis of Mozambican youth, uncertainty is experienced in moments. Payday punctuates the waiting time young people experience according to the syncopated rhythms of boredom and anticipation (Honwana 2012; Jeffrey 2010; Mains 2011; Masquelier 2013; Ralph 2008; Sommers 2012). While there is a common nostalgia for former political and economic eras marked by the security of civil service salaries or migrant labour remittances, nevertheless these Mozambican youth are no longer 'stuck in the compound' (Hansen 2005). They are not all 'caught in the structure of waiting' (Crapanzano 2003: 16). Improving fortunes have generated opportunities for wage work and the ability to plan a different future. Here, every-day resourcefulness and distant dreams are modulated by medium-term plans, literally the *planos* that people make to invest their monthly salaries in material security. These payday plans, and the capacity to aspire that they afford, constitute a form of hope. This is not an expectation or entitlement, but a recognition that external forces, factors beyond our control, limit what we can do. As Crapanzano identified, there is a necessary contingency to hope: hope's realization depends on an 'other', whether that other be a god, fate, chance, or some other human individual (2004: 100). For Marco Di Nunzio's informants, second-generation migrants living with uncertain futures in Addis Ababa, apprehension and planning ahead can be excessive with 'too much thinking' prompting stress and anxiety (cf. Mains 2011; Weiss 2009: 118–31). Yet it is the very unpredictability that uncertainty fosters that these urban hustlers embrace. Their hope, configured through idioms of chance and God's fortune, is premised on the fact that things can change in uncertain times. To seize the opportunities that luck or fate may bestow requires anticipation and mobility – a propensity to being in the right place at the right time. Being young and on the margins of urban society is recast as still having time and of still having hope – 'I have to go on thinking that I have a chance', these men say. They do not want to be 'hopeless'.

It is also the open-ended and unpredictable nature of life for clandestine Burundian refugees settled in Nairobi that presents them with the possibility for hope. As Simon Turner outlines, hope in Nairobi may exist in different modes, whether goal-oriented or open-ended, patient or active, critical or utopian, collective or individual. For these young Burundians in Nairobi, hope is having faith by joining the congregations of Pentecostal churches, but it is also about 'active waiting', especially investing in education; in such precarious conditions, hope is not about passive faith but an 'active state of mind' (Zigon 2009). This requires vigilant discipline, especially in sacrificing the enjoyments of the present so as to hold on to hopes for the future. Like the Ethiopian hustlers, the Burundian refugees espouse a complex moral calculus shaped by their understandings of faith, hope, and destiny in which life's hardships are evidence of the sacrifices necessary to 'making it' and to receiving God's blessings. The degree to which these individuals allow the agency of God a place in their lives may be limited, but their hope is shaped by a deep morality, a respect of and dedication to education, that Turner refers to as 'passionate suffering'. Yet, future options make security elusive. To choose life at the UNHCR refugee camps is perceived as a 'living death', while investing in a permanent life in Nairobi would be to concede defeat and a future in Burundi. Hence the opportunity and the chance of 'making it' are sustained by embracing the precarity of marginal status and the open-ended possibilities of hope in the city. For a future return to Burundi, the migrants' success depends on retaining a liminal and ungrounded life of uncertainty and sacrifice in the present.

The case studies presented here place a particular emphasis on contributing to 'an ethnography of the near future' (Guyer 2007). Guyer argues that as a result of analytical preoccupations with both the very short temporal focus – inspired by, for example, a fascination with the phenomenon of time-space compression (Harvey 1990) – and the very long temporal focus, as conceptualized in the notion of 'the long run' of macroeconomic projections, near temporal frames of thought and action have been overlooked. Guyer's call for an anthropology of the near future arises from a concern for empirically informed, and thus more open-ended, accounts of processes of change which address 'the reach of thought and imagination, of planning and hoping, of tracing out mutual influences, of engaging in struggles for specific goals' (2007: 409). By focusing on trajectories into the 'near future', the chapters in this section therefore bridge a focus on the immediate uncertainties of 'getting by' and 'just surviving', and the creative potential of imaginaries that draw from distant sources of inspiration.

Hence these chapters account for different ways of making sense of time and how, against these temporal horizons, uncertainty produces dispositions by which people not only 'get by' in the here and now, but 'get on' in the future. In Guinea-Bissau, for example, Vigh's emphasis is on popular understandings of how to sustain a political career or economic venture over time; Archambault shows how the monthly payday offers respite from constant uncertainties for people to invest in their futures; Di Nunzio explains that to retain hope, long-term hustlers in Addis Ababa continue to call themselves 'youth' in order to share their hopes for an alternative life-course; and Turner shows how the suffering and sacrifices endured by clandestine refugees in Nairobi are necessary to enable them to 'make it'.

What emerges from a focus on the 'near future' is an emphasis on how people position themselves – cognitively, morally, spiritually, and practically – to be open to future possibilities. This complex positionality may be what Appadurai has called the 'ethics of possibility' – those ways of thinking, feeling, and acting that increase the horizons of hope (2013: 295).

Narrating Lived Experiences of Uncertainty

The case studies collected here attempt to capture the lived experience of uncertainty in Africa. Inevitably, focusing on anticipation and that which has not yet occurred presents a series of challenges to the anthropologist. For ethnography to do justice to the experience and productivity of living in uncertain times, it must methodologically draw heavily on narrative and the individual biography. As Wagner-Pacifici (2000: 3) observes, to approach 'action in the subjunctive mood' we must turn to the general frame of narrative. Narrative storytelling represents 'a vital human strategy for sustaining a sense of agency in the face of disempowering circumstances' (Jackson 2002: 15). Like stories in which one thing leads to another and characters struggle towards an ending that is not yet certain, so in the narrative times captured in these chapters there is 'an unfolding of intention and consequence and a sense of moving towards outcomes which are imagined on the basis of what has happened so far' (Whyte 2005: 250). But how we frame these inevitably partial narratives and biographies is crucial since '...we, the anthropologists tend to become the judges of whether the hopes of our informants should be deemed prospective or deceptive' (Dalsgaard & Frederiksen 2013: 58). The need for open-ended life analysis is apparent, else our informants are presented as either victims of structural constraints or unfettered vanguards of their own destinies. To account for the contingencies of life trajectories therefore requires ethnography bent to the biographical; to adapt Wright Mills's phrase, these perspectives place ethnography at the 'intersection of biography and history'.

Several of the studies in this collection describe particular conditions of poverty, violence, pain, and oppression in contemporary African societies. But it is how people think and act in relation to the uncertainties wrought by these conditions, not the conditions themselves, that are our primary concern. What emerges from ethnography that starts from or in uncertainty is an appreciation for ways of being, a posture that confronts the unpredictable. And what we present here is an emphasis on what we might call the making of the 'subjunctive subject'. We learn that uncertainty does not always lead to trepidation and anxiety, nor does it always lead to hope, though it may. Rather, we see implicated ontologies: ways of accounting for fortune in concepts of chance and perceptiveness; the civility and vigilance required to navigate contingent personal and institutional dependencies; different ways of hoping and planning according to different rhythms of time and structures of security and insecurity; the tactics adopted in the face of domestic uncertainties; and a resolute openness to indeterminacy and the possibilities that uncertainty can uncover. In sum, the chapters offer detailed empirical evidence of the productivity of uncertainty in the conduct of social relations across Africa today.

References

Amit, V. & N. Dyck (2012) *Young Men in Uncertain Times* (New York: Berghahn Books).
Appadurai, A. (2013) *The Future as Cultural Fact: Essays on the Global Condition* (London & New York: Verso Books).
Apter, A. (2000) 'IBB=419: Nigerian Democracy and the Politics of Illusion', in Comaroff, J. L. & J. Comaroff (eds.) *Civil Society and the Political Imagination in Africa: Critical Perspectives* (Chicago: University of Chicago Press), pp. 267–308.
Bayart, J.-F. (1993) *The State in Africa: The Politics of the Belly* (London: Longman).
Berry, S. S. (1989) 'Social Institutions and Access to Resources', *Africa* 59 (1): 41–55.
Berthomé, F., J. Bonhomme & G. Delaplace (2012) 'Preface: Cultivating Uncertainty', *Hau: Journal of Ethnographic Theory* 2 (2): 129–37.
Bledsoe, C. (2002) *Contingent Lives: Fertility, Time and Aging in West Africa* (Chicago: University of Chicago Press).
Cole, J. (2010) *Sex and Salvation: Imagining the Future in Madagascar* (Chicago: University of Chicago Press).
Cole, J. & D. L. Durham (eds.) (2007) *Generations and Globalization: Youth, Age, and Family in the New World Economy* (Bloomington: Indiana University Press).
Cole, J. & D. L. Durham (eds.) (2008) *Figuring the Future: Globalization and the Temporalities of Children and Youth* (Santa Fe: School for Advanced Research Press).
Crapanzano, V. (2003) 'Reflections on Hope as a Category of Social and Psychological Analysis', *Cultural Anthropology* 18 (1): 3–32.
Crapanzano, V. (2004) *Imaginative Horizons: An Essay in Literary-Philosophical Anthropology* (Chicago: University of Chicago Press).
da Col, G. (2012) 'Introduction: Natural Philosophies of Fortune-Luck, Vitality, and Uncontrolled Relatedness', *Social Analysis* 56 (1): 1–23.
da Col, G. & C. Humphrey (2012) 'Introduction: Subjects of Luck-Contingency, Morality, and the Anticipation of Everyday Life', *Social Analysis* 56 (2): 1–18.
Dalsgaard, A. L. & M. D. Frederiksen (2013) 'Out of Conclusion: On Recurrence and Open-Endedness in Life and Analysis', *Social Analysis* 57 (1): 50–63.
Dewey, J. (1929) *The Quest for Certainty* (New York: Minton, Balch & Company).
Evans-Pritchard, E. E. (1976) *Witchcraft, Oracles, and Magic among the Azande* (Oxford: Clarendon Press).
Ferguson, J. (1999) *Expectations of Modernity: Myths and Meanings of Urban Life on the Zambian Copperbelt* (Berkeley: University of California Press).
Gable, E. (1995) 'The Decolonization of Consciousness: Local Skeptics and the "Will to Be Modern" in a West African Village', *American Ethnologist* 22 (2): 242–57.
Geschiere, P. (2003) 'Witchcraft as the Dark Side of Kinship: Dilemmas of Social Security in New Contexts', *Etnofoor* 16 (1): 43–61.

Geschiere, P. (2013) *Witchcraft, Intimacy, and Trust: Africa in Comparison* (Chicago: University of Chicago Press).

Guyer, J. I. (2007) 'Prophecy and the Near Future: Thoughts on Macroeconomic, Evangelical, and Punctuated Time', *American Ethnologist* 34 (3): 409–21.

Hansen, K. T. (2005) 'Getting Stuck in the Compound: Some Odds against Social Adulthood in Lusaka, Zambia', *Africa Today* 51 (4): 3–16.

Harvey, D. (1990) *The Condition of Postmodernity: An Enquiry into the Origins of Cultural Change* (Oxford: Blackwell).

Honwana, A. M. (2012) *The Time of Youth: Work, Social Change, and Politics in Africa* (Sterling: Kumarian Press).

Ingold, T. & E. Harram (2007) 'Creativity and Cultural Improvisation: An Introduction', in Hallam, E. & T. Ingold (eds.) *Creativity and Cultural Improvisation* (Oxford: Berg), pp. 1–24.

Jackson, M. (2002) *The Politics of Storytelling: Violence, Transgression, and Intersubjectivity* (Copenhagen & Portland: Museum Tusculanum Press).

James, W. (1995) 'Introduction. Whatever Happened to the Enlightenment?', in James, W. (ed.) *The Pursuit of Certainty: Religious and Cultural Formulations* (London & New York: Routledge), pp. 1–14.

Jeffrey, C. (2010) *Timepass: Youth, Class, and the Politics of Waiting in India* (Stanford: Stanford University Press).

Johnson-Hanks, J. (2005) 'When the Future Decides: Uncertainty and Intentional Action in Contemporary Cameroon', *Current Anthropology* 46 (3): 363–85.

Mains, D. (2011) *Hope is Cut: Youth, Unemployment, and the Future in Urban Ethiopia* (Philadelphia: Temple University Press).

Masquelier, A. (2013) 'Teatime: Boredom and the Temporalities of Young Men in Niger', *Africa* 83 (03): 470–91.

Mbembe, A. & S. Nuttall (2004) 'Writing the World from an African Metropolis', *Public Culture* 16 (3): 347–72.

Mbembe, A. & J. Roitman (1995) 'Figures of the Subject in Times of Crisis', *Public Culture* 7 (2): 323–52.

Mills, C. W. (1959) *The Sociological Imagination* (New York: Oxford University Press).

Miyazaki, H. (2004) *The Method of Hope: Anthropology, Philosophy, and Fijian Knowledge* (Stanford: Stanford University Press).

Moore, S. F. (1987) 'Explaining the Present: Theoretical Dilemmas in Processual Ethnography', *American Ethnologist* 14 (4): 727–36.

Parkin, D. (2011) 'Trust talk and alienable talk in healing: a problem of medical diversity', MMG Working Paper 11–11 (Göttingen: Max Planck Institut zur Erforschung Mulitreligiöser und Multiethnischer Gesellschaften).

Pelkmans, M. (2013) 'Outline for an Ethnography of Doubt', in Pelkmans, M. (ed.) *Ethnographies of Doubt: Faith and Uncertainty in Contemporary Societies* (London; New York: IB Taurus), pp. 1–42.

Piot, C. (2010) *Nostalgia for the Future: West Africa after the Cold War* (Chicago: University of Chicago Press).

Pratten, D. (2012) 'Retroversion, Introversion, Extraversion: Three Aspects of African Anthropology', in Fardon, R., J. Gledhill, O. Harris, T. Marchand, M. Nuttall, C. Shore, V. Strang & R. Wilson (eds.) *Sage Handbook of Social Anthropology* (London: Published with the Association of Social Anthropologists of the United Kingdom and Commonwealth), pp. 308–23.

Ralph, M. (2008) 'Killing Time', *Social Text* 26 (4 97): 1–29.

Sanders, T. & H. G. West (2003) 'Power Revealed and Concealed in the New World Order', in West, H. G. & T. Sanders (eds.) *Transparency and Conspiracy: Ethnographies of Suspicion in the New world Order* (Durham: Duke University Press), pp. 1–37.

Simone, A. M. (2004) 'People as Infrastructure: Intersecting Fragments in Johannesburg', *Public Culture* 16 (3): 407–29.

Simone, A. M. (2005) 'Urban Circulation and the Everyday Politics of African Urban Youth: The Case of Douala, Cameroon', *International Journal of Urban and Regional Research* 29 (3): 516–32.

Vigh, H. (2006) *Navigating Terrains of War: Youth and Soldiering in Guinea-Bissau* (New York: Berghahn Books).

Vigh, H. (2010) 'Youth Mobilisation as Social Navigation: Reflections on the Concept of Dubriagem', *Cadernos de Estudos Aricanos* 18/19: 139–64.

Wagner-Pacifici, R. E. (2000) *Theorizing the Standoff: Contingency in Action* (Cambridge & New York: Cambridge University Press).

Wallman, S. (1992) 'Introduction: Contemporary Futures', in Wallman, S. (ed.) *Contemporary Futures: Perspectives from Social Anthropology* (London & New York: Routledge), pp. 1–22.

Weiss, B. (2009) *Street Dreams and Hip-Hop Barbershops: Global Fantasy in Urban Tanzania* (Bloomington: Indiana University Press).

Whyte, S. R. (2005) 'Uncertain Undertakings: Practicing Health Care in the Subjunctive Mood', in Jenkins, R., H. Jessen & V. Steffen (eds.) *Managing Uncertainty: Ethnographic Studies of Illness, Risk and the Struggle for Control* (Copenhagen: Museum Tusculanum Press), pp. 245–64.

Whyte, S. R. (2009) 'Epilogue', in Haram, L. & C. B. Yamba (eds.) *Dealing with Uncertainty in Contemporary African Lives* (Stockholm: Nordiska Afrikainstitutet), pp. 213–16.

Zigon, J. (2009) 'Hope Dies Last: Two Aspects of Hope in Contemporary Moscow', *Anthropological Theory* 9 (3): 253–71.

Part One
Social Contingencies

Contingency: Interpersonal and Historical Dependencies in HIV Care

Susan Reynolds Whyte and Godfrey Etyang Siu

Introduction

The word 'uncertainty' has many relatives, each opening particular analytical possibilities. Within the extended family, we might count: insecurity, indeterminacy, risk, ambiguity, ambivalence, obscurity, opaqueness, invisibility, mystery, confusion, doubtfulness, and scepticism. Some of its cousins seem to admit of positive potential: chance, possibility, subjunctivity, hope. Uncertainty and insecurity are the most prominent members of the family. We can think of uncertainty as a state of mind, and minding, when we are unable to predict the outcome of events or to know with assurance about something that matters to us. Insecurity, the lack of protection from danger, the weakness of arrangements to support us when adversity strikes, gives rise to uncertainty. Dealing with uncertainty is often about trying to make more secure, rather than simply trying to ascertain. And making more secure usually has to do with mobilizing resources in order to exert some degree of control. Both terms are broad and often used rather vaguely, without specifying the focus of uncertainty or the source of insecurity (Whyte 2009).

We propose that another related term, 'contingency', might sharpen our analyses of the issues with which scholars grapple. Contingency means dependence on another event or occurrence about which there is some uncertainty…or, we may add, on other people, whose situations and actions cannot be known for sure. It can also mean 'true only under existing or specified conditions'. So to be contingent is to be related: to people, institutions, happenings, circumstances. In its relationality, contingency also implies time and process: one thing leads to another; events have consequences. Contingency denotes uncertainty about what may or may not occur, but it inflects uncertainty with specificity and invites us to consider connections. We usually say 'contingent upon...'. Finally, contingency has that quality of possibility that John Dewey (1930) saw in uncertainty. It is not always negative and fearsome. Contingency could imply links to people and developments that offer resources. To be contingent upon persons or happenings that cannot be fully foreseen is to lack control and be subject to uncertainty. But to try to create contingencies in the sense of making connections to possible forces for improving security is to attempt to move an uncertain situation towards greater confidence.

For the first generation of people who benefitted from widespread free access to antiretroviral therapy (ART), uncertainty, insecurity, and contingency played out with fateful clarity. We take our examples from them in order to show the interplay of different kinds of contingency, and the relation of contingency to uncertainty and insecurity. Uncertain about the invisible process of disease in their bodies, not knowing when they would die and lacking the security to sustain themselves and seek treatment, they exemplify what Bledsoe (2002) called the contingency of physical life on social relations.

The spread of HIV disease itself encapsulates contingency in the etymological sense of 'together with' – 'touch'. Transmitted through intimate touching with another person whose history you do not fully know, it gives rise to reflection on chains of consequence and lack of knowledge. Even when they discern danger – as when wives know that their husbands are 'womanizers' – people may feel insecure because they cannot control those upon whom they depend and do not have other sources of security at hand.

From late 2005 until mid-2007, a team of four Ugandan and four Danish anthropologists[1] talked to forty-eight people on ART about their life histories, and followed twenty-three of them through home visits over a year and a half. We listened to their accounts of despair, worry, secrecy, doubts, recovery, and attempts to get on with the life that the treatment made possible. We call our study Second Chances, after the common assertion in Uganda that free treatment had given them a second chance to live. But as we discovered, chanciness continued to figure even after their health improved. To simplify greatly, two kinds of contingency – historical and social – were evident in their lives.

Historical contingency draws our attention to the spread of the disease and of the means to deal with it. From the late 1980s, the Ugandan government assiduously promoted awareness of 'Slim' (HIV)[2] and its transmission. A decade later, treatment was available to those who could afford to buy it or those fortunate enough to get onto a research project. Not until around 2005 did the big donor programmes like PEPFAR and the Global Fund[3] pour in the resources to make treatment free, first at a variety of dispersed sites and later more consistently at government health units. ART became institutionalized in the treatment programmes which people joined as 'clients'. While only about 10,000 people were on ART in 2003, there was a tenfold increase by 2007 when we ended our study.

Our interlocutors, like others on treatment programmes in those years, constituted a historical generation in Karl Mannheim's (1952 [1927]) sense of having a place in history that exposed them to the same formative events. They had shared the common experience of the AIDS epidemic in Uganda. They knew AIDS as an invariably fatal disease that had claimed close family members, often after terrible anguish and prolonged suffering. Many had tried to pay for their own treatment before it became available for free, sacrificing family welfare, and missing their medicine when they had no money (Whyte et al. 2004; Byakika-Tusiime 2005). They had lived through a time when people did not want to go for an HIV test because uncertainty was preferable to confirmation of a fatal disease for which there was no security of treatment.

When ART became widely available, news of its life-saving powers spread rapidly throughout the population. For the HIV-positive people who managed to access treatment, a kind of generational consciousness emerged – an awareness that they differed from their predecessors, for whom there was no Second Chance. Narratives of salvation through the miraculous effect of ART helped to maintain consciousness of their unique historical location. So did the health education talks emphasizing that 'medicines are your life' which were a part of their regular clinical visits. Historical contingency was evident as well in the way a few worried about whether their treatment programmes would continue. Yet, at that time there was surprisingly little general discussion of sustainability, donor policy, or the rights of therapeutic citizens.

What preoccupied people were *social contingencies*, that is, their interdependencies with others. Therapy programmes understand themselves as having agency. They reach out and give treatment. But we were struck by the way our interlocutors themselves spoke as agents who had achieved treatment. And by and large they described their achievement not as an individual accomplishment, but as a series of steps facilitated or impeded by other people. Whether they were talking about how they first went to test 'in order to know my life', how they managed to get onto an ART programme, or how they were sustained through times of illness and doubt, they spoke of specific relatives, friends, and acquaintances. That is not to say '*the* family' or '*the* community' as policymakers put it, but particular members of their own circle of contacts. This inclination to explain the turnings of life in terms of connections to, or dependence upon, other people may be in part a conventional form of discourse, but it remained strong despite the tendency in biomedical treatment to assign individuals responsibility for their own bodies and therapies.

Researchers have long recognized the social basis of response to illness in Africa. John Janzen's (1978) notion of the therapy-managing group in lower Zaire emphasized the social rather than individual nature of treatment-seeking. The broader the group, the more different treatments were tried. The vulnerable were not necessarily those who went to traditional healers, but those whose therapy-managing group was so limited that they did not receive any kind of treatment (Feierman 1985: 83; Feierman 1981: 402–3). Having someone connected to biomedical health work within your therapy-managing group is so key that Ugandans regularly ask people going to a health facility: 'Do you know anyone there?' The value of what Bourdieu would have called social capital was evident in an epidemiological study in Guinea-Bissau. Among children admitted to the paediatric ward in Bissau's main hospital, those whose mothers knew a doctor had a risk of dying within thirty days that was 48% less than those whose mothers did not know any physician (Sodemann et al. 2006). In Ugandan English this kind of social capital is referred to as 'technical know who'.

The recognition of the importance of connectedness can be taken a step further to examine the dimension of uncertainty in interdependence. There is an element of chance in relying on another person to help you. He may be transferred or turn indifferent; she may fall ill or die. Being dependent on persons rather than reliable institutions introduces an element of fragility. It was Caroline Bledsoe, in her book *Contingent Lives* (2002), who brought into focus the uncertainty of social contingency. In her study of women's conceptions of fertility and ageing in West Africa, she showed how they thought of the life-course not in terms of chronological ageing, but rather as the outcome of chains of dependency. Contingent developments rather than linear time explain bodily ageing.

> ...the success with which a woman can prevent or contain future bodily harm depends on her investing broadly and deeply in social relations. Indeed, the word *contingency* connotes a sense of social ties that underlie all aspects of life, including the physical growth, development, and decline of the body (25).

She shows that vulnerability to others upon whom women depend is invested with uncertainty in that it is difficult to predict or control the agency and circumstances of those others. 'The fact that one person is proximate to another implies that the acts of one will likely have repercussions for the other. These...may be beneficial... But the repercussions of proximity also can be deleterious' (Bledsoe 2002: 20).

James was a university student who was articulate about the importance of connections. Godfrey once remarked that he was impressed by the networks James had built among staff at Mulago, the national referral hospital, and James explained: 'You know, maintaining life is not the responsibility of one person, and those other people who help you maintain it should not be your enemies'. He clearly saw the potentially beneficial aspect of contingency. His domestic situation was based on kinship connections. He was staying with the family of his maternal cousin Tito, together with other relatives, including Tito's brothers. As Godfrey learned, it was a precarious arrangement since no one in the household had a salary; they were thankful for some support from Tito's mother-in-law. But there came a time when Tito made it clear that the household could no longer maintain James, especially with his extra feeding needs after starting on ART. James was sickly and had lost weight. His dependence on his cousin was proving a source of uncertainty rather than security. James's friend Kenneth told Godfrey that Tito was actively discriminating against James; this contingency had become deleterious. It was Kenneth who took the initiative to get another relative to accommodate James.

Social contingencies are always multiple in that you are dependent on several other people, and the sources of uncertainty are correspondingly several. Historical contingencies are not singular either, as we shall see in the story of John below. But even with this multiplicity of contingency, it is still possible to trace sources of uncertainty and thus to reach a more detailed understanding of how beneficial and deleterious possibilities follow on from relationships.

Railway Connections

John was a railwayman living in the Kampala railway housing estate known to anthropologists through Ralph Grillo's (1973) early research on African trade unions. Like many others, he had discontinued his education for lack of funds, but he was fortunate to get a job with help from his brother and other relatives who worked in Uganda Railways. Starting modestly as a porter, transferred here and there all over the country, he helped support his parents and his brothers and their families, even before he rose to a position of greater responsibility and got a railway house in Kampala. Godfrey visited him eight times, and spoke to him on the phone occasionally, over the time from 2006 to 2007.[4]

John's account of the doubts and worries of his therapeutic journey was full of both historical and interpersonal contingencies. In 2001, he developed a cough and weakness and feared that he had tuberculosis. He first went to a private clinic in Kampala, where he was referred to the Joint Clinical Research Centre (JCRC), the major AIDS treatment facility in the city, for an HIV test. 'But being a man from Jinja, I decided not to go to this place because I did not know it and I was alone. I thought of where else to go and I decided to have the test done back in Jinja'. Although he had good railway connections, John's health contacts were weak. He tested positive in Jinja, but there was no one to help him do anything about it.

A year later, he was at death's door. He lost weight and appetite, developed a cough, and his stomach swelled up 'like a person who has been poisoned'. At last his brothers and wife decided to take him to Mulago, the national hospital. But they did not know anyone there and it was a terrible experience, as he told Godfrey:

> My brother! The way I was handled there! You cannot believe. Those people rejected me. I was sent away. They saw my health condition and maybe thought, 'After all this one is dying'. They said, 'This one should be taken home because he has no hope'. So we left the hospital and came towards town. I was badly off and my brothers were considering returning me to the village just to wait for my death. But they disagreed with my wife – she said no. Even me I said no, as I still had some senses. We appeared stranded [undecided] on where to go as the vehicle headed to the city centre. Since it was a hired vehicle, the driver challenged us to decide quickly. But this driver was too good... He was too sympathetic to my situation and expected that I should be taken to another hospital. But my brothers did not seem to want. So this driver took personal responsibility and decided to drive to Nsambya Hospital. The driver said, 'At least I should take you to Nsambya and dump you there, rather than leave you go to the village'.

In John's telling, it was the taxi driver who tipped the scales and prevented him from being taken to the village to die. From there on, the story was a chain of connections, from Dr Xavier, who treated him at

Nsambya Hospital with some medicine whose name he did not know, to the private clinic of Dr Xavier's brother. When he finally went to JCRC, the major AIDS treatment facility to which he had originally been referred, he found Dr Xavier again.

All this time he had been paying for treatment; he used to collect his salary and go straight to buy his medicine. His life depended on his job and his wages. They in turn were affected by national and international developments.

> My employers, Uganda Railways Corporation, used to notice my poor health – all the time I was ill, sometimes for long, and sometimes I even failed and got stuck somewhere on my journeys. They saw that I was affecting their work and the board sat to discuss plans to lay me off. The decision to stop me was to be made, but I can tell you, God is good. That very day, the government announced that workers should not be laid off due to poor health. So rather than come to dismiss me, the personnel officer called me and said to me: 'You have been coming to my office because of your sickness, so get this form and fill it. We are going to start paying for your treatment'. I had not expected this kind of news. I was overwhelmed and I knelt down to thank the madam. I said, 'Madam, I don't know how to thank you. You have saved me'.

This policy change allowed John not only to keep his job, but to continue treatment at JCRC, the country's best AIDS clinic, at no cost to himself. At the time Godfrey met John in 2006, he seemed to be among the most fortunate of all the people we followed. But he was worried.

The government-owned Uganda Railways Corporation was to be privatized and many employees would be laid off. A few months later, Godfrey found him preparing to relocate to the village, though not because of the privatization. He had been interdicted – suspended from service and put on half pay pending investigation of an accident for which he was held responsible. He worried about how the interdiction would affect his treatment but feared to ask, thinking it was better just to continue going to the clinic as if nothing had happened. The uncertainty about his medicine coincided with other unknowns: Would he be able to keep his house in Kampala? Could his children continue school there? How could he manage on so little salary? The brothers who depended on him and his job were also concerned. With this blot on his record, he was sure to be fired when the work force was cut down in connection with the impending privatization.

John said that life was a 'gamble', the common term in Ugandan English for the insecure state of having no money and desperately trying out any opportunity to get some. He encouraged his wife to stay in the village where she could cultivate and do some small business. But she and their baby were both HIV positive, and he had little money for treatment and for buying milk, a necessity since positive mothers were told not to breastfeed. He could only hope for the termination package that might allow him to invest somehow so that his family might survive.

The next time Godfrey met John, he had just been through an interview, together with hundreds of others, with the new management. He was convinced that this was just a formality and that the South African company that had bought the railway would dismiss them all. Worse still, when he went to collect his medicines and told the receptionist that he was from Uganda Railways Corporation, she snapped at him, 'Oh, so you are the people!' and demanded his identity card. Panic struck while he waited, trembling. The dispenser told him that these were the last drugs to be covered by his employer, as the corporation was being sold. He would have to pay for the next ones. Since he was on a very expensive second-line treatment, he knew he could never afford it. Confirmation that the situation was hopeless came when he went to ask for help from the manager of Uganda Railways. The manager told him to forget about it. He himself was in the same boat of losing access to treatment. How could they expect the corporation to pay for their care when it was collapsing? He would have to go back to the village to die.

Still he tried. His brother working in Jinja agreed to contribute some money towards buying the next supply of medicines. Meanwhile, Godfrey was also trying to find out if there was any way he could get free second-line drugs. When Godfrey contacted John a month later, his life had taken even more dramatic turns. His sickly youngest child had narrowly survived a severe bout of illness. While the child was in hospital, his wife went into labour and delivered another baby, who also could not breastfeed because of the mother's sero-positive status. He had run out of drugs and his brother could not provide any more money, so he went to beg help from JCRC. They put him on a waiting list, but fearing to miss any more medicine, he went to his original treatment source, Nsambya Hospital, which sent him back to JCRC for a referral letter. Surprisingly, when he went to request it, the doctor announced that JCRC would start providing him with free second-line treatment. What he did not know was that at this time the huge American AIDS programme PEPFAR was channelling money into JCRC to enable the roll-out of free treatment in Uganda.

Not all the news was good. Uganda Railways had informed him that he was not eligible for the coveted termination package because his interdiction had been resolved as a dismissal. He believed that some malicious person had organized this development because others with similar cases had been excused and received severance packages. 'My problem is that I don't have godfathers like they do'. He was considering asking his MP to intervene on his behalf.

Perhaps he did have godfathers (several relatives worked for the railways) or maybe he was just amazingly lucky. The newly restructured Rift Valley Railways rehired him and doubled his salary, with full knowledge of his health condition. They did not tell him anything about medical care, so when he fell ill again and was admitted to hospital, he asked to be discharged almost immediately, figuring he could not afford to pay. But the railway staff doctor intervened and explained that the company would cover all expenses. The last time Godfrey visited John in May 2007, he was working, and his job provided the security of salary, health care, and housing. Now it was the work itself that gave cause for concern. It was demanding to supervise the train crew on long journeys without rest. The goods train travelled at awkward hours, it was hard to get regular meals, and his health was not reliable. He worried about having to miss work because of illness, and he thought that his colleagues were backbiting him. He heard that some even feared to make a long journey with him because he might collapse and die in their hands. He tried to show that he was not as weak as they thought, but his appearance belied him.

The Ethos of Contingency

Contingency colours interactions, as became evident to us in the course of our fieldwork. We realized that people saw us as potential connections, coming as we did from the university and with links to Europe. Benjamin, who was paying for his drugs, asked Godfrey if he could connect him to someone who could help subsidize his treatment. When Godfrey said he was only aware of what Benjamin already knew – that treatment was free at some places – Benjamin replied, 'You never know, keep trying'. This phrase seemed to capture perfectly the sense of possibility with which people tested out potential connections. Benjamin encouraged us to keep our eyes open for possible benefactors, and perhaps he was also encouraging himself to keep looking and hoping.

This disposition of hopeful 'you-never-know-keep-trying' recalls Johnson-Hanks's term 'judicious opportunism'. Writing of young educated women in Cameroon and their hesitation to specify future plans, she says: '[T]he activity, therefore, is not to develop a good plan and follow it but rather to respond effectively to the contingent, sudden, and surprising offers that life can make' (Johnson-Hanks 2005: 376). But the ethos of contingency, as we saw it, is more than taking an opportunity unexpectedly offered; it is being constantly on the lookout for opportunities. This kind of watchfulness for positive possibility is the other side of the vigilance and apprehension about negative potentiality of which Henrik Vigh writes in his chapter of this volume.

For our interlocutors, the positive or negative nature of potentiality was often unknown and only became clear over time. The privatization of the railway was first a disaster and then a blessing for John. Being dependent on persons who may help or hinder you in the future is associated with a disposition of 'civility'. You avoid open confrontation, even when you feel you have been wronged, in order to maintain the relationship. Examples are many. A few years ago (after this study had come to an end), Jinja District ran out of AIDS medicines. People who had been told they must never miss a day of medicine were turned away empty-handed when they went for refills. At one rural health centre, the ART patients decided to walk peacefully to the District Health Office to request politely that the DHO pressure National Medical Stores to supply the drugs. The patients went first to the head of their health centre to request her permission, not wanting to take any steps that would alienate her. She forbade them to go and went discretely herself to National Medical Stores and came back with just enough drugs to get her patients through a month. She feared that even a peaceful manifestation of need might be interpreted as a criticism and cause offense to someone in a position of power. So she preferred to make a small effort behind the scenes herself.

Civility is expressed in the very common phrase 'I just kept quiet' when people tell of how someone important to them had wronged them. What this means is that open criticism is often suppressed at intimate, institutional, and broader political levels. Privately, complaints about health workers are lively and indignant. But no one dares to accuse them of laziness and corruption to their faces, because you never know when you might need them. So the ethos of contingency is attentiveness to future possibilities that might help secure values, as well as endanger them. This entails checking out people with potential resources and keeping resentment in your heart, which in turn adds to the general sense that there are invisible malcontents among us.

The ethos of contingency is one of tentativeness, which is a particular kind of uncertainty. It is about discerning and trying various possibilities, while recognizing their provisional, undetermined nature. It requires recognizing relationships, dependencies, and conditions that mediate what is important to you for better or for worse. The uncertainty lies in the inability to predict the conditions on which you are dependent.

Impersonal and Personal Contingencies

The treatment that kept John alive was historically contingent: it depended upon the policy of the Uganda government, the big bilateral and multilateral AIDS relief programmes, the neo-liberalization that privatized the railway, the worker insurance of the South African company, and the procedures of therapeutic institutions. He experienced these somewhat abstract forces as unfamiliar and mostly unknowable sources of fortune and misfortune. When he could, he tried to put a face on their features: the good Dr Xavier and the personnel manager before whom he fell on his knees. Or he imagined an inimical personal agent, like the malicious hand in the denial of his termination package. But by and large, these were forces seemingly beyond his control. There was no mobilization of railway employees to protest the privatization, nor did AIDS patients demonstrate for their rights as therapeutic citizens. Uncertainty arose because John felt he was at the mercy of anonymous forces with which he could not directly engage. He did not know what implications the privatization of the railways would have for the treatment upon which his life depended. He did not even dare to ask, not wanting to draw the attention of the JCRC staff to his changed circumstances. Uncertainty was preferable.

This is not to say that workers or medical patients in Uganda are always politically naive or uncritical. Phillip, who was on treatment from a faith-based organization, was deeply worried about whether he would be able to stay on in the modest one-room house the programme had rented for him. It was crucial that he maintain residence in the parish catchment area. He made the intellectual connection to the national and international forces at play. Corruption might mean that the donors would cut off aid to the treatment programme: 'They misused this money from the Global Fund – you see, they are killing us indirectly'. But this insight did not help him resolve the uncertainty about his accommodation.

John, like all of the other people we followed, tried to secure his situation mostly through his relations with other people. They did not necessarily provide security (e.g., John's brother could not afford to keep him on the expensive second-line treatment). But personal relations seem more susceptible to influence than abstract forces. Interdependencies are explicit, and you can better comprehend the chanciness and the chains of consequence, as John did in recalling the conversation in the taxi on the fateful day he was sent away from Mulago Hospital as a 'gone case'.

Personal contingencies and the uncertainties they might hold were pronounced in connection with speculation about infection. Women recounted how they did not know what their men were doing on the side; they remembered hearing that a former wife had a baby who died before she herself passed away. They told of partners who had sickened with mysterious symptoms; they still were not sure whether it was HIV. It was not only contingent men who were sources of uncertainty. An army officer we call Mark told of a girlfriend with whom he always stayed when he was on missions in the west away from his wife. Once when he came to her home, her family deceived him that she was away. Later it turned out that she had died. Some said it was witchcraft worked against her because she befriended other women's husbands. But when he inquired, the soldier found that she had been sick for a long time and had never told him. The symptoms, when he finally heard about them from others, made him suspect AIDS. 'You know, you may have a friend but you can never learn who they are! I stayed with this girl for more than five years as a friend but she kept a secret from me, which I think I am still annoyed with...' Mark confided, upset at the memory and breathing hard.

For most of our interlocutors, however, the contingency of how they acquired HIV was a matter of the past, not relevant anymore. 'It has already happened' was a common remark. Although some, like the soldier Mark, still speculated and resented, and others asserted that they really did not know how they had become infected, these were no longer matters of urgency. What preoccupied them were the contingencies of the immediate future. Mark was concerned about telling his wife, who had also fallen sick, that he was the source of her infection. He had asked the doctor to secretly test her blood and then to put her on ART without revealing why she should take medicine every day. He was uncertain what effect it would have on their marriage when he revealed the chain of consequences that led her to be hospitalized.

Impersonal historical contingencies and personal social ones influence one another. The historically contingent advent of new health technologies like HIV testing and ART created new kinds of uncertainty. How is my life/health? (The word is the same in many Ugandan Bantu languages.) Will I be able to live on treatment? Will it make me sicker? Will the medicine be available where I can get it? The unprecedented response to the epidemic created new social dependencies on organizations concerned with HIV/AIDS. Free ART is institutionalized in such a way that each patient must become a client of a specific treatment programme. To be a client is to belong to an organization, to return regularly for medicine refills and check-ups, and to have one's paperwork in proper order at one's clinic (Whyte et al. 2013). As we saw in the case of John, he could not simply switch to free treatment at Nsambya Hospital once he was registered at JCRC. The relationship of institutional dependence was often elided with one of personal dependence – on familiar and friendly health workers. Many of those we followed expressed worry that they might be transferred away from the relative security of the clinic and health workers they knew. Those on the large and amply resourced research project run by Centers for Disease Control had heard that their programme would be ending and felt uncertain about what shifting their clientship elsewhere might mean.

In addition to the vital relations of clientship upon which people felt that their life/health depended, other new possible personal connections emerged as part of the historical shift that the first generation experienced. A plethora of NGOs mushroomed to offer support to positive people and to widows and orphans. They, as well as the treatment programmes themselves, took on 'volunteers' to carry out their work. Although the volunteers were not on salary, they received occasional 'motivation' in the form of lunch and travel allowances and opportunities to participate in workshops. The tentative ethos of contingency as possibility informed these types of sociality. The chance to collect a little money, to receive some training, and, most of all, to position oneself in a domain where a real job might materialize, was highly valued. But it was only a chance and required more education than most had. Here too, it was generally believed that you needed good connections to get the chance.

Interdependence and contingency characterize most people's lives in Uganda. Will my uncle continue to pay my school fees? Will the 'owner of my pregnancy' take responsibility? Will my son send money this month? The response to HIV has underlined these contingencies and introduced some new ones. That is to say, the historical contingencies of the epidemic and the roll-out of free treatment played into existing social relations. Our interlocutors told how the disease and its treatment increased their dependence on selected family members, in whom they confided and who helped them through periods of illness. Some moved in with relatives; some stayed with family members when they went to collect their medicine refills. These social relations provided a degree of security, especially in the first months on ART as people were getting used to the medicines and gaining strength. But by the same token, tensions or changes in circumstances could introduce uncertainty about the future.

Gender relations have been affected by new questions and doubts. The advent of testing technology focused uncertainty on what a positive test would mean for the durability of a partnership. As we have already mentioned, some of our interlocutors were so concerned about this that they dared not tell their partners that they were HIV positive. At a more general level too, testing and treatment problematized gender roles. Siu and colleagues (2012) explored the relation of HIV tests and treatment to notions of masculinity in a gold-mining village of eastern Uganda. They found that men made a connection between ART and the ability to work hard, a core dimension of masculinity. But the implications of testing and treating for their manly images were not fixed; in some situations men on treatment were seen as better able to work, in others they were seen as weaker and more vulnerable than their workmates. The implications were partly contingent upon the supportiveness of their personal work relationships; they were also dependent on institutional considerations in that some donor-supported programmes facilitated shifting to less physically demanding occupations. Also here it was evident that both personal and institutional contingencies were at play. They could be specified and examined using ethnographic methods.

Conclusion

John's story, like those of the other ART 'clients' we followed, exemplifies the contingencies of personal relations and large-scale political and institutional developments. C. Wright Mills (1961: 6) famously wrote that sociology and anthropology should concern themselves with the 'intersection of biography and history'. Ethnography allows us to do this in a particular way. By following the lives of persons over time, we are able to describe them not only as biographic individuals, but as socially embedded actors. We can see how they appropriate institutions and how they are affected by historical tendencies, some of which are beyond their own purview. At crucial points in his therapeutic journey, John relied on the support of his brothers, who helped at some points, but failed him at others. His experience with treatment institutions was mixed. Mulago Hospital sent him away, and JCRC refused to give him free treatment when Uganda Railways was privatized. He tried to secure continued support from the Railways Corporation through a personal approach to the manager, but without success. He was not aware of the PEPFAR programme that made it possible for JCRC to offer him free second-line treatment when his brother could no longer help. When he was 'rescued' by his new private employer, Rift Valley Railways, he did not fully comprehend their policy. He gained a degree of security even though he was not certain about the grounds for his good fortune.

John was unusual in having an employer who paid for his hospitalization; the last annual census found that only 16% of the Ugandan labour force was working for regular wages (Uganda Bureau of Statistics 2006). The majority of employees are civil servants whose contracts do not include fee-for-service health care. But he was typical in being dependent for ART on an institution that was funded by external donors. Ultimately, his life was contingent upon a policy that provided regular, reliable treatment. He could not influence the impersonal institutions (and ultimately the US Congress, which allocated the funds for PEPFAR). But he could try to personalize his relationship to his treatment provider, and he could put a human face on the institution that employed him, just as he did when he knelt down to thank the personnel manager of Uganda Railways Corporation.

Distinguishing historical and social contingency allows us to explore how large-scale transformations, such as the influx of resources for antiretroviral therapy, affects the nature of social relations within a generation. Moreover, we can trace how social relations mediate the working out of historical changes, as when people gain access to treatment programmes through someone they know. In both cases there are elements of consequence and connection that cause people to feel uncertain about what will happen. In both cases, contingencies are multiple, and different sources of uncertainty may seem to conflate. But at least the distinction sets a course for tracing dependencies and linking worlds of personal social experience to trends beyond immediate grasp. This is a task for which ethnography is well suited. It allows us to locate uncertainty (Whyte 2005) and to follow its transformations as one contingency replaces or is overshadowed by another.

Notes

1 'We' were Godfrey Etyang Siu, Phoebe Kajubi, David Kyaddondo, Hanne Mogensen, Lotte Meinert, Jennipher Twebaze, Michael Whyte, Susan Whyte. The study followed a decade of working together at Child Health and Development Centre, Makerere University, on an Enhancement of Research Capacity project funded by the Danish International Development Agency. A book (Whyte forthcoming) presents our study more fully.

2 'Slim' was the popular name for HIV disease in Uganda in the era when no treatment was accessible and patients lost weight drastically before they died.
3 The US President's Emergency Program for AIDS Relief is the largest programme ever launched against a single disease. Uganda is one of the main recipients. The Global Fund to Fight AIDS, Tuberculosis and Malaria is a multinational financing agency which has also provided major support to Uganda, although it held back for a period because of mismanagement of funds.
4 John's story and a discussion of his therapeutic journey and his work situation are presented more fully in our book, *Second Chances* (Whyte forthcoming).

References

Bledsoe, C. (2002) *Contingent Lives: Fertility, Time and Aging in West Africa* (Chicago: University of Chicago Press).
Byakika-Tusiime, J., J. H. Oyugi, W. A. Tumwikirize, E. T. Katabira, P. N. Mugyenyi & D. R. Bangsberg (2005) 'Adherence to HIV Antiretroviral Therapy in HIV+ Ugandan Patients Purchasing Therapy', *International Journal of STD & AIDS* 16: 38–41.
Dewey, J. (1930) *The Quest for Certainty: A Study of the Relation of Knowledge and Action* (London: George Allen & Unwin).
Grillo, R. D. (1973) *African Railwaymen: Solidarity and Opposition in an East African Labour Force* (Cambridge: Cambridge University Press).
Janzen, J. (1978) *The Quest for Therapy in Lower Zaire* (Berkeley: University of California Press).
Johnson-Hanks, J. (2005) 'When the Future Decides: Uncertainty and Intentional Action in Contemporary Cameroon', *Current Anthropology* 46 (3): 363–85.
Mannheim, K. (1952 [1927]) 'Essay on the Problem of Generations', in Kecskemeti, P. (ed.) *Essays on the Sociology of Knowledge* (New York: Routledge & Kegan Paul).
Mills, C. W. (1959) *The Sociological Imagination* (New York: Oxford University Press).
Siu, G. E., D. Wright & J. Seeley (2012) 'How a Masculine Work Ethic and Economic Circumstances Affect Uptake of HIV Treatment: Experiences of Men from an Artisanal Gold Mining Community in Rural Eastern Uganda', *Journal of the International AIDS Society* 15.
Sodemann, M., S. Biai, M. Jakobsen, M. S. Aaby & P. Aaby (2006) 'Knowing a Medical Doctor Is Associated with Reduced Mortality among Sick Children Consulting a Paediatric Ward in Guinea-Bissau, West Africa', *Tropical Medicine and International Health* 11: 1868–77.
Uganda Bureau of Statistics (2006) *The 2002 Uganda Population and Housing Census, Economic Characteristics* (Kampala: UBOS).
Whyte, S. R. (forthcoming) *Second Chances: Surviving AIDS in Uganda* (Durham: Duke University Press).
Whyte, S. R., M. A. Whyte, L. Meinert & B. Kyaddondo (2004) 'Treating AIDS: Dilemmas of Unequal Access in Uganda', *Journal of Social Aspects of HIV/AIDS* 1 (1): 14–26.
Whyte, S. R., M. A. Whyte, L. Meinert & J. Twebaze (2013) 'Therapeutic Clientship: Belonging in Uganda's Projectified Landscape of AIDS Care', in Biehl, J. & A. Petryna (eds.) *When People Come First: Critical Studies in Global Health* (Princeton: Princeton University Press), pp. 140–65.

Whyte, S. R. (2005) 'Uncertain Undertakings: Practicing Health Care in the Subjunctive Mood', in Steffen, V., R. Jenkins & H. Jessen (eds.) *Managing Uncertainty: Ethnographic Studies of Illness, Risk and the Struggle for Control* (Copenhagen: Museum Tusculanum), pp. 245–64.

Whyte, S. (2009) 'Epilogue', in Haram, L. & C. Yamba (eds.) *Dealing with Uncertainty in Contemporary African Lives* (Stockholm: Nordiska Afrikainstitutet), pp. 213–216.

Charity and Chance: The Manufacture of Uncertainty and Mistrust through Child Sponsorship in Kenya*

Elizabeth Cooper

Introduction

Uncertainty is commonly conceptualized as psychosocial enigma. As a consequence, it is prone to being analysed as a cultural phenomenon, both in the meanings that different people attribute to it and how people respond to it. In this, different cosmologies of fortune, destiny, and chance have been carefully considered by anthropologists, as have the various avenues of people's inquiries and petitions, including religion and science, for example (da Col 2012; Haram & Yamba 2009; Evans-Pritchard 1937). These contributions have been important for unsettling any potential ethnocentric prejudice that would claim that there is one way in which people understand (or should understand) how and why our lives can surprise us.

This chapter analyses uncertainty in a different way. In this, uncertainty is not found to be primarily cultural in conceptualization, but rather as a by-product of a particular political economy. I accept as a useful working definition of uncertainty 'a lack of absolute knowledge' and 'inability to predict the outcome of events or to establish facts about phenomena and connections with assurance' (Whyte 2009: 213). However, I argue that this definition does not mean that uncertainty is

*This research was funded, in part, by a Social Sciences and Humanities Research Council of Canada Doctoral Fellowship and Postdoctoral Fellowship, a British Council Chevening Scholarship, the Godfrey Lienhardt Memorial Fund for Research in Sub-Saharan Africa administered by the University of Oxford's Institute of Social and Cultural Anthropology, the Peter Fitzpatrick Travel Scholarship administered by St Antony's College, and a research grant from the British Institute in Eastern Africa.

necessarily a condition characterized by mystery and incomprehensibility. Rather, as this chapter's case study illustrates, some conditions of uncertainty can be perceived and analysed in concrete and immediate, rather than tenuous or indistinct, ways.

The case study at the centre of this chapter concerns experiences of uncertainty created through the operation of a child sponsorship programme in a village in western Kenya. The focus on charity as a particular system of inequitable control over the allocation of resources – or 'chances' as people in the study context say – provides an example of how differentiated access to knowledge makes possible different types of causative analysis of what is behind uncertainty. This chapter is therefore an effort to analyse uncertainty in terms of the political economy of control over resources, including knowledge.

My study is premised on the idea that taking people's experiences and perceptions of uncertainty seriously can open important avenues for studying the particular forms, distributions, contingencies, and effects of power. Such methodological potential has been demonstrated in Javier Auyero and Debora Swistun's ethnographic study of people's uncertainty about environmental contamination and risks in an Argentine shantytown. In that study, Auyero and Swistun (2008) examine how uncertainties about the local environment's toxicity are embedded in residents' lived histories and 'relationally anchored' to their embodied, everyday routines. However, rather than limiting their analysis to community members' experiences and perceptions of toxic uncertainties, Auyero and Swistun also extend their analytical lens out and 'up' from the immediate community, and in so doing, they account for how local residents' uncertainties are, in fact, generated by a 'labour of confusion' among powerful outside actors, including state officials, environmental scientists, and health practitioners. That study thus demonstrates that the problematization of uncertainty can be a productive starting point for tracing horizontal as well as vertical relations of affect and effect. We learn from that example that the purposeful and extended study of uncertainty – what we might think of as the institutional ethnography of uncertainty – can offer far more than an account of what people are uncertain about and why; it can also be the means by which we account for how particular inequalities are structured and maintained, and the differentiated consequences of this.

My analysis relies on some distinctions between uncertainty, insecurity, and contingency as different, albeit closely related, kinds of conditions. Susan Reynolds Whyte (2009: 213–4) has suggested a conceptual framework that recognizes uncertainty as a state of mind characterized by a lack of absolute knowledge, insecurity as a social condition associated with limited resources for action, and contingency as an existential condition arising from the state of being 'dependent on, or affected by, something else that cannot be fully foreseen or controlled'. Reflecting on these distinctions, Whyte suggests that '[d]ealing with uncertainty is perhaps not so much about making certain, as it is about trying to make more secure' (Whyte 2009: 214). My case study of the effects of child sponsorship programmes on how people perceive what is uncertain, and why, demonstrates this idea. As the analysis below describes, while the uncertainty prevalent in the operation of child sponsorship programmes – and indeed charity more generally – interests people, its propensity to deliver erratic and inadequate support means that people do not count on such interventions for their security. As such, in this context, people's interests in charity tend to be more opportunistic than committed. People's greater concern with their security is focused on access to livelihood resources that are understood as more intelligible, responsive, and consistent, including local, interpersonal (often kin-based) relationships of care and patronage. At the same time, this study reveals how the element of contingency in the allocation of charity's chances has significant existential implications, particularly in terms of people's understandings of who (including oneself) can affect one's chances in life, and how. Organizational restrictions that impede the possibilities of social contingency (Whyte and Siu this volume) between the people engaged in these transnational relations pose the serious existential effect of manufacturing an uncertainty that diminishes people's understandings of individual and collective efficacy.

   The study suggests that one implication of child sponsorship programmes is that children and adults understand charity, and indeed externally initiated interventions generally, as unpredictable, unaccountable, and ultimately untrustworthy. I find that this judgement is in part the result of deliberate inequities of power in the structure and practice of child sponsorship programmes, yet such judgement is most commonly expressed as suspicions of corruption among some Kenyans of other Kenyans. At the same time, this idea of charity as untrustworthy also tends to be understood in terms of individual children's personal luck – or chance, as local people choose to translate it. (The Dholuo term used is *hawi*, which translates as luck, chance, fortune, and blessing.) I suggest that what allows for the potentially paradoxical coexistence of cynicism regarding corruption and hope related to chance is the very structure of sponsorship programmes. First, foreign sponsors are held at such distance from sponsored children and their families that they are understood by people in Kanyathi to be unknowing and innocent; they are conceptualized as pure givers of chance. Meanwhile, the international organizations' stringent efforts to limit personal relationships and direct accountability between sponsored children and foreign sponsors (and even between local staff and international staff) mean that it is only by chance that a child's good fortune might indeed slip through this tightly controlled system.

In what follows, I first explain how I pursued this study, and I review the history and organizational structure of transnational child sponsorship charities. I then account for how people in one area of western Kenya have recently perceived and interacted with such interventions as uncertain. This leads into my analysis of how such perceptions and interactions shape particular ideas and practices related to chance, mistrust, and trust. This analysis highlights how the contingencies that people can identify and act upon, such as their immediate, interpersonal relationships, are appreciated as more meaningful than those that are inaccessible. The inaccessible and unaccountable determinations of child sponsorship cause such interventions to be regarded as untrustworthy in both practical and ethical terms.

The Study

The case study analysed in this chapter rests on the experiences of several different children and their families as well as the volunteer community outreach workers and regional programme officers involved with the child sponsorship programmes of World Vision and ChildFund (formerly Christian Children's Fund), which are active in the western Kenyan city of Kisumu and its environs. I had not originally planned to study child sponsorship programmes. However, as I conducted an ethnographic study about children's lives in a village on the outskirts of Kisumu that I call 'Kanyathi', I learned that several children I had come to know were registered in sponsorship programmes. I therefore made child sponsorship one line of inquiry of my broader study. Specific to this interest in child sponsorship, I conducted focus group discussions with a group of thirteen girls (between the ages of eleven and fourteen) and a group of twelve boys (between the ages of ten and fifteen) that were sponsored by World Vision, and I conducted individual interviews with eight girls and boys sponsored by the two different organizations. I was already familiar with these children from my time spent doing some volunteer after-school composition classes as well as living as neighbours in the village. As well, I interviewed seven parents or guardians of sponsored children. I also conducted interviews with four Kisumu-based staff of the two organizations and 'shadowed' two organizations' community outreach workers over several days as they conducted their outreach activities in and around Kanyathi. I was permitted to read sponsors' and children's letters at the Kisumu office of one of the organizations, and I also attended one organization's special event in Kanyathi at which cards from sponsors were distributed to children and children wrote their reply letters. These sponsorship-focused research activities were one small part of a larger ethnographic project that I conducted in Kanyathi over sixteen months between 2007 and 2009 (Cooper 2011), and three months of additional fieldwork in Kanyathi in 2011 and 2012. I therefore consider the findings concerning child sponsorship in the broader social and historical context of everyday life in Kanyathi.

A History of Changing Chances

Transnational child sponsorship has been around since the 1930s[1] and still has a large share of globalized child-focused charity.[2] Its defining feature is the pairing of individual children 'in need' with individual sponsors who make monthly financial donations to the charity with which the children are registered. Up until the late 1990s, these paired relationships had a direct material basis: individual sponsored children received economic assistance, often in the form of the payment of school fees and the provision of particular material goods, such as mosquito nets, blankets, clothing and shoes, and food, for example. Such direct benefits to individual children are no longer the case, however. Instead, sponsors' financial contributions flow into a general fund from which community-based projects are financed. These include infrastructure investments, such as latrines and water pumps, as well as some informal education and training courses for children (focused on health and child rights, for example) as well as adults (such as income-generating activities).[3] Yet, despite the lack of individualized material assistance, the pairing of individual children and individual donors continues. These relationships are primarily comprised of the exchange of information about a particular child by the organization to the child's matched sponsor, as well as letters from the child to the sponsor and the option for the sponsor to write letters to the child. All communication is filtered through the organizations' offices, however, with strict controls on the exchange of information that would allow for children and sponsors to communicate directly. All of the charities remove any personal contact information, such as email and postal addresses and telephone numbers that would allow sponsored children to directly contact their sponsors.

The charities also reject letters in which children make direct requests for assistance from their sponsors.

Child sponsorship comprises one long-standing charitable initiative in Kanyathi and the encompassing region. The mission-associated charity that is now called ChildFund (previously Christian Children's Fund) began child sponsorship in Nyanza Province in the 1960s; World Vision began its child sponsorship programming in the area in the 1970s; and Plan began child sponsorship programming in Kisumu in the 1990s. In 2012, approximately 13,000 children in the local Kisumu area were registered with three different child sponsorship programmes: approximately 9,000 with Plan in Kisumu West and East districts (combined population of 620,000); 3,000 with World Vision in Winam Division (population: 350,000), of which approximately 700 live in Kanyathi's local sub-location (population: 19,500); and just over 900 with Child-Fund in Kisumu East District (total population: 145,000), of which approximately 200 live in the village of Kanyathi and its surrounding five kilometres. There are concentrations of sponsored children among particular pockets of these larger populations. For example, in the government primary school in Kanyathi, which had a total pupil population of 679 in 2009, there were over sixty children registered with World Vision and approximately twenty with ChildFund. As well, there are many former 'sponsored children' living in Kanyathi.

The 1980s and early 1990s are remembered as the heyday of child sponsorship in western Kenya, and it is against those experiences that current initiatives are compared. Sarah,[4] who volunteered with one of the Christian Children's Fund's (CCF) local partner organizations in the 1980s and was later employed by CCF (now ChildFund) from 1985 until 2004, was well positioned to summarize the history of changes, both ideational and practical, to child sponsorship programmes in Nyanza. She recounted to me that until 1988 there was 'full sponsorship': 'Families were taken care of in terms of food, shelter, medical care, and all of the children's school fees. [...] It was 100% giving and little participation'. After 1988, however, things changed: 'This was the introduction of cost sharing', Sarah explained. 'There was a lot of emphasis on community participation'. This meant both a reduction in the amount of financial and material assistance provided to sponsored children and their families by the organization as well as the expectation that families must also provide a certain amount of financial or in-kind support for their children's schooling. These changes in the parameters of sponsorship occurred around the same time that Kenyans were hired instead of foreigners to staff the organization within Kenya. Sarah described this coincidence as very unfortunate: 'Local people remembered white missionaries giving everything and then they were suspicious of the local Kenyans because now what was being offered had also changed'.

Over the years several other changes were made to the eligibility criteria for sponsored children and the kinds of assistance offered. These changing criteria reflect changing notions of childhood vulnerability and organizational efficiency, as well as moral virtue. For instance, in the late 1990s, the rules were changed so that only students who qualified for national or provincial schools would have their secondary education funded; others would be 'dropped'. Then in 2003, when the Kenyan government introduced 'free' primary education, sources at several child sponsorship organizations recount that they were advised and agreed to no longer sponsor children's primary school fees because officially these fees no longer existed. School enrolment became a condition of sponsorship, although it is well known that there continue to be costs that families are required to pay for their children's education, which can mean that children of the poorest households are unable to attend and are also ineligible for sponsorship. Also in the early 2000s, the charity became more interested in sponsoring orphaned children and children that local staff referred to as 'potential orphans', that is, children with an AIDS-affected or otherwise ailing parent. In Kanyathi, the village where my study was based, ChildFund's long-time community outreach worker pointed to several other criteria that blend ideas of vulnerability and virtue, including the ineligibility of children born out of wedlock or living with unmarried mothers but the eligibility of children living with widowed mothers. Most recently, the organization also changed its criteria to only enrol children less than five years of age.

The most significant change in the experience of child sponsorship programmes, however, occurred in 2005–2006 when the organizations' uses of sponsors' funds changed. From that point, all of the monies raised through individual sponsors' monthly payments would be pooled in one common fund to pay for community-based projects, such as the installation of water wells or latrines. Individual children and their families would not be allocated direct financial or in-kind assistance on a regular basis. This became the standard practice among all of the international child sponsorship charities. According to Sarah, this was an unfair policy and practice: 'They advertise a link between an individual sponsor and individual child. On the website the policy is the same, but in practice it is not an individual child sponsorship programme. [...] So we are not being straight with the sponsor, and we are not changing the life of that child. I think it's unfair to the sponsor and unfair to the child whose photo was taken and was promised help'. As a long-time insider to a child sponsorship organization, Sarah's account and critique of how child sponsorship programming has changed in Nyanza is better informed than most. Yet, her most emphasized point, that the many changes in how these organizations operate has made it difficult for people to understand and trust them, resonates strongly with the perspectives of children and adults in Kanyathi who have personally been enrolled in sponsorship programmes.

Contrived Disconnections

My discussions with a group of girls and a group of boys sponsored by World Vision revealed a lack of knowledge concerning how the organization had changed from providing individuals with material assistance to funding community-based projects. For instance, when I asked the group of girls what they understood as the purpose of World Vision, their initial answers comprised a list of material donations: 'They provide us with bags'; 'They took our pictures'; 'The give us blankets'; 'And mosquito nets'; 'Plates and cups'; 'Rubber shoes – they gave all of us those'. So I asked what the girls had received during the last year (which was 2008), and to that question the reply was '[n]othing. They were not calling us last year'. Another girl elaborated that '[t]hose other things we got before. Now they don't give us things'. When I followed up to ask what being sponsored means in the girls' lives now if they do not receive things, they only mentioned that they can be called by the organization to come to a meeting where they are given juice or sodas. In responding to my question about the purpose of such gatherings, the girls became stuck for an answer. One said they 'fellowship' (pray) together and another said that sometimes they write letters to their sponsors. A discussion with boys sponsored by World Vision yielded very similar responses. One nine-year-old boy who had just been registered as sponsored for a year described: 'There is nothing they have brought for me, so I feel bad about it'. An older boy voiced his criticism of the present structure: 'I've felt bad each time when they come and they give us a soda – nothing we can see, like a goat. They should do better than sodas'. Another boy chipped in: 'As you know, [the neighbouring village where meetings are often held] is quite a distance from here, so we walk all that way for nothing but a soda. You feel it's not good'. One more boy added: 'Sometimes our parents will even tell us not to go to those meetings because there is nothing we get from them'. The feelings of disappointment that the children described indicate how poorly understood and endorsed the recent changes have been among the very children who are used by the charity to raise funds.

Another critical element noted in Sarah's history of changes in child sponsorship programming was how the convergence of the 'hand-over' from foreigners to Kenyans in the charity's local administration with the reduction in direct assistance to children and their families generated significant suspicion. Many children and adults still believe that foreign sponsors want and try to send children direct assistance, but that these efforts are stymied by Kenyan personnel. In replying to my question about what children's family members say about them being sponsored by World Vision, one girl replied: 'They say that when our sponsors send things the World Vision people take the things and give us just a little and they remove the phone numbers too'. I asked who does this and the girl stated: 'People in Nairobi. Some of them here in town [Kisumu] too'. Another girl later described: 'My disappointment has been that when the *mzungus* [foreigners] send us something, they [Kenyan World Vision staff] take it. That is bad'. Parents expressed very similar suspicions about Kenyan-based corruption. One mother of three sponsored children said that she did not like that the staff did not allow children to have access to the phone numbers or email addresses of their sponsors so they are unable to contact them. She told me that when some parents had asked why their children could not have their sponsors' contact information, the local staff had replied that if the children had that information, they might want to go and look for their sponsors and then get lost. But the mother said the parents did not believe that: 'We think the reason is that sometimes more is sent for the child but they [World Vision] keep that back. That's why we can't know the sponsors or we would learn for ourselves'.

These are very significant critiques of the operation of child sponsorship charities. They reveal how an organization's purposeful design to both replace direct assistance to individual children and families, as well as to carefully insulate foreign donors from the children and families with whom they are matched, leaves the charity's Kenyan personnel exposed to other Kenyan people's frustration and blame. Encapsulating this contrast in believing in the goodness of foreign sponsors and the badness of Kenyan employees, one boy described: 'The sponsors themselves are good. The problem is only with the office here because that is where the things meant for us go missing. A good sponsor should be that person who comes with those people that give those things he sent so he can see that the things are truly getting to the sponsored child'.

This contrasting confidence in foreigners and disparagement of locals feeds a broader public discourse about the inability of Kenyans to secure their own prosperity, which may itself contribute to undermining the efficacy of collective efforts. That this idea is being learned at a young age by many, and integrates easily with a broader discourse, suggests its potential for shaping sustained opinions and attitudes.

A Local Political Economy of Charity and Chance

As the local actors that mediate access to the charities' chances, the role of community outreach workers brings into play contingencies of personal relationships and judgements, and by extrapolation, a discernible local political economy of chance. These individuals, who live in the same community as the children who may be sponsored, are the ones who are delegated the power to select one child for sponsorship from many others, and therefore they are the local agents through which that chance works. It is through what these individuals see and hear, and what personal interpretations and inclinations these inspire for them, that relationships between children in the village and the transnational charities are made possible. As they walk through the village, writing down a name of a child to consider, or searching for a home to deliver a package, or apologizing for bringing nothing, they personify people's various hopes and frustrations with the limited possibilities of this kind of charity. And they know what this embodiment feels like: they feel the eyes of the village on them, and they describe carrying the same hopes and frustrations in their hearts as they pursue their work.

We can consider this through the case of Malcolm, who began volunteering as a community outreach worker for World Vision in Kanyathi and some other nearby villages in 2000. Malcolm had previously earned money as a private photographer of local events in the area. Most commonly, he would be hired by families to photograph their burials, weddings, or other special occasions. When World Vision 'came to the ground', as Malcolm put it, looking for people to help them with the recruitment of children for sponsorship, they found that he knew about many different children and families in the area because of his photography work. During his first years with World Vision, he helped the organization to register 300 children from the area for sponsorship. In 2009, Malcolm recalled: 'They saw I knew the children here so well so they gave me chances every year to add some. Now there are 612'.

I asked Malcolm how children come to be registered for sponsorship. Malcolm explained children's and relatives' approaches, as well as his own role, all in terms of getting chances and testing luck:

> Mostly it is needy children or their relatives who just come to me and ask, 'If you get a chance, can you help my child?' So when I get a chance, I can take that child. But I tell them [the parents]: 'The project is not helping much, but every once in a while the child can get a balloon – just a balloon. Do you still want me to join him?' Because some children get a balloon sent from their sponsors, but some don't.
>
> And no one refuses.
>
> They want their children in because they hear about the GINs – that is, Gift Notifications. They want to know their child's luck. Maybe they've heard of a child who got some money, so they think maybe their child too can be lucky.

The odds are stacked against a child's luck: of the more than 600 children Malcolm had registered in his district, only two children received 'GINs' (Gift Notifications, meaning that the sponsor has volunteered to send something extra to be received by the child) in 2009. Nevertheless, what these few children received were relatively significant contributions towards their families' welfare: in 2009, one child received KSH 5,500 (USD 69) and the other KSH 7,000 (USD 88). These monies were used to purchase for each child's family a combination of livestock (one family bought a calf, the other a goat), mattresses, blankets, and some house-building materials, all of which Malcolm took photographs to send to the children's sponsors to evidence their purchase. Meanwhile, children registered with ChildFund have better chances: of the 128 children sponsored through ChildFund in Kisumu West district in 2009, thirty children had what are called 'active sponsors' who regularly (for example, once or several times each year) sent money or specific orders for purchases to be delivered directly to the child's family. The other hundred children have what local staff call 'dormant sponsors'; these make their monthly contributions to ChildFund, which are directly deposited in the organization's pooled fund for community projects, but they do not send anything extra to be specifically directed to their sponsored children. However, again, the few examples of 'active sponsors' had an important impact for both the individual families that benefited as well as other community members' perceptions of how child sponsorship might yield a good chance. In one widely cited example from 2008, a child's sponsor sent KSH 300,000 (over USD 400) with which ChildFund oversaw the construction of a new house for the child's family. Why that child and her family had been recipients of this assistance was explained by other sponsored children and their relatives in terms of their personal good fortune as well as the noble benevolence of their sponsors. However, according to Simon, the community outreach worker who was involved, that chance had been promoted by his photograph and description to the sponsor of the family's previous dwelling; the local staff's intervention had helped to guide the sponsor, although it was still the sponsor's 'good heart' that was believed to have really made the difference.

Children and their families recognize how rare the chances for receiving individual gifts are. But, as Malcolm put it, they are interested to at least test a child's luck. In pursuit of this, there are some actions children or adults may take. They can petition community outreach workers to register certain children, for example. In this, families may rely on their social networks to solicit the support of a local outreach worker, and they will describe their family's life in terms of impoverishment and their child's life in terms of vulnerability. The first step towards entering the child sponsorship lottery, then, is not regarded as pure chance. While children and adults recognize that child sponsorship programmes are for 'the needy', 'orphans', and 'the ones who are struggling to keep up', they also have many examples of how contingent children's registration can be to personal relationships. For example, in response to my question as to how World Vision staff chooses children for sponsorship, one girl replied: 'Sometimes both of your parents have died and you are living with a relative and that relative can know someone who works for World Vision and she can take your picture to them and ask for assistance. So you can get sponsored like that'. Other tactics include demonstrating one's good character through attendance at church services and village meetings (*barazas*) at which the outreach worker is present. One mother started volunteering with World Vision so that her request for the organization to sponsor more of her children might be approved. (It was: three of her children were eventually 'sponsored' although none had proven very lucky, as no direct assistance had yet been received.) As well, the outreach worker for ChildFund consults with the local primary school's committee and the government of Kenya's appointed assistant chief for the area to identify vulnerable children that he might register for sponsorship.

While each of the organizations has criteria for the kind of children it deems vulnerable and worthy, and therefore eligible for sponsorship, the judgements of the community outreach workers are also influential. As Simon, the community outreach worker with ChildFund, explained: 'Sometimes it can be difficult to know who is needy. Sometimes you can just tell by seeing them – they look poor – but for others you can't tell because they are dressed well. But I know from knowing the families'. In most cases, both organizations' outreach workers found that their judgements regarding which children were worthy of sponsorship were trusted and endorsed by their respective organizations. Only sometimes the community worker's recommendation is overruled. As Malcolm described, 'We can send a name and description of a child for sponsorship to the Nairobi office, but then the name does not come back. For example, the Nairobi office decides that child is not vulnerable'.

The local personnel of these sponsorship organizations know that they are watched carefully, sometimes with hope, and often with suspicion, by members of the local community. They see themselves bearing the brunt of families' frustrations with the lack of direct assistance available through sponsorship as well as the lack of accountability between children and their sponsors. When I asked Simon how relations were between ChildFund (and their local community-based partner organization) and local families, he acknowledged: 'There is much suspicion that the office is eating the sponsors' money'. World Vision's representative, Malcolm, also described the challenges of his intermediary role:

> It is sometimes difficult. You can go to town to pick up the mail without eating anything and then you deliver those things and the parents think those things that were to come to their child you have eaten. They think I have taken and eaten what was there for their child.[5]

I asked him how families felt about the community projects that are funded through sponsorship monies. Malcolm described that parents without children in the sponsorship programme felt these were 'okay' but parents with sponsored children do not like such projects. He explained: 'They say, "How can my child's name be used to go collect money from outside for these things and yet he is not getting any help?" They can be quite frustrated about this'. He explained that the only adults who appreciate him in his community are those whose children have a sponsor who has sent a gift – 'like a calculator or a T-shirt' – which he has been able to deliver. When I asked what recommendation he would suggest for the programme, Malcolm was very clear: 'They should try to give direct benefit to the children. Then all of the children would be happy'. The community-based worker's preference for direct assistance to children clashes with the preference among the charity's more remote decision makers for 'community-based' projects, as discussed further in the last section.

Certainly, in the community, the outreach workers are regarded as the charities' gatekeepers. A mother summarized her acceptance of the outreach worker's refusal to divulge the contact address for her daughter's sponsor: 'They are the ones who found this sponsor, so what can you do?' Malcolm understood how powerful some of his neighbours consider him: 'Some parents think I am the one who chooses which child will receive a gift'. Meanwhile, he also acknowledged the importance of his role as his community's agent and described feeling pride and commitment in this: 'Those children are yours. You don't want your children to lose their sponsors. So it's in our hearts to do this job. We don't want to see the children dropped. When your children and your local area benefits, you feel proud, and so we just continue even if without a salary for now'. ('Volunteers' receive occasional remuneration, however, this is not predetermined and therefore not predictable, which has caused some charities' volunteers to threaten strike actions.) The fact that one of the former community outreach workers for ChildFund became the government-employed assistant chief for the area further indicates how the role of a gatekeeper to charitable chances entwines with the broader local political economy. I speculate that his past ability to grant sponsorship – at a time when this meant the provision of material goods to sponsored children's families – provided him with a form of patronage with which he was able to build local political support for his endorsement as a chief.

Access to charity seems to come as a result of two different types of chance: the first chance is akin to opportunity, and the second chance is luck. Whereas the first step towards access to charity is locally regarded as determined by contingencies of personal relationships and meeting an interpretation of vulnerability, the second step concerning whether or not a child will actually receive charity through his or her sponsorship is attributed to pure chance. This is where a local idea of chance interweaves with, and is supported by, the unpredictable and unaccountable workings of child sponsorship. In conveying the attitude that follows from a child's registration for sponsorship, a parent may say: 'We will try our luck' (*Watamo hapwa*).

Conditions of Mistrust in Life's Chances

The notion that a person's life chances are influenced by his or her personal luck or fortune (noun: *hawi*; construct possessive: *hap-*) is quite widespread among people living in Kanyathi. It is common that a person will defer to chance in his or her forecasting of what might happen, even with something that might appear quite concrete. For example, if a person has been promised a job, or a student has won a bursary to advance her or his studies, she or he is not likely to make confident statements about the materialization of this opportunity. Instead, the person will likely make a statement along the lines of 'We will see' or 'I will just try', perhaps with the additional qualification that 'I will see my luck' (*Abiro neno hapa*).

There is scepticism woven into such statements as well as a learned ambivalence. Both seem an appropriate response to local experiences of unevenly met expectations of outside intervention in the region, whether in the form of charity or development projects. The history of the local area has not been a smooth trajectory of 'development' nor of a steady plummet of 'decline' (Cooper 2011: 71–92). The uses of the land and nearby lake, as well as human productivity, have changed with changing speculations, often made by outsiders and not by the local population. In their life histories, men and women and girls and boys described how they have struggled to adapt to keep pace with their changing environments. Certainly, the new developments have stirred hopes of accessing new resources, including new economic opportunities. And some individuals have benefited in various – usually temporary – ways. However, there have been many experiences to caution against naive optimism that new projects will guarantee local people's economic security and well-being.

To take but one of many examples from Kanyathi's recent history, when a Norwegian NGO cabled in electricity – over the tops of people's homes and businesses – to service their enclosed compound near Kanyathi with its primary and secondary schools and boarding houses for the 'rehabilitated' street children they sponsor as well as some privately paying students, local villagers speculated it was just a matter of months before they too would be connected to the grid. However, over four years later, this had not happened, and even the local government school and clinic were still without electricity in 2012. Nor had the NGO sponsored any children from Kanyathi to attend its private school. Indeed, when the locally elected councillor visited the NGO directors to directly ask them to take in a few specific vulnerable children from the local area, she was refused. When I later asked the Norwegian director about the NGO's interest in the people who live around where the institution is located, he described that after the post-election violence in early 2008 (during which two other NGO-run children's homes in the Kisumu area were attacked by local people), the NGO had, over the course of one day, fed 800 people a meal, and several months later the NGO had taken approximately forty old and sick people from the village to their office headquarters in Kisumu to feed them a meal. 'They were all very happy with that', he concluded.

On a regular basis, however, the NGO's activities were beyond the reach of local residents, and the local villagers saw themselves excluded from this neighbour's concerns and 'development'. In fact, people told me that the only thing that had changed for them as a result of the opening of this NGO's school in their midst was their experience of a higher frequency of Landcruisers driving up the village's road to the NGO's gated compound. These vehicles, as symbols of socio-economic mobility and differentiation, figure prominently in local villagers' suspicions about what was happening to their world and their uncertain role in it. The anxiety was matched by an appropriately unpleasant sensory phenomenon. As one man said to me about how the villagers experience these particular neighbours as they sped past in their vehicles: 'We just swallow their dust'.

This example of disillusionment, as well as the relative indifference with which children and adults experience child sponsorship programmes, reflect a prominent – if often unspoken – local critique of externally imposed charity as incapable of fulfilling people's principal concerns with their long-term socio-economic security. Local attitudes towards charity are relegated to slim hopes of a possible sudden boon, such as a house construction, or, more likely, an instance of minor assistance, such as receipt of a mosquito net or a meal. As a result of this low threshold of confidence in its economic value, charity is regarded as relatively frivolous. Moreover, charity's overall efficacy is further undermined by its seemingly arbitrary and locally unaccountable mode of operation as, for example, often occurs in the determination of what certain people identified as 'needy' will be given without those people's own meaningful participation. In this, the conceptualization of charity in terms of uncertainty and chance reflects apathy in people's perspectives towards it. More confidence is invested in those endeavours and relationships that might promise more enduring and accountable security for people – such as investments in their own income-generating activities as well as their own kin relationships, for example.

One critical issue at the core of child sponsorship charities' poor endorsement by local communities seems to emanate from the lack of trustworthy relationships, and by this, I mean relationships characterized by interpersonal accountability and even reciprocity. The fact that the English word 'sponsor' has made it into daily lexicon among Dholuo speakers in Kenya is telling of the exoticism that characterizes foreign patronage. For example, a child might state '*An gi* sponsor' or '*Amanyo* sponsor', which translate as 'I have a sponsor' and 'I am looking for a sponsor'. The use of the foreign word, instead of its translation with a Dholuo word, denotes a conceptually different category. For, indeed, there are common terms and phrases used by Dholuo speakers to refer to a local person who serves as a patron. *Jatayo* literally translates as 'a person who guides' and is used to describe a person who uses her or his own hands to help a toddler to learn to stand and walk, as well as someone who provides advice and/or material assistance or opportunities. For example, a grandson who has been given a plot of land by his grandfather can specify '*jatachna ma kwarwa*' (the grandfather who guides me). Or an adult who has secured a job for a younger person can identify that young person as '*ng'a matayo*' ('the person I have guided'). This terminology can be used for relatives as well as nonrelatives (*jatayo majalibamba*). Other phrases that are commonly used refer to people who 'stand for' others as patrons or representatives (Cooper 2012). However, a foreign benefactor is always a 'sponsor'. The different category seems to reflect the limited expectations invested in a foreign patron: the relationship with a foreigner is more purely understood as material, and not as personal as a relationship with a local patron who is interested in 'guiding' the individual he or she is helping. We may consider that a relationship that privileges the meaning of guidance assumes a more long-term and vested interest in the other's success and in this it implicates potential reciprocity. The strangeness of the word 'sponsor', meanwhile, seems to suggest a more superficial and alienated relationship.

The alienation that can manifest in relationships of charity, and particularly as a result of a lack of equality and accountability in these relationships, has been described by other scholars as well. In her classic study *Imposing Aid: Emergency Assistance to Refugees,* Barbara Harrell-Bond (1986) argued that much of aid's ineffectiveness is the result of not taking local people's perceptions and capabilities into account and consequently overlooking potentially important opportunities to support people's more secure livelihoods. Other studies of humanitarian relief assistance have come to similar conclusions (for examples, see de

Waal 1989; Hyndman 2000). In analysing charity in terms of gifts and giving, some anthropologists have found Marcel Mauss's analysis of gift exchange relevant (Bornstein 2005, 2012; Bornstein & Redfield 2011; Fassin 2001; Harrell-Bond et al. 1992). In this, the social construction of moral categories and practices of relationships are brought into focus. In an analysis of relief food assistance to refugees, for instance, Harrell-Bond et al. (1992) conjure Mauss's observation that the recipient of a gift is somehow debased, and particularly so if the idea of returning it is not entertained. Dider Fassin's study of a French programme for granting emergency financial assistance also notes the way in which charity is organized to be, above all else, 'discretionary', which spurs his recommendation for further examination of 'the workings of justice in charitable practices' (Fassin 2001: 473). Meanwhile, Erica Bornstein's study of child sponsorship in Zimbabwe points to the irony that '[t] he transcendent aspirations of philanthropic practice not only failed to transcend difference, they may have magnified and reconstituted economic disparity' (Bornstein 2005: 95). These are instructive observations for a critical appraisal of the dispersed and long-term implications of charitable interventions.

A large part of these other studies' critiques, as well as the local critique that exists among people in Kanyathi concerning child sponsorship charity, centres on the lack of power that local community members have in accessing resources or even in holding those who control decisions over access to account. However, it is too simplistic to characterize charity as a polarized system of all-powerful 'givers' and powerless 'recipients'. There are, in reality, many nodes and links in the workings of a transnational organization's power, and these are significant for how they affect people's understandings not just of charity, but also of the broader structures of power that charity often signifies. I have already considered how the role of community-based outreach workers is embedded in personal relationships with their fellow villagers. As a result of this more immediately accountable link in the charity's chain of power, the distinction between sponsorship as an acquired opportunity, won through the contingency of personal relationships, and sponsorship as pure luck, decided through unknown and unaccountable people and interests, is blurred. In this blurring of the interpersonal and the institutional, the accountable and the unaccountable, and notions of opportunity and luck, we can see how the 'rules' of a charity – that is, its policies and the practices enforced to ensure their adherence – can generate a pervasive uncertainty about what, and who, can be trusted to affect life's chances.

The perspectives of the child sponsorship charities' managing personnel in the regional offices illuminate another critical link in how charity's
chances are mediated and the existential implications of this structuring.
According to two different organizations' officers, the charities' recipient
countries' managers (including those in Kenya) are advocating for a complete abolishment of direct benefits to individual children and families.
This is intended 'to end feelings among children without individual sponsors of being discriminated against', explained a programme officer. These
charity managers believe that the chances that still exist for the lucky
few to receive charitable assistance directly from their individual sponsors
sow discontent among other community members and suspicion towards
the Kenyan staff of their organizations. The personnel in the headquarter
offices, therefore, would prefer all sponsors' donations to only be used for
community-based programming. This not only contrasts with the preferences of the community outreach workers who would like to see 'direct
benefits' to the children and families they live among, it also conflicts
with what some sponsors prefer. For example, while World Vision Australia has now ended the ability of sponsors to send 'their' children money
or gifts, World Vision USA has not because of their sponsors' preferences.

'Sponsors are different', explained one charity's regional manager
to me. 'Some are intellectual. Others are emotional'. The 'emotional'
sponsors still seek a more directly interpersonal form of charity, which,
according to that manager, prevents the charity from operating in
a more rational way. This struggle between the 'emotional' and the
'rational' may indeed be at the root of the many different perceptions
of this form of charity as untrustworthy. The two inclinations turn on
very different ideas of accountability: the 'emotional' emphasizes the
integrity of interpersonal relations, while the 'intellectual' subscribes to
a more impersonal and institutional-centric 'audit culture' (Strathern
2000). Such differences can cause confusion and contention, especially
when they are left unresolved, as is the case of the existing discrepancies
between the hopes of sponsors and sponsored individuals and the governing practices of the organizations. Further, the deliberate co-optation
of the 'emotional' for the 'rational' in child sponsorship campaigns
invites uncertainty not only about the practical effects of child sponsorship, but also uncertainty about their ethical virtue.

Conclusion

This case study of how child sponsorship can be understood in terms
of uninformed, unpredictable, and unaccountable chance – pure and

simple luck – suggests that people's experiences and ideas of uncertainty and fortune do not always need to be attributed to a cultural concept. It suggests how local experiences and perspectives of uncertainty and chance can also be analysed to ascertain what different interests and power structures might engender them. Chance, in this case, is not an indigenous philosophical idea. It is 'a different way of knowing' only because it is a way of knowing emergent from a position of not being able to know. In this, the ideas of chance that children and adults in Kanyathi associate with child sponsorship highlight a particular kind of powerlessness. Yet, at the same time, the use of chance as an explanatory framework can obfuscate an attribution of power inequities, and thus serve to depoliticize the actions that perpetuate these. Where luck is recognized as the central problem, questions of power are left aside.

In Kanyathi, people's understandings of child sponsorship programmes as charitable lotteries did not reflect a tendency to depend on outsiders' assistance. To the contrary, the largely unfair, uneven, and unpredictable nature of sponsorship specifically, and outsider-fuelled charity and development initiatives generally, did not nurture an incautious dependence, but instead a cautious detachment. People had learned through their many experiences of being helped temporarily, only to be 'dropped' without recourse later, not to invest significant confidence and hope in outsiders' assistance. Ambivalence was a safer perspective to maintain. Ambivalence allowed for individuals to still feel hope when opportunities presented themselves, but this allowed for a hope in chance only; that is, there was a hope in testing one's luck, but not a confidence in things going to plan.

On the one hand, this seems a sensible detachment. Everyone understands that it is very unlikely that a child will get a sponsor that will consistently provide wealth to that child and his or her family. And therefore there is little hope invested in the outcomes of a child being registered with World Vision or ChildFund or Plan for potential sponsorship. The notion of chance is present, but this idea is not distracting for adults, and it seems even children are only temporarily preoccupied with what being sponsored might mean for their futures. Many have been disappointed and have learned to accept this disappointment without much protest.

While such learned ambivalence and detachment are evidently warranted and sensible in children's and adult's everyday interactions with sponsorship programmes and even other charity initiatives, these sentiments might also signify a potential to greater cynicism and its consequences. With so many lessons from recent personal experiences of the unpredictable starts, stops, and changing conditions of chances to access external assistance, people have learned not to trust either the longevity or the integrity of charity or development. This distrust could very well suggest a rationale of exploiting the availability of any small chances as quickly and as much as possible. When people have learned that they do not have influence over what chances might be available, and further, that no chance is certain except what can be grasped in the present moment, is it really fair to decry seizing such chances as corruption? Charitable interventions that are unaccountable and unresponsive to local people's influence might very well be encouraging such cynicism about how opportunities are realized.

In this chapter I have sought to demonstrate the analytical potential available in tracing beyond what people feel uncertain about so as to examine how these uncertainties have been generated and their cumulative implications. This approach illuminates that child sponsorship charities' activities in western Kenya are not only evaluated in terms of their present activities, but also in terms of local histories and memories. As well, while these particular systems create particular suspicions, they are also embedded in a broader context of suspicion. The few 'chances' of child sponsorship, and the asymmetrical charitable relationships of these specific programs, cannot be understood as isolated experiences. They are experienced and comprehended as part of the way the world works and one's place in it. In this, even these small initiatives inform local logics of practice, including logics of practicing subjectivities and sociality in Kanyathi.

Notes

1   The international charity now called Plan claims to have instigated the first international child sponsorship charity in 1937 when it appealed to British people to donate a shilling a day to fund the care of children affected by the Spanish Civil War (www.plan-uk.org/about-us/our-history/). ChildFund traces its beginning back to 1938 when it began as China's Children Fund to raise funds through sponsorship to assist children displaced by the second Sino-Japanese War (www.ChildFund.org/about_us/mission_and_history/ChildFund_History.aspx). World Vision first ran a child sponsorship campaign in the 1950s to assist children affected by the Korean War.
2   In 2011, the charities ChildFund, Plan UK, and World Vision received through their international child sponsorship programmes financial contributions of USD 165,741,558, USD 39,459,224, and USD 38,109,167 respectively (ChildFund 2011; Plan UK 2011; World Vision 2011).
3   It is rather difficult, however, for the newcomer to some child sponsorship to understand that this is how the charitable assistance is organized. Some child

sponsorship charities' promotional materials tend to be convoluted and less than clear in their explanations of how sponsored children do not, in fact, receive any individualized (including household- or family-based) forms of support (see www.childfund.org/child-sponsorship/sponsor-a-child.aspx and www.worldvision.org.uk/child-sponsorship/?gclid=CIbTuObY4rACFUUhtAo dESoPzQ). Other charities, such as Plan, for example, are more direct in their communication about how child sponsorship donations do not go directly to sponsored children.

4 All individuals' names are pseudonyms.
5 'Eating' is a common idiom for corruption in Kenya (Wrong 2009).

References

Auyero, J. & D. Swistun (2008) 'The Social Production of Toxic Uncertainty', *American Sociological Review* 73: 357–379.

Bornstein, E. (2012) *Disquieting Gifts: Humanitarianism in New Delhi* (Stanford: Stanford University Press).

Bornstein, E. (2005) *The Spirit of Development: Protestant NGOs, Morality and Economics in Zimbabwe* (New York: Routledge).

Bornstein, E. & P. Redfield (2011) 'An Introduction to the Anthropology of Humanitarianism', in Bornstein, E. & P. Redfield (eds.) *Forces of Compassion: Humanitarianism between Ethics and Politics* (Santa Fe: School for Advanced Research Press), pp. 3–30.

ChildFund (2011) Small Voices, Big Dreams. 2011 Annual Report (ChildFund International).

Cooper, E. (2011) Who Cares for Orphans? Challenges to Kinship and Morality in a Luo Village in Western Kenya (DPhil dissertation, Institute for Social and Cultural Anthropology, University of Oxford).

Cooper, E. (2012) 'Sitting and Standing: How Families are Fixing Trust in Uncertain Times', *Africa* 82 (3): 437–456.

da Col, G. (2012) 'Introduction: Natural Philosophies of Fortune – Luck, Vitality, and Uncontrolled Relatedness', *Social Analysis* 56 (1): 1–23.

de Waal, A. (1989) *Famine that Kills: Darfur, Sudan, 1984–1985* (Oxford: Clarendon Press).

Evans-Pritchard, E. E. (1937) *Witchcraft, Oracles and Magic among the Azande* (Oxford: Clarendon Press).

Fassin, D. (2007) 'Humanitarianism as a Politics of Life', *Public Culture* 19 (3): 499–520.

Haram, L. & C. Yamba (2009) *Dealing with Uncertainty in Contemporary African Lives* (Stockholm: Nordiska Afrikainstitutet).

Harrell-Bond, B., E. Voutira & M. Leopold (1992) 'Counting the Refugees: Gifts, Givers, Patrons and Clients', *Journal of Refugee Studies* 5 (3-4): 205–225.

Harrell-Bond, B. (1986) *Imposing Aid: Emergency Assistance to Refugees* (Oxford: Oxford University Press).

Hyndman, J. (2000) *Managing Displacement: Refugees and the Politics of Humanitarianism* (Minneapolis: University of Minnesota Press).

Mauss, M. (1990 [1925]) *The Gift: Forms and Functions of Exchange in Archaic Societies* (New York: W. W. Norton).

Plan UK (2011) Annual Report and Accounts (London: Plan).

Save the Children (2012) Results for Children: An Update from Save the Children (Save the Children).

Strathern, M. (2000) 'Introduction: New Accountabilities', in Strathern, M. (ed.) *Audit Cultures: Anthropological Studies in Accountability, Ethics and the Academy* (London & New York: Routledge), pp. 1–18.

Whyte, S. (2009) 'Epilogue', in Haram, L. & C. Yamba (eds.) *Dealing with Uncertainty in Contemporary African Lives* (Stockholm: Nordiska Afrikainstitutet), pp. 213–216.

World Vision (2011) Annual Report (World Vision).

Wrong, M. (2009) *It's Our Turn to Eat: The Story of a Kenyan Whistle-Blower.* (London: Fourth Estate).

The Quest for Trust in the Face of Uncertainty: Managing Pregnancy Outcomes in Zanzibar

Nadine Beckmann

Introduction

'Giving birth is like bingo', a young woman from my neighbourhood in Zanzibar Town told me. 'You have a fifty-fifty chance of survival'. This poignant statement reflects widely shared sentiments about the dangers and unpredictability of pregnancy and childbirth among Zanzibari women and defies claims in the field of public health that women are not aware of the risks of birth.[1] While the perceived risk of maternal death does not accurately reflect the actual risk of dying in childbirth, it nevertheless signals a situation in which maternal and child death is relatively common. The facility-based Maternal Mortality Rate (MMR) in Zanzibar was estimated in 1998 at 377 per 100,000 live births (UNICEF).[2] Main direct causes of death are unsafe abortions, eclampsia, haemorrhage, and obstructed labour. The 2006 Reproductive and Child Health Situation Analysis shows that surgical deliveries are only available at the hospital level, however, manual vacuum aspiration is not routinely available even in hospitals (Hussein 2006). The general lack of emergency referral is a major constraint to the availability of emergency obstetric care on the islands.[3]

A major public health strategy to improve maternal and infant health is focused on increasing women's use of biomedical antenatal care and delivery in a health-care facility. And indeed, antenatal coverage in Zanzibar is good, with 99.4% of women attending at least once during pregnancy, and 48% visiting two to three times (NBS 2011: 129). 35.5% of women received two tetanus toxoid vaccinations and 89.5% of mothers were protected from tetanus during their last childbirth (NBS 2011: 133). The situation is thus better than in mainland Tanzania. Home deliveries have reduced from 63% in 1999 (NBS 2000) to 50% in 2004 (NBS 2005). According to the Tanzania Demographic and Health Survey

2010, 67.5% of women in Zanzibar's larger island, Unguja, delivered by a skilled provider (i.e., doctor, clinical officer, assistant clinical officer, nurse/midwife, MCH aide), but rates of health facility-based delivery vary considerably according to administrative region, ranging from 23% in Zanzibar North to 73% in Urban West (NBS 2005: 15). Postnatal care coverage remains relatively low at 36.2%, with disparity between Unguja (43.5%) and Pemba (23.7%) (NBS 2011: 138). Abortion is the leading cause of admission in female general/surgical wards (MoHSW 2006), yet post-abortion care is not available in all health facilities. Induced abortion is illegal, though available against payment of a bribe, and the abortion case fatality rate is 2.2%.

While the increase of biomedical reproductive care use seems promising, quality of services is often poor, and the reputation of hospital care has suffered in recent years with the introduction of cost-sharing models at a time of deteriorating health-care conditions in the wake of economic crisis and structural adjustment from the 1980s (Lugalla 1997; Putzel & Lindemann 2008) characterized by staff shortage and constant lack of even basic medicines. Doctors sometimes openly admit that some of their equipment is of poor quality. In a conversation I overheard, for example, the government hospital Mnazi Mmoja's head gynaecologist advised a foreign visitor to bring her own intrauterine device (IUD) because the Chinese IUDs they use were substandard and often faulty.

Recent rapid privatization of health services has resulted in an increasing range of choices but also heightened uncertainty. After two decades of socialism, the ban on private medical facilities was lifted in the mid-1980s. Subsequently, private clinics, hospitals, and pharmacies emerged all over the islands but particularly in the urban centres. Privatization turned health into a marketable commodity, a fact which traditional healers, who used to offer their services for free or a nominal fee, also recognized. As a result, today there is virtually no free professional health care anymore, neither in biomedical nor in alternative health sectors (Beckmann 2010). The costs of private health care are prohibitive for a majority of Zanzibaris, but the quality of care is not necessarily better than in the public sector, where user fees have also been introduced in 2004. Moreover, the marketization of health has raised uncertainty about providers' trustworthiness, and diagnoses are often mistrusted as ploys to make money. De facto, neither public nor private health facilities offer optimal care; private hospitals often look nicer and staff tend to be friendlier, but few have surgical facilities, and emergency cases are referred to the government hospital Mnazi Mmoja.

Much has been written on the precarious nature of maternal health delivery and the complex choices between 'traditional' pregnancy and childbirth care and hospital-based, biomedical care (Obermeyer 2000a, 2000b; Roth Allen 2002). This chapter deals with women who are generally invested in a belief in the superiority of biomedical care, and have financial resources to pursue it, but who still face significant uncertainties and try to navigate different options in the quest for establishing trust and reducing the dangers of pregnancy. It explores a semantic field that includes the notions of uncertainty, trust, and secrecy. These notions link people's practices and beliefs to a context of increasing privatization of health services, which acts as an additional recourse to older known ways of curbing dangers and enhancing well-being.

The data derive from several years of ethnographic fieldwork in Zanzibar and mainland Tanzania since 2004,[4] during which I lived with a local family in Zanzibar Town. The case studies I present are of two sisters from an urban family that originates from the Hadhramawt in Yemen and belongs to the trading middle class. They are well educated, having left secondary school after completing form four and undergone some vocational training. Both work in the family business, are part of a large family network of traders, and have access to cash resources for health-care expenditure.

Uncertain Outcomes

Children are highly desired in Zanzibar and regarded as a blessing, and it is expected that the first child will be conceived within the first year of marriage, followed by subsequent births ideally spaced by several years. Successful reproduction is closely connected to reaching full social status, and childless women – and men – are pitied. For women particularly, the ability to bear children cements their position within a marriage and the wider community. A lot is at stake in ensuring reproductive success. When visiting a woman who had had several stillbirths, her visitors barely enquired about her health. Instead they tried to comfort her by saying she should not worry about her husband marrying another woman – surely he loved her enough to excuse her sub-fertility. The preference for multiple children is reflected in a consistently high total fertility rate for Zanzibar of 5.1 births per woman (National Bureau of Statistics 2011: xix).

At the same time, pregnancy is widely regarded as very dangerous, the time of danger culminating in childbirth and the post-partum period. Common rhetoric portrays pregnancy and childbirth as a highly precarious process whose outcomes are never certain and that often ends in death: 'You either die or you don't, you can never be sure', '*Uzazi hamna uzoefu*, there is no getting used to giving birth, you can never predict how it will end', and 'Having children is dangerous. These days, many women die in childbirth', women (and many men) often commented when talking about childbirth, expressing the extreme unpredictability and anxiety associated with this central female duty. Everybody can recount relatives, neighbours, or friends who experienced childbirth-related crises, including maternal death, stillbirths, and infant death, and these stories are often discussed among women. In the space of three months in the summer of 2011, for example, in my immediate surroundings, one neighbouring woman suffered her third late-term stillbirth in a row due to pre-eclampsia, one of my host sisters experienced severe post-partum haemorrhage, and the other needed an emergency caesarean section, as did an employee of the same family, one of my key informants had a miscarriage (and a late-term stillbirth a year later), and an old family friend's daughter suffered severe complications and lost her baby four days after birth. At the same time, the wife of a prominent doctor in Zanzibar died giving birth in one of the island's private hospitals despite her husband's presence, a case that was often discussed to underline the unpredictability of a healthy pregnancy outcome, even under qualified medical care – but also to highlight the poor state of biomedical health care in the islands.

Visits to the maternity ward do not help to dispel these concerns. On one of my visits in August 2011, the antenatal ward is full of women walking around or lying in beds, moaning and praying in pain. It is hot and there is an acrid smell of blood and body fluids. The fans are switched off and the windows closed because nobody wants to catch *upepo*, 'wind', which is believed to bring chills and illness. Relatives are not allowed inside and are constantly chased away, even from the hallway outside, but cats go in and out, and there are no mosquito nets to protect the women from mosquitos and flies. Two women are bound at their hands and feet to the beds, one has her baby delivered right there, with just a partition placed in front of her bed. Several women have bloody catheter bags hanging from between their legs, some bursting full, but nobody bothers to change them. There are moans and screams, prayers and calls for the doctor: 'Doctor, doctor, help me!', and several younger women cry for their mothers. The woman next to me just lies on her back and breathes heavily; she seems to be unconscious. The one next to her wails loudly: 'What have I done, please just kill me! You are my elders, why are you behaving like this?' and then keeps repeating

'*Salaam aleikum*' (a common Islamic greeting that translates as 'peace be unto you') again and again. 'She has become mad from giving birth', my informant says quietly: 'To give birth is a great challenge (*mtihani*), you can easily become mad or get a heart attack'. The atmosphere is tense; patients are scared and relatives want updates on their loved one's progress, but few dare approach the nurses who are stern and unforgiving to those who bother them with questions. 'At night it's especially bad', I am told, 'the doctors are cruel at night! They beat their patients if they're unruly, and tell them to carry their own bags to the delivery room. If the woman says: "I can't", they shout, "You can't? Yes, you can!"' On the other hand, staffing levels are constantly low. During the night of Mamu's crisis (see below), for example, the nurses claimed they had delivered almost 80 babies. 'We are tired', a nurse exclaimed, 'of course you get impatient!'

Common perceived dangers around childbirth and the post-partum period include excessive blood loss often connected to anaemia (*upungufu wa damu*, literally 'reduction of blood') during pregnancy, fever (*homa*), fits (*kifafa*, literally epilepsy, but in terms of pregnancy it refers to pre-eclampsia and eclampsia, the most common causes for perinatal mortality worldwide[5]), and madness (*wazimu*). There is a strong concern about blood, which reflects broader cultural and religiously influenced ideas about the creative and destructive qualities of women's blood. Especially during the post-partum period, the mother's loss of blood is closely monitored by questions and inspection of her underwear and sanitary pads. The frequency of changing sanitary pads is used by healthcare staff, too, in order to assess the severity of bleeding after delivery.

Mamu: Managing the Dangers of Childbirth

A number of practices in response to birth-related crises are widely shared, both among the urban and the rural population, as the following case shows. Mamu, a 32-year-old woman of third-generation Hadhrami origin, gives birth to her fourth child in 2011, a year after an abortion due to an abdominal pregnancy. When her waters break, she goes home to her mother's house, following Zanzibari tradition, and I watch over her throughout her labour. Walking relentlessly in a circle in the upstairs sleeping quarters, she calls Dr Aisha[6], a midwife and nurse in the government hospital whom she had been consulting for her previous pregnancies, too. Dr Aisha tells her to come to the hospital straight away, but Mamu declines: 'I'm not coming yet, there's still time'. Over the next hour, her labour progresses quickly, aided by drinking hot tea and honey, both to increase the heat in her body, and castor oil ('to soften the stool', she says). She manages the pain by constant walking and hitting herself on the thigh, as recommended by her mother, who periodically comes to check on her. In between contractions, which now come every one to two minutes, she prays silently, sometimes bending over with pain. She still refuses to go to the hospital. After about two hours, she finally asks me to call her husband to get the car and we drive to the maternity ward, where Dr Aisha receives her. We have to buy a file and bring all the childbirth supplies: a syringe and a dose of oxytocin, a plastic sheet (to avoid soiling the hospital bed), four pairs of rubber gloves, sanitary pads, and *kanga* cloths for the baby. A relative slips the ward staff some money. About half an hour after arriving at the hospital, Mamu gives birth to a healthy daughter.

We bring Mamu some *uji* (porridge) and water, but she is eager to go home. The hospital policy dictates that mothers should stay in the hospital for twenty-four hours after giving birth, which had been reduced to six hours due to the shortage of beds. Nevertheless, Mamu pleads with Dr Aisha to let her go, and after an oxytocin injection to stop the bleeding we are on our way back home, one hour after she gave birth. While her husband recites the *shahada,* the Islamic creed, into the baby's ears, and her mother feeds the baby honey and bitter aloe – to show her that 'life is both sweet and bitter' – Mamu rests on the bed and chats with the family members who came to congratulate her. After a couple of hours, her sister and I take her to the bathroom to shower. Suddenly, her face loses all colour and blood gushes from between her legs and I can just about catch her when she collapses in the shower. We drag her onto a bench in the hall and she seems better. But suddenly her face turns ash grey and her eyes roll back. She chokes and starts shaking as if in a fit. Everybody is wailing and praying at the same time. 'My child is dying! This is exactly how her aunt died, I was there, I saw her, she's dying!' her mother screams. Someone calls Dr Aisha, who cannot come, but orders Mamu back to the hospital immediately. In the meantime, Mamu's mother prays the death prayer and spits *maji ya zamzam*, holy water from the Zamzam well in Mecca, which her father had brought home from his last Hajj, at her face. She later recounts again and again how this was the decisive action that helped Mamu back to life. An aunt who is a nurse advises to put Mamu's feet up but offers no further first aid. Milk, strong coffee, and *maji ya zamzam* is given to Mamu to drink, and her feet and head are rubbed with *habasoda* oil (oil of black caraway seeds, an important, powerful substance in Islamic medicine), while a friend lays her hand on Mamu's head and prays fervently. Slowly, Mamu regains consciousness and silently joins in the prayer. A neighbour advises rubbing the feet with lime juice to keep the feared *maradhi ya baridi* (literally 'cold diseases' – denotes a number of illnesses, including anaemia, intermittent fevers, paralysis, and vegetative states) at bay. 'What kind of blood did she lose?' her mother asks me. 'Bright red blood', I respond. 'That's *damu ya mwili*', (literally 'blood of the body') she wails in horror. This kind of blood is different from the dark, almost black, and often thick 'dirty' blood that comes from the uterus and must leave the body. *Damu ya mwili* is thin and bright red. It is the blood that carries life force. Losing even small quantities of this blood is considered life-threateningly dangerous.

Finally the men bring a chair to carry her to the car and we drive back to the hospital, where she is immediately put on a drip and given a curettage. She is hospitalized for a night and slowly gets better over the following week, although she remains weak and dizzy from the blood loss. During this time she is closely observed by her family members, and her strength is built up through the traditional blood-increasing foods provided during the post-partum period.

While post-partum haemorrhage is feared as one of the most common causes of childbirth-related deaths, blood that flows from the uterus is considered dirty at the same time, and controlled bleeding is therefore necessary for a healthy recovery. Menstruation is widely regarded as an opportunity for women to regularly rid their bodies of dirt (*uchafu*), and a number of practices and medicines are dedicated to cleaning the vagina, which is seen as a place where dirt accumulates easily (and thus a seat of infection and disease). Both menstruation and sexual intercourse confer on the woman's body a polluted state (*janaba*) in which she is prohibited from praying or touching the Qur'an. From menarche on, girls are taught to perform the ritual ablutions necessary to cleanse the body after menstruation. New brides are reminded to wash their vaginas with hot salt water after having sex, and never to have sex during their menstruation, due to the dangerous polluting character of menstrual blood. Traditional midwives (*wakunga*, plural; *mkunga*, singular) sell herbs that are placed inside the vagina to cleanse it of polluting remnants after menstruation.

Because of the harmful potential of blood that originates in the womb, sexual intercourse is strictly prohibited for the seven days of menstruation and during the first forty days after childbirth (*arobaini*), although the last rule is often not adhered to and the period of abstinence is sometimes limited to the phase in which the woman is still bleeding. If conception takes place from sexual intercourse during menstruation, the child is believed to contract epilepsy (*kifafa*), be disabled (*mlemavu*) (for example, through trisomy 21 [*kichwa kubwa*]), or can develop outside of the woman's uterus, causing prolonged labour, severe pain, and even death of the mother at the time of birth. An old traditional midwife explained this as follows: 'Every month the dirty blood from the uterus gathers in one of the ovaries, one month on the right side, the other on the left. During menstruation the bladder bursts and the blood flows out of the body. If you have sexual intercourse, then the man's semen will block the way, the blood cannot leave, and a child can start to grow outside the uterus. Often these children are very big, because they are not constrained by the uterus, and have to be born by caesarean section, or it might be born "feet first" [*miguu mbele*, i.e., in breech position], causing great problems for the mother and the child'.

During pregnancy the menstrual blood stops flowing and contributes to 'feeding' the foetus: '*mtoto anakula damu*, the child eats blood', women often complain when they feel weak and tired during pregnancy. *Upungufu wa damu* (anaemia, also called *ukosefu wa damu*, 'lack of blood', or *safura*) is considered one of the most common and serious pregnancy problems, and pregnant women's blood levels are constantly monitored by their relatives, who look out for paleness, weakness, dizziness, feeling cold, and shortness of breath. This concern is underlined by blood tests performed in antenatal care facilities, which measure the woman's haemoglobin levels. Anaemia is very widespread among women in Zanzibar and increases the risk of post-partum haemorrhage (Kavle et al. 2008). Therefore, iron and vitamin supplements like Hemovit are routinely prescribed by health-care providers, and families try to provide blood-increasing foods (*chakula cha kuongeza damu*), such as milk and dates, green vegetables, and Lucozade for pregnant women.[7]

Because the menstrual blood is not shed for nine months, the woman's body is considered full of dirt at the end of the pregnancy. This dirt must be expelled through controlled bleeding, which is induced by a range of techniques that create heat in the mother's body: she is placed inside a hot room, wrapped in warm clothes, and is only given 'hot' food and drinks to consume. She is served special food, such as spicy porridge (*uji mtamu*), chicken soup, and octopus soup, that must be light and fluid (*vyakula vyepesi*), because her stomach is still said to be soft (*laini*), but at the same time should be hot and spicy (e.g., strong ginger tea and large amounts of black pepper as a seasoning[8]) to make the blood flow. She is also washed with hot water and placed on a traditional Swahili bed, or alternatively a chair with a hole in the seat, while burning coals with fumigations (*mafusho*) are placed underneath. This is supposed to 'dry up' (*kukausha*) the uterus through maintaining a steady but slow flow of blood over a longer period, preferably for at least twenty days. Strong and painful massages with *habasoda* oil carried out twice a day by the *mkunga* and firm binding of the stomach with several pieces of *kanga* cloth are said to help with making the still-soft body firm again and shrinking the belly. The ultimate goal is for the cleansed body to regain strength and to 'contract' (*kukaza*), reflecting a concern with 'openness': 'The vagina needs to be washed with hot water after sex and after childbirth, so that it contracts and gets tight again, so it doesn't stay open [*ikaze, isikae wazi*]', explained the *mkunga*. 'If it remains open [*wazi*] it invites disease'.

In addition to the physical dangers of excessive bleeding, fever, and infection, the post-partum period is also spiritually dangerous, because in an impure state the woman cannot pray and thus cannot protect herself (*kujikinga*) from malevolent attacks, while the smell of the blood is said to attract the spirits (*masheitani*), whose food is human blood. Therefore, women who had suffered from spirit possession episodes commonly do not want to visit a woman in the first days after giving birth, because they 'cannot stand the smell of the post-partum blood' (*Ile harufu ya mzazi, damu inanuka, hii siwezi*). Fumigations (*mafusho*) with strong-smelling substances, such as dried leaves, onion, or garlic peel, *habasoda*, *mvuje* (asafoetida, an important and powerful local medicine), and *ubani* (frankincense) are used to cover the smell of childbirth blood and thus deter spirits.[9] 'Every occasion has its smell', Bi Fatuma, an old *mkunga* explained. 'The smell of weddings is *udi*, a scented incense [from the Arabian *oud*]; for funerals, you use *ubani*, frankincense. And for birth you use *mafusho* and *mvuje*, a herb that is *dawa kubwa*, strong medicine. So when you pass by a house, people can tell by the smell what is going on: "*nasikia harufo ya mtoto*, I'm smelling the scent of a baby"'. Some women also use protective amulets (*hirizi*) and black bracelets which contain a small pouch filled with *mvuje* for protection against spirit attacks, both on themselves and on their children. This practice is not shared by everybody, however; some consider it superstitious (*shirk*) or a matter of custom (*mila*) and thus un-Islamic.

A Leap of Faith

Mamu's example demonstrates both the dangers of childbirth and the many beliefs and practices used to manage uncertainty about a positive outcome. It shows how in the absence of reliable emergency and postnatal medical care, women draw upon a number of long-standing practices throughout pregnancy, birth, and the post-partum period in an effort to reduce the dangers of childbirth and strive for safe delivery. These practices are rooted in local understandings of the body, the agency of spirit and divine forces, and the knowledge of other women experienced in childbirth matters.

These beliefs are widely shared in Zanzibar, and discussions among those involved in Mamu's care reflect this sense of common understanding. They represent what Parkin has termed 'trust talk': talk about (and response to) an illness by the patient, healer(s), and members of the wider community, each 'speaking from established roles and cooperating in a common search for repatriation or remedy' (Parkin 2011: 12).

Especially the use of Islamic remedies and a strong belief in the effectiveness of prayer are shared and practised by all of my informants, rural and urban, poor and wealthy. Trust is first and foremost placed in the hands of God and in long-standing practices. In this sense, trust is a form of faith – or rather derives from faith, as the shared linguistic root of the Kiswahili terms for trust, faith, hope, and security suggests. Trust, as a leap of faith, requires a lack of transparency, of full information; rather than being based on complete knowledge of all relevant factors, trust relies on a basic confidence in the reliability of tried and tested practices and the divine power that underlies every action. Thus, 'paradoxically trust rests on, but also tries to surmount uncertainty' (Parkin 2011: 9).

While trust and confidence refer to expectations that can be frustrated, faith also implies an element of pragmatism based on the notion that one has to try to make the right choices and find the person or practice that is most trustworthy and thus likely to lead to a positive outcome. Zanzibari women, and their wider social network, try to establish a sense of security in the face of deep uncertainty by taking an active but pragmatic approach in pregnancy, according to their means. They try to eat a number of foods that are believed to increase the amount and quality of blood in the body;[10] pray and follow Islamic rules more closely; avoid provoking envy or anger; engage in exercise, which maintains the baby's health during pregnancy by circulating the blood, and after childbirth helps contract and tighten the body softened from pregnancy; and 'open the way' for the baby's birth through sexual intercourse close to the due date.[11] At the same time, they acknowledge that certainty and full control over their pregnancy cannot be achieved.

Additionally, those who can afford it consult specialists. These are not easily trusted, however. Rapidly increasing privatization and marketization of health services has exacerbated existing uncertainties about the quality of care and the ulterior motives of health-care professionals, both in the private and public sectors, and including non-biomedical healers and carers. Moreover, biomedical authorities, who are often socially distant from the patient, alienate the patient's experience and codify it into judgements of cause and effect (Parkin 2011: 13). 'Trust talk' here turns into 'alienable talk', where different viewpoints create contradictory suggestions and claims and may lead to accusations and counter-accusations (Parkin 2011: 12). Experts are thus carefully tested through hiding previous diagnoses in consultations, as the following case demonstrates.

Establishing Trust through Secrecy: Nassra

Mamu's younger sister Nassra was in her late twenties and newly wed when she fell pregnant. Like her sister, she does not belong to the rural poor; her family are urban traders and have worked their way up to a comfortable middle-class status. While financial resources were not unlimited, she could afford good quality food, as well as locally available private health care and medicines. But even under these nearly ideal circumstances, she was extremely anxious from the beginning of her pregnancy, a feeling that was exacerbated by her experience of Mamu's post-partum complications. Throughout her pregnancy her comments conveyed her heightened anxiety and uncertainty. Whenever asked how she felt about the baby, or whether she was looking forward to being a mother, she claimed: 'I don't care about the baby right now, only about my health. You never know if you are going to survive...' She avoided all information about the baby's development; she neither wanted to know about the foetus's size, nor hear its heartbeat. Instead, her focus was entirely on the changes her body went through and all the aches and pains she experienced. In order to alleviate some of her uncertainty and anxiety, Nassra took an active approach and, in addition to the widely shared and trusted practices, frequently consulted a number of different experts on pregnancy and childbirth.

Not surprising considering the high frequency of sexual intercourse especially in the first weeks of marriage, Nassra fell pregnant one month after her wedding. One day, she felt dizzy and went to a large private hospital, Al Rahma, to get checked for malaria. No malaria was found, but instead the doctor told her she was pregnant. 'I was shocked', she says. 'I didn't even cry, I was so afraid'. On the next day, she told her sister Mamu, who advised her not to tell anybody else, but took her to another private hospital, a mother-and-child clinic specialized in pregnancy care (the Mama na Mwana clinic), where she had an ultrasound, which cost

TSH 20,000. The pregnancy was normal, but she was diagnosed with cystitis and prescribed antibiotics. Before taking them, she went to a private pharmacy and pretended to buy the same antibiotics for a pregnant friend, to test if they were safe. The pharmacist informed her that the antibiotics she had received from the mother-and-child clinic were not safe during pregnancy, so she did not take them. Instead, she went to another doctor and asked about antibiotics during pregnancy. Here, she was prescribed a different antibiotic (amoxicillin), which, the doctor reassured her, was especially for pregnant women. He also gave her some general advice on personal hygiene (always wash from the front to the back when going to the toilet), diet (eat fruit and vegetables to increase your blood), and exercise (don't sit too much and don't bend your stomach). Several doctors, including one in Mnazi Mmoja, added the benefits of prayer to this general advice – the physical movements of standing up, bending over, and getting down on the knees would work to turn the baby around – which resonated well with a strong local belief in Islamic prayer as treatment for illness.

These were only the first of frequent and numerous visits to different health-care providers. On average, Nassra sought expert advice about two to three times per week, most of the time for a fee, for issues including headaches, constipation, nausea, backaches, worry about the baby kicking/not kicking, dizziness, fatigue, fast heartbeat, shortness of breath, heartburn, and general reassurance that everything was well. She consulted at least four different private clinics, besides registering with the government hospital antenatal clinic (ANC).

While the majority of women have to make do with whatever services they can access, those who can afford private health care tend to prefer this arrangement, especially when the pregnancy does not fulfil societal expectations. Women who get pregnant while their last child is younger than two years, for example, often complained of being scolded in the public ANC for not spacing their childbirths correctly. I have also witnessed moralizing questioning in the public hospital about the marital status of the mother and open contempt if she was unmarried, and a doctor voiced suspicions of adultery in the case of a woman who claimed she had only fallen pregnant seven years after getting married (which was a lie). Women therefore tend to keep secret any information they think may invite judgement and often recount their pregnancy history along socially acceptable lines. Many of my informants also used false names when registering with the hospital, not trusting hospital staff to treat their information confidentially and reflecting a general concern about keeping private information secret. This means that doctors often have a very limited understanding of the patient's medical and social history, as details that may be important for diagnosis are left out, including the use of other biomedical or traditional medicines, pre-existing conditions, or undesirable behaviours, such as earth-eating.[12] Yet, despite the moralizing and harsh treatment women often experience in the government health sector, it is considered important to register with the ANC in order to get a 'clean' maternity card so that delivery can take place in the hospital without problems.

Making Connections

The most important strategy in securing good quality care within the public health system is to connect with somebody who works in the hospital. In discussions about their interactions with the health-care system, women – and men – constantly emphasized how vital it is to have a relative or friend among the staff: 'You need to know somebody in the hospital, and also pay them a bit, then they look after you really well, *wanakushughulikia vizuri*, and they will let a family member visit you'. The need to know someone in the hospital to get good care is even more pronounced in the sister island Pemba, a stronghold of the political opposition, which has frequently been punished by the government for its oppositional politics through inducing shortages of medicines, water, electricity, and qualified personnel. In general, party politics play an important role in people's perceptions of hospital care in both islands: poor quality of care, lack of drugs, and harsh treatment by health-care providers are closely associated with the hospital as an extension of the ruling party. The mistrust of government health facilities goes as far as accusing health staff of deliberately mistreating patients and killing infants during birth through poor treatment or medical neglect. Many patients, especially those affiliated with the opposition party, thus consider it vital to have a relative or close friend among the health staff to look out for them while in the hospital.

Therefore, when it was time for Nassra's first ANC visit, Mamu took her on a visit to Dr Aisha's home, her own trusted maternity-ward nurse. Mamu had known Dr Aisha through connections via her extended family and had delivered her last children in her care. Mamu describes her as very capable (*hodari*), warm, and friendly. Mamu bases her judgement on her previous positive experiences with Dr Aisha but also on the fact that she is an older woman who has been working at the hospital for many years and – crucially – that she never asked for payment. Together with Dr Aisha's pious demeanour, this makes her a person of high morality and thus particularly trustworthy. While Dr Aisha indeed seems to be a caring and professional nurse, she also knows that Mamu's family will not be stingy; for her last delivery, Mamu gave her an envelope with TSH 20,000. Dr Aisha refused, which increased Mamu's trust in her, and she insisted that she accept the present. So we pay her a visit in her home, at first politely enquiring over her health, her little niece's progress, and about her other relatives, just like in a normal visit among friends. Only towards the end of our stay, Mamu mentions that Nassra is pregnant too and would like to come to the ANC. Dr Aisha sends us home with her private mobile phone number and instructions to arrive at the hospital early the next morning. When we get to the antenatal clinic on the following day, Nassra calls her on her mobile phone and Dr Aisha meets us outside, channels us through the crowded waiting room, bypasses the long queue, and makes sure Nassra is treated well and without delay. On every further visit with the ANC, Nassra follows this routine.

Secrecy: Testing and Trying

Despite all the different options for treatment, it is often difficult to get the care needed. For example, one night in her sixth month of pregnancy, Nassra was very sick, so her husband took her to the government referral hospital, Mnazi Mmoja, at 3 a.m. In Mnazi Mmoja they were told there were no doctors because it was a Sunday. So they went to the private Al Rahma hospital, where they found a doctor, of course for a fee. There she was told to have a blood test, but there were no needles. After a long odyssey, they managed to buy a needle and take some blood. She was diagnosed with mild malaria and prescribed an injection, the painkiller Panadol, Omeprazil, and a blood-building tonic. But Nassra did not trust the doctor's expertise enough to take the medicines. Instead, she called Dr Aisha, who advised her not to get the injection, but to use Fansidar, a different antimalarial, instead. Her husband tried everywhere, but this drug is only given out in the government hospital Mnazi Mmoja, where it has to be prescribed by a doctor. When she went to Mnazi Mmoja the next morning, there were still no doctors available because of a bank holiday, so instead she went to see Bi Nafisa, an old midwife who claims to be biomedically trained but also performs spirit rituals. She is widely known in Zanzibar as an experienced midwife and 'doctor' and impresses her patients by writing English words in their patient booklet and performing physical examinations, which combine biomedical procedures, such as measuring blood pressure and taking blood, and inspections of the eyes and tongue. A woman in the waiting area told me how she had tried to trick Bi Nafisa by simulating pain, but one glance at her face and tongue sufficed for her to uncover her fib. Nassra was ambivalent about

Bi Nafisa, as her expert reputation is tainted by her involvement with spirit healing, which many consider an un-Islamic cultural practice, thus making her morally ambiguous in Nassra's eyes. As with all consultations, Nassra did not tell Bi Nafisa of the test results from the hospital, but pretended to have come straight to Bi Nafisa, and only described her symptoms. Bi Nafisa measured her blood pressure and palpitated her abdomen, diagnosing that the baby was already in birth position. She prescribed multivitamin tablets, folic acid, vitamin B1, and Buscopan.

In addition to these formal and semiformal biomedical facilities, Nassra also consulted a number of 'traditional' and alternative pregnancy experts, despite the fact that she and her family tend to subscribe to a more essentialist version of Islam, where most traditional forms of diagnosis and treatment are regarded as un-Islamic, and she herself considers traditional healing largely as an expression of backward, superstitious rural belief. However, in her opinion, these practitioners are not necessarily less trustworthy than medical doctors – in her experience, the latter often also have questionable qualifications and hidden motivations. Thus, in her quest for some sense of security, she spread the net wider and tried out different routes.

In addition to herbalist treatments and a traditional midwife who took on her post-partum care, Nassra also decided to test a famous 'miracle healer' who is frequented by some of her relatives, particularly her brother's wife. He is known for his success in treating reproduction-related issues, such as infertility and childbirth problems, and his patients claim that he is a trained medical doctor who became proficient in herbal and spiritual treatment. Indeed, he uses biomedical terminology and drawings that resemble anatomical renderings of body parts in his diagnoses and prescriptions, although these do not hold up to medical scrutiny. Nassra was suspicious of 'miracle healers', whom she regards as quacks of questionable moral disposition, but nevertheless decided to test his skills, because she trusts her relatives who swear by the effectiveness of his treatments. As a first trial, she therefore asked him about the position of her baby (which had presented in breech position on the ultrasound a couple of days earlier) and about the due date. 'That way I will know if he has any knowledge', she explained. We arrived at his practice late in the evening. A large billboard on the gate reads 'Dr Haji Ali Haji, miracle doctor and herbalist, cures every disease'. His large, tiled, up-market house and the number of patients waiting outside the treatment room speak of his commercial success.

When Nassra and I entered the treatment room she sat down on the floor and asked her questions. He told her to undress her upper body and diagnosed by pressing on her belly. 'The baby is in breech', he stated, and showed her some exercises to turn the baby around, making her sit on all fours and contract and relax her belly in a cat-like fashion. He also assembled some plant medicines from his shelves with instructions on how to use them, and Nassra left TSH 6,000 on a small stool on the way out, as instructed by other patients beforehand. Upon her return home she recounted her experience to her mother and sister, who are themselves doubtful of this 'miracle healer', and decided not to take the medicines, but to try out the exercise, because his diagnosis did match what she had been told in the hospital. Her subsequent consultations with Dr Haji followed a similar course, him pressing on her belly and feeling the baby, her asking questions. She remained suspicious of his skills because often his answers did not seem to resonate with her own experience, and she never used any of the medicines he gave her.

At home, finally, Nassra sought advice from older women in the family and relied heavily on praying and adhering to Islamic values. She was told to follow *dawa za kisunna*, (literally, 'sunna medicine'), such as eating seven pieces of date at daybreak, following the prophet's example (*sunna*). She was also put on the same treatment regime as her sister: *tende na maziwa* (a thick brownish milkshake with dates which seems to taste terrible) was prepared for her, as well as a brew of *mpambawake*, the powerful blood-increasing tree medicine, and she obediently followed these treatments.

Despite all her efforts in gaining some sense of control, however, Nassra's pregnancy ended in an emergency. About three weeks after my departure, Nassra noticed that her underwear was wet: 'I thought it was urine, I thought my bladder had burst!' She wore a sanitary pad and went to the shop. Out of shame she did not tell anybody at first, but when she went to the bathroom she saw that the pad was soaked, to the extent that water would flow out when wringing it. Scared, she told Mamu, who said, 'That's a sign of labour, you're ready to give birth!' Mamu called Dr Aisha who told her to come to the hospital for a check-up. Since Dr Aisha was away that day, Nassra saw a different doctor, who checked and scolded her for coming in too early. She was sent home with instructions only to come back when she was in pain and bleeding. So Nassra left, and for the next two weeks water kept leaking out. She said, 'I drank four bottles of water every day and rarely went to the loo! But I didn't feel any pain, and there was no bleeding'.

On the fifteenth day, Dr Aisha passed by the shop by chance and was shocked to find that she was still leaking water: 'You haven't had the baby yet?!' She prescribed a drug to help induce labour and told Mamu to take her to the hospital the next morning, after making sure she took the two pills.

Despite the medication, Nassra still did not go into labour. Since she had not felt the baby move since the morning, Dr Aisha told her to go to the hospital immediately. Once at the hospital, the gynaecologist shouted at Nassra because she had not come earlier. The doctor grabbed her belly and squeezed it hard, to check if the baby would move. She then asked Nassra where the heartbeat was, but Nassra was not sure and pointed first to one side then to another. The doctor shouted at her: 'Are you playing games here?' By now, the baby's heartbeat was very faint, and the doctor told her she needed an emergency caesarean section. Nassra was very scared, and declined at first, pleading with the doctor: 'Let me try, I can do it!' She says, 'I was really thinking: should I stay or should I run away? I went to the loo, and was already halfway outside the hospital'. Only Dr Aisha's calm and patient explanation of the process helped convince her: 'First you wear this green gown here. Then you go into the operating theatre, and you sit down on the table. Don't be scared of the machine, they're not going to use it. Now sit forward, and they will give you an injection in your back, so you won't feel anything'. She finally agreed to have the caesarean section, and both she and the baby were fine. But without Dr Aisha's chance visit, and her patient and friendly care, Nassra would not have gone back to the hospital, and her baby would likely not have survived.

Nassra's story shows women's use of secrecy and 'trying out' in their attempts to gain more confidence and thus security when navigating the terrain of different public and private, formal and informal health facilities and providers. At each visit, she took care to hide diagnoses and treatments she had received from other specialists, reflecting both women's distrust of the various health-care options and their active endeavour to gain more confidence and security. At the same time, their deliberate creation of uncertainty through obscuring of certain symptoms, previous diagnoses, and treatments means that the consulted health providers never gained a full picture of their condition, which in turn could make present diagnoses less informed and diminish the chances for a successful outcome.

Nassra's case also shows the cost of such treatment. Her sister summed up the dilemma that patients face when she discussed their visit at the old private midwife: 'Bi Nafisa is very knowledgeable (*hodari sana*), but now she has started to take money: before you just gave her something small, now she charges TSH 8,500 for the first visit, and 7,000 for the next ones. The medicine comes on top of that and has to be bought in the pharmacy'. This expense not only raises suspicions about the midwife's intentions, but also adds to the range of treatments Nassra had pursued in the last weeks, which included payments for each consultation, prescriptions, blood tests, and ultrasound examinations. This commodification of health care has led to a general loss of trust in the health professions, and patients constantly suspect ulterior motives in their interactions with doctors of any kind. It has also led to a further deterioration of the quality of public health care, since many doctors have started their own practices, where they spend much of their time and energy (Beckmann 2010). As Mamu succinctly states: 'The doctors get such a small salary that they don't spend any energy at the public hospital, they don't "care" [*hawajali*] for the patients. They spend all their time at the private hospital, where they make money – how are they going to have energy for the public hospital? When are they going to rest?'

Secrecy and Morality in Uncertain Times

The introduction of business interests into health care, and the close entanglements of biomedical institutions with politics, have given rise to rumours about deliberate neglect of patients or even the killing of babies in the hospital. A woman who had a stillbirth and was hospitalized for one week recounted to a scandalized audience of neighbours and relatives: 'Many babies die in the hospital. When I was in Mnazi Mmoja, about twelve babies died. And many babies are killed by the doctors, so that the mother can survive. They get an injection in the head! When the mother is in a bad state, they tell her: "We have to kill your baby so that you survive". The doctors here are negligent [*wazembe*]; they don't care'.

These rumours reflect broader concerns about loss of control and a general lack of trust in a world with new and increasingly uncontrollable dangers. When asking about the reasons of a woman's high blood pressure and stillbirth, for example, her relative explains: 'These days the food we eat is bad, it has many chemicals [*vyakula vina chemicals nyingi*]. In the old times, plants were grown over many months, but today they are rushed [*kuharakishwa*] with the help of chemicals. This led to many new diseases. Diabetes [*sukari*], for example, used to be a rich people's disease [*maradhi ya tajiri*], but today even children and poor people get it; the same with hypertension [*presha*], even young people get it'. These reflections resonate with concerns over extensive social, economic, and political transformations over the past decades, which are frequently portrayed in terms of moral and cultural decline. Rapid immigration and expansion of tourism, neo-liberal reforms and increasing marketization of basic services, the spread of modern media and communication technologies, and economic decline have led to a profound sense of uncertainty both about individuals' and families' prospects, and about the continuity of Zanzibari society as a whole (Beckmann 2009). Life has become harsher, ruled by politics and profits, rather than by moral values of kindness, modesty, and restraint, people often complain.

In such difficult times, trust is hard to establish and in some respects has become a drawback: where success in life has become connected to savvy and ruthlessness, trusting others has acquired a whiff of gullibility and backwardness. This is especially the case when dealing with the institutions and agents of power, be they connected to the state or to the powers of the market. People have learned from experience that these socially distant forces are unreliable and largely beyond individuals' control and have little faith in their workings. Trust is therefore primarily invested in those who are socially close, and the establishment of personal ties with people within institutions of power, such as the hospital, reflects this notion. My informants' encounters with socially more distant health-care institutions and practitioners were characterized by scepticism and warranted a careful routine of testing and evaluating, which was achieved through handling the encounters with secrecy.

Parkin (2011) analyses the relationships between patients and healers, which have been captured in medical anthropology in a number of ways, from 'encounter' to 'negotiation'. An encounter usually implies a hierarchical relationship, in which the patient is subordinate and submits to the healer's diagnosis and recommended course for treatment, while negotiation leaves scope for questioning the healer's opinion. 'Negotiation and unquestioned acceptance', Parkin points out, are 'best seen as points on a possible continuum [...] and as overlapping tendencies [...] rather than as essential and fixed elements' (2011: 10).

The patients in my paper neither submit nor negotiate – they exercise agency by 'testing' different healers' capacities and intentions and carefully weighing the different diagnoses and treatments in their quest for security and a greater sense of control. This sense of control is achieved through establishing a measure of confidence as a basis for whom to trust. In a context of heightened uncertainty, such as a quest for trust – which is a social project, revolving around social interactions – is only possible through managing the encounters with secrecy: by approaching care providers with scepticism and testing the trustworthiness of their diagnoses and treatment recommendations through hiding knowledge acquired through previous consultations with other experts, my research participants constantly triangulate in their attempts to determine the most promising treatment course. Women's paths to safe motherhood are therefore shaped by a triangular interconnection: a condition of uncertainty over the best way to manage the dangers of childbirth leads them to search for trust (in the form of trustworthy advice), which they try to establish through secrecy by testing and trying different professional and lay recommendations. This secrecy, in turn, deliberately generates more uncertainty.

Issues of secrecy and mistrust characterize life in Zanzibar. Secrecy is a central value in Zanzibari society, and private, domestic matters must always be kept secret (*siri*). This reflects an Islamic concern with concealment of one's inner affairs, including matters concerning family life (and especially intergenerational disagreements or issues between husband and wife), as well as one's innermost feelings, desires, and aspirations. Feelings and conduct that violate the practice of social conformity in particular should not be disclosed, but should remain concealed at all times due to the fear of *aibu*, shame (Larsen 2008). Other people's ability to shame and insult a person depends on their knowing about the life and activities of the insulted and his or her family. Thus, to have *siri* (secret) is considered prudent and sensible in order to maintain the family's honour (cf. Swartz 1991, for Mombasa).

Secrecy is considered an essential protective feature of good pregnancy care, and women usually try to hide their pregnancies from all but the closest relatives for as long as possible. Wide, loose-fitting garments help in concealing the growing belly, and women take pride in having been able to 'surprise' friends and neighbours with a newborn baby, while nobody had suspected a pregnancy. I have never heard the words 'I am pregnant' spoken by anyone; subtle clues are used to point those who need to know in the right direction. Unusually snappy and sharp behaviour, for example, is a widely used means to convey the message to the husband, and men are instructed in their premarital wedding instructions to look out for this behaviour as a sign of pregnancy.

Even quite mundane everyday or morally not contentious matters are often kept secret, and people make up stories about where they have been, what they have done, who they were with, or what they believe. In fact, skilful storytelling, joking, and pulling a person's leg are valued and admired and are an important means to teach others a lesson. As a result, there is a pervasive feeling that nobody can be trusted to tell the truth. Whenever I asked somebody, 'Who do you trust?' the answer was always the same: 'Nobody, except perhaps my father/mother' (usually not both). A long history of intelligence-gathering and reporting on neighbours and family members makes those close to or working for the government particularly suspicious in the islands, which have a long history of oppositional politics. Pervasive corruption both in and outside the health system and experience of bad quality of services have made people wary in their interactions with the health system and constantly doubt the diagnoses they are given. The truthfulness of a diagnosis is here assessed by judging the morality and intentions of the person, rather than merely his or her position or qualifications.

Contingency, Social Closeness, and the Creation of Confidence

Trust thus depends on who it is that gives the advice. In addition to consulting and 'testing' maternity-care professionals (both for their skills and their moral disposition and intentions), Nassra, for example, used every opportunity to ask those close to her for advice, on how to sleep (on your side), how to get up, what to eat, what to avoid, which movements to do, what exercises are best, which sexual positions to use, and so on. She consulted Bi Fatuma, the old woman who provides traditional post-partum care; her mother; her sisters; the widely respected, knowledgeable, and successful neighbour; and all the relatives who kept coming in. Whether or not she followed their advice largely depended on her assessment of the person's trustworthiness and knowledgeability. Advice coming from her husband, for example, was quickly discarded, since he clearly has no experience with childbirth. Her mother had given birth herself, but is not trusted too much, because she is old and somewhat backward in her belief in a number of un-Islamic traditional practices, while Mamu serves as her main confidant and is highly trusted due to her position of authority as an older sister who shared experiences of pregnancy, but also because of Mamu's piety and largely essentialist Islamic belief, which discards the majority of 'traditional' healing practices as mere custom (*mila*) or even superstition (*shirk*). Dr Aisha shares this strong Islamic belief, which is reflected in her behaviour and reputation as a pious, moral person. Combined with her medical qualification and experience, and her position as a socially close contact within the public hospital, these factors make her the most trusted medical expert involved in Nassra's care.

Ultimately, it is this connection with people, and the ability to weigh different, often contradictory advice from different individuals, institutions, and professions, which is the balancing act people in Zanzibar have to strike in navigating the health landscape. This social contingency, the relationships with and dependency on others, is often decisive in directing matters towards a positive outcome, as Nassra's experience of childbirth demonstrates. While contingency in its relational form necessarily implies uncertainty, a lack of control over the person upon whom one depends, Whyte and Siu (this volume) demonstrate its positive potential. The deliberate creation of contingency by forging links with those who may help improve security is an 'attempt to move an uncertain situation towards greater confidence' (Whyte & Siu this volume).

Zanzibari women's understanding that contingencies can have significant effects on outcomes at the same time increases and decreases their sense of security and confidence in the course of their pregnancies. Connections to strategically important persons within the health system are widely recognized as vital for good care and increases patients' confidence considerably; but those who do not succeed in making these connections know that their care will likely be poor.

At the same time, contingency upon others of course cannot guarantee success – particularly in a context where secrecy is highly valued and trust is elusive – but, in the face of uncontrollable forces, such as powerful state and market institutions, people turn to those who are close to them, whose intentions and motivations appear more easily knowable. Forging relationships with people inside the health system – trying to 'put a face' on abstract forces (Whyte & Siu this volume) – is one way to gain greater control over the highly uncertain and unpredictable process of reproduction and highlights an 'ethos of contingency', a 'disposition of hopeful 'you-never-know-keep-trying' (Whyte & Siu this volume).

Conclusion

Pregnancy and childbirth in Zanzibar is a dangerous endeavour. Strategies to control the risks include an active quest for care that can be trusted. In the private and family realm, trust derives from a firm faith in God and use of long-standing remedies. In the more socially distant, institutional encounter with professional health-care providers, trust is harder to establish and impeded by an increasing marketization of health and long-standing political interconnections.

While biomedicine's claims to effectiveness rest on the assumption that its remedies work directly on the body, regardless of belief or personal connection, patients know from experience that its practitioners are closely entangled with state and market forces, which are widely regarded as untrustworthy. They thus try to establish some sense of trust by building personal relationships and careful testing, drawing on practices of secrecy. Ultimately, personal connections are vital: contingency upon personal connections ensures survival, much more so than money and drugs.

Notes

1   Cf. Obermeyer 2000a for a critical discussion of this claim in Egypt.
2   The 1998 study seems to provide the most recent verified numbers (e.g., the Ministry of Health in Zanzibar keeps referring to this number and study). The 1996 and 2004 DHS did not have adequate statistical sample sizes for Zanzibar to conclude MMRs. However, there are some newer numbers cited in some WHO documents (MMR of 362 for Zanzibar according to the Country Cooperation Strategy brief of 2011), and a 2011 update on MDG goals 4, 5, and 6 issued by the Ministries of Health for Tanzania mainland and Zanzibar suggests that 'available data indicates a fall in the maternal mortality ratio in Zanzibar since 1998 and a dramatic decline between 2008 and 2009 from 422 to 279', based on 'data from intensive surveillance of maternal deaths at all health facilities'. The methodology for these data, however, is not comprehensively explained.
3   Zanzibar is a small island archipelago off the Tanzanian coast with a population of approximately one million people. The two main islands are small, and health facilities are in close reach compared to parts of the mainland.
4   Substantial fieldwork periods included an initial fifteen months stay from July 2004 to October 2005, and regular follow-up visits of varying lengths in July/August 2007, May to October 2008, December/January 2010, June to September 2011, and August/September 2012.
5   According to an epidemiological study in Zanzibar's referral hospital, Mnazi Mmoja, in 2007, of a sample of one hundred women, nine had pre-eclampsia (four mild–moderate; five severe), and two had eclampsia. The prevalence of eclampsia and severe pre-eclampsia in Zanzibar was thus forty and ten times higher, respectively, than in the UK, pointing to the comparatively low quality of antenatal care in Zanzibar (Tufton and Patel 2011: 69).
6   Not her real name. Dr Aisha is also not a medical doctor, but rather a nurse and midwife in the maternity ward.
7   For a more detailed discussion of traditional treatments for anaemia, see Young and Ali 2005.
8   Black pepper causes heat, but not of a blood-producing kind; its heat can be dangerous as it makes the blood leave the body. In women this can result in stronger menstrual bleeding, which is dangerous for the uterus (*ni hatari kwa mfuko wa uzazi*) and can make the woman feel dizzy (*kuona kizunguzungu*). Because of this blood-expelling effect of black pepper, it is consumed in large amounts after childbirth in order to purify the womb.
9   The baby and the baby's clothes are also fumigated thoroughly, and most babies have their forehead painted with *wanja* (kohl), an additional deterrent for spirits and witchcraft attacks.

10 Pregnancy is a time of heat (*joto*) and therefore all heat-inducing substances must be avoided until the time of childbirth, when heat helps with the progression of labour. Therefore, care is taken to avoid 'hot' foods such as pepper, honey, ginger, etc., during pregnancy.
11 During the earlier stages of pregnancy, sex is mainly regarded as important to keep the husband content and 'at home'.
12 Eating soil is described as a common craving among pregnant women and also regarded as a treatment for anaemia.

References

Beckmann, N. (2009) 'AIDS and the Power of God: Narratives of Decline and Coping Strategies in Zanzibar', in Becker, F. & P. W. Geissler (eds.) *AIDS and Religious Practice in Africa* (Leiden: Brill Publishers), pp. 119–54.
Beckmann, N. (2010) 'Markets for Health, Markets for Sickness: The Commodification of Misery', in Van Dijk, R. & M. Dekker (eds.) *Health and Healing in Africa: New Arenas and Emerging Markets* (Leiden: Brill Publishers), pp. 201–227.
Kavle, J. A., R. J. Stoltzfus, F. Witter, J. M. Tielsch, S. S. Khalfan & L. E. Caulfield (2008) 'Association between Anaemia during Pregnancy and Blood Loss at and after Delivery among Women with Vaginal Births in Pemba Island, Zanzibar, Tanzania', *Journal of Health, Population and Nutrition* 26 (2): 232–240.
Larsen, K. (2008) *Where Humans and Spirits Meet: The Politics of Rituals and Identified Spirits in Zanzibar* (Oxford & New York: Berghahn Books).
Lugalla, J. L. P. (1997) 'Economic Reforms and Health Conditions of the Urban Poor in Tanzania', *African Studies Quarterly* 1 (2): 19–37.
MoHSW (Ministry of Health and Social Welfare Zanzibar) (2006) Zanzibar Health Sector Reform Strategic Plan II 2006/07–2010/11 (Zanzibar: Revolutionary Government of Zanzibar).
NBS (National Bureau of Statistics) [Tanzania] (2000) Tanzania Demographic and Health Survey 1999 (Dar es Salaam, Tanzania: NBS and ICF Macro).
NBS (National Bureau of Statistics) [Tanzania] (2005) Tanzania Demographic and Health Survey 2004 (Dar es Salaam, Tanzania: NBS and ICF Macro).
NBS (National Bureau of Statistics) [Tanzania] (2011) Tanzania Demographic and Health Survey 2010 (Dar es Salaam, Tanzania: NBS and ICF Macro).
Obermeyer, C. M. (2000a) 'Risk, Uncertainty, and Agency: Culture and Safe Motherhood in Morocco', *Medical Anthropology* 19 (2), 173–201.
Obermeyer, C. M. (2000b) 'Pluralism and pragmatism: knowledge and practice of birth in Morocco', *Medical Anthropology Quarterly* 14 (2): 180–201.
Parkin, D. (2011) 'Trust Talk and Alienable Talk in Healing: A Problem of Medical Diversity', MMG Working Paper 11-11 (Göttingen: Max Planck Institut zur Erforschung Mulitreligiöser und Multiethnischer Gesellschaften).
Putzel, J. & S. Lindemann (2008) Tanzania: An Analytical Narrative of State Resilience (Crisis States Research Centre, London School of Economics).
Roth Allen, D. (2002) *Managing Motherhood, Managing Risk: Fertility and Danger in West Central Tanzania* (Michigan: University of Michigan Press).
Swartz, M. (1991) *The Way the World Is: Cultural Processes and Social Relations among the Mombasa Swahili* (Berkeley: University of California Press).

Tufton, N. & R. R. Patel (2011) 'Prevalence of Hypertensive Disorders in a Prenatal Clinic in Zanzibar', *International Journal of Gynaecology and Obstetrics* 112 (1): 69–70.
Young, S. L. & S. M. Ali (2005) 'Linking Traditional Treatments of Maternal Anaemia to Iron Supplement Use: An Ethnographic Case Study from Pemba Island, Zanzibar', *Maternal and Child Nutrition* 1: 51–58.

Food Security, Conjugal Conflict, and Uncertainty in 'Bangladesh', Mombasa, Kenya

Adam Gilbertson

Introduction

In Kenya, informal settlements or 'slums'[1] are urban residential spaces characterized by poverty, high population density, lack of infrastructure, substandard housing, tenuous land rights, and high rates of HIV/AIDS and other infectious diseases. Often, these areas exist as the '...physical and spatial manifestation of urban poverty and intra-city inequality' (UN-HABITAT 2003: xxvi). In these environments, households are important units for food security as they are the loci where decisions about employment, income, expenditure, and resource distribution are negotiated and where food storage, preparation, and consumption take place. According to the Food and Agriculture Organization of the United Nations (FAO), food security is defined as existing '...when all people, at all times, have physical, social, and economic access to sufficient, safe, and nutritious food which meets their dietary needs and food preferences for an active and healthy life' (FAO 1996, 2003). Although the proportion of residents in Kenyan informal settlements who are food insecure is unknown, previous research from Nairobi suggests that many (if not most) residents struggle daily with problems related to food (see APHRC 2002, 2002a; Amuyunzu-Nyamongo & Taffa 2004: 6; and Amuyunzu-Nyamongo et al. 2007).

Within informal settlements, most of what is eaten must be purchased (APHRC 2002; Gulis et al. 2004) at small kiosks, shops, cafés, or larger marketplaces. For the residents of one of Mombasa's most populous informal settlements, 'Bangladesh', or 'Bangla', experiences of household food insecurity are related to failures of entitlement (Sen 1981), which mean people regularly lack the money needed to purchase food from these venues. The inability to access sufficient food on a daily basis means that entire households, or certain household members, may be forced to eat less (or less-preferred) food, skip meals, or go for whole days without eating. Seeking commonalities in experiences of food insecurity across cultures, Coates et al. (2006: 1442S–45S) identify four 'universal', 'core' domains of experience. These are 'uncertainty and worry about food', 'inadequate food quality', 'insufficient food quantity', and 'concerns about social unacceptability of food'. Although consideration of each of these domains is essential to understanding food insecurity as a lived experience, the first, and probably the most common indicator of food insecurity, that of uncertainty and worry related to food, is the focus of this chapter.[2]

To begin, I offer a brief introduction to my research methods and field site and present households as units for food security research in terms of membership and headship, power relations, economics, and gendered divisions of labour related to food. Next, I consider and describe the most common type of conjugal relationship within Bangla. Following this, I introduce experiences of food insecurity, uncertainty, and conflict in this informal settlement before considering the importance of food to the negotiation of power within conjugal households. Thereafter, I address how experiences of food insecurity and uncertainty contribute to the instability of household units. Finally, I offer a brief conclusion and discussion of my findings.

Appadurai's (1981: 501) work from south India depicts food as 'both the medium and the message' of conflict and power within households, and Nichter (1981) similarly considers food as an 'idiom of distress'. My findings also support the notion that food and eating represent emotionally powerful expressions within conjugal relationships in Bangladesh, Mombasa. However, I contend that within an informal settlement, where many households are chronically food insecure, the threat of hunger draws greater attention to food in the household, deepening its significance in negotiations of power and as a medium of expression. Furthermore, I argue that in addition to the stress and worry which accompany experiences of food insecurity, problems with food contribute to a sense of domestic uncertainty and to the instability of household units by causing interpersonal conflict and by inspiring spouses to call into question their partners' fidelity.

Field Site and Methods

Bangladesh, Mombasa, is located on the mainland west of Mombasa Island in Changamwe, along the Nairobi-Mombasa (A109) road. The area surrounding this settlement is known as Mombasa's industrial zone, and there are factories, refineries, and processing plants which stand as testament to this distinction. Although local unemployment rates are high, many of those who are fortunate enough to find employment in these factories as unskilled labourers, mechanics, seamstresses, or security guards live in Bangla. The population of this informal settlement is estimated to be 10,000 to 15,000 residents.[3] The density of population varies across the settlement: some spaces are open and easy to navigate, whilst in other areas, houses and other structures are built so closely together that they resemble a maze of endless corridors, doorways, blind corners, and dead-ends. Here, there is very little privacy and neighbours see or hear most of what goes on within households.

To an outsider, what is most striking about Bangla is the diversity of its landscape. The juxtaposition of cramped living, abrupt edges, decay, rust, and refuse alongside open spaces, rolling hills, sea vistas, green *mashamba* (gardens; singular: *shamba*), and the flowing contours of red clay paths set this informal settlement apart from those found in Nairobi. The amount of open land available for building or for *mashamba*, and access to resources such as clean water and electricity, vary across the settlement. Whilst households located near the central market tend to have access to electricity, those located in the periphery do not. Against this backdrop, vulnerability to flooding, erosion, 'land grabbing' and eviction, crime, and violence are also unequally distributed.

Bangla's residents claim various ethnic group affiliations, including Giriama, Kamba, Kikuyu, Kisii, Luhya, and Taita. However, the majority of residents are Luo economic migrants (or the progeny of migrants) who came to Mombasa from western Kenya. The most commonly spoken languages are Kiswahili and Dholuo (the Luo language), as well as other native languages and English.

Between July 2009 and December 2010, I spent approximately fifteen months conducting my doctoral fieldwork in this informal settlement. The methods I utilized included participant observation, semi-structured interviews, focus group discussions (FGDs), and questionnaires which included formal measures of food insecurity, such as the Household Food Insecurity Access Scale (see Coates et al. 2007). In total, 109 interviews and three FGDs were conducted with men and women identified through 'snowball' or convenience sampling. Twenty-eight households completed questionnaires. I utilized translators for interviews not conducted in English (that is, Kiswahili or Dholuo). Informed consent was obtained from all participants and interviews were recorded and transcribed. All qualitative data were translated as necessary and coded for post-fieldwork analysis.

Households and Headship

The collectives of individuals who live together and constitute a 'household' are often locally synonymous with *familia* (family), but this is not always the case since some households are united by factors other than kinship, including friendship and/or financial hardship (for example, the inability to afford rent alone). In Bangla, there is no single household form; instead, households are heterogeneous units whose memberships may shift with necessity and changing conditions over time. In addition to co-residence, households are recognized as distinct units through a second marker of domesticity: eating together from food usually cooked on the same *jiko* (a wood-, charcoal-, or paraffin-burning stove).

Heads of households are expected to ensure the food security and general well-being of household members. In conjugal households, the recognized head is almost always the husband, although under certain conditions (for example, if a husband is incapacitated), a wife or another member may fill this role. In such situations, whether or not the wife would be recognized as head (as opposed to operating as a de facto head) was a matter of contention among my interviewees. Household heads expect to have the most *sauti* (voice) in household affairs and to be the ones who make important decisions. Examples of these types of decisions include those relating to food expenditure, household upkeep and security, education, employment, family planning, and where and how a household lives. Although dynamics vary among different domestic arrangements, in male-headed households it is not unusual for husbands to consult with their wives before making a final decision.

Most of the men and women I interviewed considered male headship and female subordination 'natural' and aligned with 'traditional' and 'African' expectations of gender roles within families, as well as those set out by the Bible or Qur'an. Intra-household gender-based inequality is therefore common, but power relations are complicated, and norms do not go unchallenged. Whilst husbands usually wield the most influence, power is also held to varying degrees by wives and others, especially by those who contribute income. In this way, power is negotiated and held in tension among household members. Women in male-dominated households tend to be aware of their influence and are skilled in its application. This finding agrees with critiques outlined by Guyer (1981) regarding the use of the 'household' in research in Africa and Silberschmidt's point (1999: 8) made with reference to the Kisii that, '…stereotypes of male domination and female subordination can be misleading'.

Power, as it relates to household headship, was defined by my interviewees primarily as *mamlaka* (authority) and *uwezo* (ability). *Mamlaka*, like headship, exists only in relation to other people and is closely associated with a man's role in the household, his ownership of the house and its contents, and his ability to provide for his family. Indeed, my interviewees' explanations for whether or not a woman could have *mamlaka* were inconsistent. Some insisted that *mamlaka* is a husband's domain; others agreed that wives have *mamlaka* in relation to their children but not to their husband, or that *mamlaka* is something that husbands can give their wives. Nevertheless, some women promptly cited examples of households, such as that of Mama Rukiya, where the wife is the breadwinner and (de facto) household head. Mama Rukiya ran a profitable food kiosk, which, in addition to income for her family, provided breakfast and lunch for her eldest son Elijah and his brothers, whilst her husband, Boniface, was inconsistently employed. Citing similar examples, some interviewees explained that when a wife is the provider, she is the one with the most *mamlaka* in the house. According to my key informant and married father of four, Barnabas, 'definitely she can be having *mamlaka* because you have to respect that, the duties she's doing. So if you reduce her as nothing, she can run away, and you'll be in problem'.

For both men and women, being 'listened to' or 'heard' by spouses and others in the household (for example, children and relatives) is a key component of *mamlaka*. For most married women, this means that their husbands consult with them, take their advice, include them in discussions, and let them make certain decisions. For men, at least in the privacy of our interviews, this issue was more about respect and an idealized sense of absolute control: that his decisions are adhered to and not questioned or undermined. Some men also referenced education and knowledge or 'wisdom' as components of *mamlaka*.

Uwezo is a component of household power which is understood in relation to an act, as in the ability to do 'X' with respect to the household; for example, '*uwezo wa kuamua*' (the ability to decide). *Uwezo* most often emerged in my fieldwork as a reference to having money in order to provide for the needs of the household and, secondarily, to the most common ways people acquire money: through employment or small businesses. The ability to provide for a household – paying for rent, clothing, school fees, and especially for food – is an essential characteristic of household authority. Thus, the concept of *uwezo* is connected to relations of dependency which underpin the concept of *mamlaka*. Semantically linked, *mamlaka* and *uwezo* are nearly interchangeable in certain contexts. Robert, a married man whose wife and children lived in western Kenya, told me: 'If you are somebody who cannot produce even food, it means *huna uwezo kupata chakula* [you do not have the ability to get food]; nobody will know that this man is our father. Even children, they will not identify you as their father, because you have no *uwezo*'.

Although my informants consistently made clear that 'ability' cannot be separated from *pesa* (money), and that 'you can be the decision maker because you've got resources', men and women also supported the notion that authority is innately masculine and that men may have *mamlaka* without having *uwezo*. By this they meant that a husband may have the authority or right to do something, although he is without the means to accomplish it. Such an understanding suggests that *mamlaka* is inherent to the social identity of adult males as fathers and husbands. These views, however, were not universal among my interviewees, with as many others arguing that a man who cannot provide, who does not have the financial 'upper hand' over a wife, will have his authority and influence reduced (if not usurped entirely) in the household. As Barnabas put it, '…the power which we are talking about in the relations between you and your wife depends on how much money you have'. Similarly, Robert told me: 'To have power [*mamlaka*]…I must be able to manage, or to feed those my people. That is when I will have that power. I can't have power just talking, bragging.… I'm the head of the family but I can't feed them?' According to Moses, a divorced and recently arrived migrant, '…it is just in terms of money, if you are not financially capable, then you don't have to make most of the decisions because decision-making nowadays depends on what you have in your pockets; that is when you will be heard'.

In general, despite the traditional cultural norms of (respective) gender expectations which support male dominance and authority in the household, as a woman's contribution to household income increases, so does her relative influence (see Oppong 1970; also Hartmann 1981). Whilst some men are grateful for their wives' financial contributions, others see this threat to their authority as unacceptable, with some employed men going as far as to refuse to allow their wives to work. Husbands who are unemployed (and hungry) may have less say in the matter. Silberschmidt (1999: 7) argues that the failure of men to fulfil socio-cultural expectations to provide, which in large part constitute their '…social value, identity, and sense of self-esteem', threatens their authority and in some cases reduces their role in the household to that of 'figureheads'. Such conclusions are consistent with my findings, especially concerning *mamlaka* and *uwezo*, where it is not only a man's lack of ability to provide, but his wife's ability to do so, her *uwezo*, which is problematic. According to Barnabas:

> ...men are expected to be the most authoritative people in the families, or having more *uwezo* and *mamlaka*. But with modern civilization, I think, things are changing because now the money factor is influencing everything. If you slap even a woman she can jail you for the rest of your life, when she has got money. So your powers as a man, or your physique, you have to put it in your pocket and humble yourself.

Echoing these sentiments, Robert told me:

> If a wife, if [...] she is earning better than you, is when she can aggravate everything and challenge you, that *shilingi* [Kenyan shillings]. Because she'll ask you about any money you failed to produce... that cash. And if she has got that cash, then even the children will know that *mama* is the head of the house now. Our father is dormant nowadays'.

Difficulties for husbands may be exacerbated if local economic environments favour women and the modes of production more readily accessible to them. Changing social, political, and economic conditions which have brought (or forced) increasing numbers of women into the role of breadwinner have been described by Silberschmidt (1999, 2001) and Prince and Geissler (2010) in western Kenya and by Boonzaier (2005) and Strebel et al. (2006) in South Africa. In Bangla, many female interviewees found work more easily than their husbands because the jobs and enterprises in which they were prepared to engage (for example, washing clothes or plaiting hair) were more available, were better supported by local market demand, and required little start-up capital and expertise.

In addition to *mamlaka* and *uwezo*, some interviewees noted the importance of *nguvu* (strength) to defining power within households. In Bangla, it is common for husbands to threaten their wives (and to follow through) with beatings, usually in the form of slaps or kicks, in order to ensure their orders are followed or to 'correct' their wives' behaviours. Thus, the role of men's strength, physical size, and their history of (and tendency towards) violence in the household, and the intimidation this combination inspires, must also be considered in terms of how power is negotiated. In general, men tend to have the advantage over their wives in terms of physical strength, and women in Bangla tend to be the more consistently and severely abused partners in domestic relationships. However, it would be misleading to portray women as only victims of violence since wives sometimes physically abuse their husbands. For example, Lester, an economic migrant from Nairobi who had lived in the area for two decades, admitted that his wife, Darla, who had recently forced him to move out of their house, had attacked him multiple times over the years. These abuses included biting, stabbing him with a knife, and clubbing him over the head (and knocking him unconscious) with an empty Guinness bottle.

Marital Relationships: 'Come-We-Stay'

Whether monogamous or polygamous, the marriages which form the basis of conjugal households are rarely united through formal weddings since traditional marriages in Kenya represent the culmination of long courses of interfamily negotiation and exchange (Fredericksen 2000). Such procedures and formalities are often beyond the financial means of residents and are usually unmanageable otherwise, especially for migrants whose marital negotiators (parents and/or other elders) live in western Kenya. More often, men and women become informally 'married' when they begin living and sleeping together. In so doing, both partners come to accept certain marital obligations and expectations.[4] For men, these include providing for the material needs of the household, especially in terms of rent and food; for women, expectations include that she will cook, clean, care for the children, and be available, sexually, to the man.

Referred to as 'come-we-stay' relationships, these unions are not officially recognized, and couples are not afforded the same legal rights as those in formal marriages.[5] Locally, however, these relationships are readily recognized: soon after commencing to live together, friends and neighbours will refer to the couple as *mke* (wife) and *mume* (husband). This is despite the fact that their respective families may regard these marriages unfavourably, or may see them as illegitimate, especially if no bride price has been paid. Without the exchange of bride wealth, neither spouse's family may be particularly invested in the relationship. As a result, partners in come-we-stay relationships may be less committed than those in marriages united by traditional practices and exchanges. These unions therefore tend to be prone to sudden dissolution and the threat of one's *mke* or *mume* 'running away' is a common concern. Describing the social precariousness of these relationships with reference to the couple's respective obligations as husband and wife, one male participant insisted that '...it is like they are living on a contract basis or a basis whereby you can part way[s] anytime. You can get divorced anytime'.

Whilst some authors emphasize economic necessity and a lack of alternative options as the primary reasons for the prevalence of come-we-stay unions, reducing them to 'survival tactics' (Mweru 2008: 340; see also Preston-Whyte et al. 2000) utilized by women to garner financial support from men, others seek a more balanced explanation. Referencing the predilection of youths to seek out these unions, Fredericksen (2000: 216) states: 'Young Kenyans' reasons for entering into such unions were no different from those of young Danes or Americans in the same situation: a combination of love, sympathy and convenience...'. Although some women (and men) seek out these unions for financial benefit or convenience, most relationships which may appear to be based on material pragmatism are often more complicated and mean much more to those within these relationships.

Household Food Security, Uncertainty, and Hunger

In Bangla, household food security is understood to exist when every member has 'enough' acceptable, if not preferred, food to eat each day without the worry of how or from where this food will be acquired. Describing what it means to have enough food, Barnabas referenced the related concepts of quantity and *kushiba* (to be satisfied), which he described as 'to eat until now you don't want any more'. To this he added that having enough is 'to eat and everyone gets satisfied; not you eat the portion that you are given. You eat the way you want. Yeah, that is enough food'. Making clear how food security is always dependent on the *uwezo* of the provider(s), Moses told me:

> ...enough food is eating what you want to eat at any particular time and having it to your satisfaction. That is what I understand by having enough food. You eat what you want to eat. Okay, for example, if I now feel that I should eat meat and I'm capable of going for that meat, then that one is enough food. If I feel that I should eat a quarter of a kilogram and I can afford that quarter of a kilogram and eat it, then that is enough food for me.

Daily access to 'enough' food therefore depends mainly on the ability to purchase it. Due to the vagaries of climate, especially rainfall, this remains true even for the minority of residents, including Barnabas, who own *mashamba* and are able to grow some of their own food. When I discussed experiences of food insecurity (that is, not having enough food) with interviewees, conversations always turned to a lack of money. For instance, Nialla, an HIV-positive married mother and *chang'aa* brewer,[6] told me, *'Pesa ni kila kitu* [money is everything]... If you want to have anything in the house, you have to have money'. Isaac, a married father, local businessman, and landlord, likewise offered that '[i]n the slum, money is all that matters', whilst Barnabas explained: '...the day you miss to get something [money], you just go hungry. Most people in Bangladesh are just hand-to-mouth'.

Experiences of uncertainty, expressed as *wasiwasi* (worry) or sometimes *hofu* (fear), concerning whether or not there will be enough food at home, were common among my research participants. This sense of uncertainty was closely associated with the economic realities of life in an informal settlement. These include widespread poverty and unemployment; the high price of rent, school fees, and health care; the difficulties of saving money; dependency on a partner's income; and the regular failure of small businesses, such as pulling *mikokoteni* (carts for transporting goods; singular: *mkokoteni*) or selling fruits and vegetables to produce profits. For example, Robert, who relied on *kibarua* (casual labour) to earn a living – work which is notoriously unreliable – told me, 'If I wake up in the morning, even before I sleep, I start worrying, what will I eat tomorrow. [...] Where will I get money...to buy food?'

Anxieties concerning food insufficiency are well founded since the members (including children) of households which cannot access enough food may have no other choice but to eat less (or nothing) and go to bed hungry. Highlighting feelings of uncertainty and unhappiness in his account of the impacts of food insecurity, Moses offered:

> When there is not enough food, there is just fear of hunger because you know, okay, if you've got little *unga*,[7] I just know if I cook this one lunchtime, and maybe if I get a little for supper, then tomorrow I may not have something. And if you are somebody who is not employed, like myself [...] so that one can just, okay... If I have a little *unga* that is not enough until tomorrow, then I must be upset.

Describing experiences of *njaa* (hunger) and emphasizing the attention it demands, and the pain and sense of powerlessness it may instil, Barnabas's wife, Diana, told me:

Njaa...we can say it is a pain. [...] It is a painful thing which comes [...] the cause is because of lack of food. And *njaa*, it is a very bad thing which you cannot control. [...] ...it is a painful thing which you cannot resist and you cannot control it without having food. I think that is *njaa*. Yeah. [...] [When someone has *njaa*]...he can think where to get food, but nothing else.

Experiences of food insecurity, especially those involving the pain of *njaa* (or even just the threat of hunger), tend to inspire or to exacerbate conflict between husbands and wives (and other household members). Explaining what happens when households lack food, Robert offered: 'If there is no food in the family, there is a lot of *kelele* [noise; uproar] and fighting. Even children and women are so harsh, you can't.... Lack of food causes a lot of chaos in the house. Because even a woman, you cannot ask her anything; she'll answer you very rudely. If you have got nothing to give her to buy food, she'll be very rude...if she is hungry'.

For Diana, the potential for food insecurity to contribute to experiences of physical, verbal, and emotional abuse was a deeply personal and disturbing subject. In one of our interviews, she offered the following from her own experience:

Because if there's no food...like me and Barnabas [...] ...if you don't have anything to eat in the house, maybe Barnabas doesn't have money or...if he doesn't have money anyway, so [he] is *yaani* [that is], is looking for flimsy excuse so he can enter the place he want, maybe start quarrelling a lot, *yaani*, talking a lot without any sense of if somebody can see that thing. It doesn't have meaning of quarrel. So it brings a lot of problem, even the children are crying, there is no peace. Like this Mosi [her two-year-old son], he don't know to put the hunger, to stay with *njaa*. He can't know if, if he doesn't have food. He just want food. 'Food, I want *ugali*, I want *ugali*, I want *uji* [porridge]'. He don't know if it is not there. So it cause problem.

Diana explained how hunger puts her and Barnabas into undesirable moods which, for Barnabas, might be expressed through beating their children, causing Diana further suffering:

Even children. If they [have] done a small mistake, maybe like Rachel [her eldest daughter], they like to swing, they tie rope on the trees, then they swing, we call it *bembea* in Swahili. So if the father found that thing done, he can tell them, 'Lie down, everyone five cane crooks. Five canes'. Yeah. He beat them surely until he feel 'yeah, I'm fed up' [until he has had enough].

Speaking more generally, yet likely continuing to base her comments on her own experience, Diana again highlighted the effects of hunger on husbands and how it causes them to become angry very quickly, making them more likely to become abusive:

> If there is no food, first of all, you can't have peace in your house. There is no peace. Because if...even somebody like your husband has found a spoon there, [on] the floor [in the dirt and out of place] [...]. He can start beating you that far because he's hungry, he don't have money, he can beat you very bad.

Although he did not reference his own behaviour or that of his wife at home, Barnabas agreed that food insecurity can lead to physical insecurity and abuse among those who are suffering from hunger. At first telling me, 'Hunger and anger, these things are inseparable' and that 'hunger will give birth [to] anger...naturally, whether you like it or not', Barnabas subsequently provided a more elaborate description of domestic insecurity and hunger which identified uncertainty and violence as key components of these experiences. He said:

> Eh, people are very cruel and there's no happiness. And anything can happen. There are people who you hear are cutting somebody with *panga* [machete] on a very flimsy issue. [...] ...you know, the wife may say 'Don't play with an angry dog'. These aren't even...to human beings *bwana* [mister]. They don't want any joke. Yeah, it's raising anger very fast; a very small thing, you just want to put violence on somebody.

Food and Power within Conjugal Households

In conjugal households, partners must work together and coordinate their efforts in order to make ends meet and feed their families. Providing, cooking, and sharing food as meals are activities which are necessary to ensuring that everyone receives enough food to eat every day. Whilst morning and afternoon meals may be eaten together, separately, or skipped entirely, depending on the practicalities of employment and whether or not food is available, evening meals are more important and mark a time for all household members to come together. As Barnabas explained, uniting for evening meals offers 'a way for a man to keep his family together'. More than for other meals, wives expect their husbands to provide them with food for dinner; in return, husbands expect their wives to cook what they provide 'well' and 'on time' – that is, to the husband's liking and promptly after his arrival home in the evening.

According to Mama Rukiya, if a man brings home food which his wife does not cook well, the man will start quarrelling with her and feel that he has wasted his money because the food is '*chafu*' (dirty) or burnt. As an example, she offered that a man will not be happy if he brings home half a kilogram of meat but his wife cooks it with too much water. Or perhaps the *ugali* is not cooked long enough and is '*mbichi*' (raw), so it cannot be eaten.[8] In agreement, Ezekiel, a father of three, offered: 'Yeah, good food brings respect and it shows love in the family because when my wife is not able to cook on time, when she's not able to cook what I need, then that love won't be there'. For Lydia, an HIV-positive woman in an HIV-discordant relationship, the importance of looking after a husband in this way was clear: '...if you want to influence him, as in to keep him in the house, then you have to take good care of him stomach-wise and cleanliness'.

Therefore, whilst providing food, cooking, and sharing meals are important to household food security, unity, and collective well-being, these acts are also closely related to the negotiation of power within marriages (see also Ellis 1983; Murcott 1986; Charles & Kerr 1988; Counihan & Kaplan 2004; and DeVault 2008). As Diana explained, '...maybe husband, he's the one who giving money to that household. Maybe he is giving you money every day. He's the one maybe that say, "I want this food today to be cooked like this. Maybe I want rice and chicken, yeah, to be cooked the dry fry. And maybe *ugali*". So that is now *mamlaka* between the way he will give you to follow and the money he give you'. Making a similar case for cooking as a way wives may gain *mamlaka*, Ezekiel offered:

> ...timely cooking, good cooking, I'll be punctual in my house. And she'll have some authority of questioning me, 'Today why are you late? Your food is getting cold, today you have come back early, why? You know I cook your time...at such times', these things. I will also invite my friends to come and taste what my wife is cooking. If they leave my house happy, my wife also remains happy. And in that way, she'll have some control.

Described as a 'bad omen, bad luck' and '…the beginning of bad things', a wife's refusal to cook represents one of the principal ways women may either punish their husbands for failing to meet expectations or undermine their husbands' authority when wives are unhappy with how they are treated. Other strategies include wives refusing to have sex or to speak with their husbands, disobeying their husbands' requests or commands, and by being wilfully unhelpful. Taken together, these actions offer women opportunities for empowerment and chances to 'claim' or reclaim power in the household. For example, Elijah recalled a time when his mother, Mama Rukiya, refused to light their *jiko* one evening. Describing the ensuing struggle of wills, Elijah explained how his father, Boniface, did not allow anyone else to light the *jiko* because he wanted his wife to light it as an act of submission in deference to his authority. Although Mama Rukiya was successfully able to refuse her husband's order to light the *jiko*, this act of defiance meant that the entire household spent the night without eating.

Tactics such as refusing to cook are more often called upon by breadwinning wives, like Mama Rukiya, who are less economically dependent on their husbands. As Moses suggested: '…maybe she washes clothes in Mikindani or Magongo,[9] or she does some other jobs, when she comes, maybe she does not want to cook, [or] maybe she will cook but deny the husband…'. Referencing this latter strategy of cooking for everyone except their husbands, an approach to which wives commonly turn when their husbands fail to provide money for household expenses (especially food), Mama Rukiya described how women 'get fed up feeding *wanaume wa kurandaranda* [idle, loitering, jobless men]'. In response, they prepare meals for themselves and their children early, before their husbands come home. Following these surreptitious meals, wives will clean and put away the dishes before their husbands can find evidence that they have eaten. When the 'idler' eventually arrives home, he finds that there is nothing to eat. Highlighting her dissatisfaction with her own husband's failure to provide, Mama Rukiya added, seemingly as a jab at Boniface, that 'some decent men fear coming home empty-handed because they know they will be asked what they have brought home for [the family] to eat'. According to Diana, the reasons women refuse to cook include the desire to express their worth and that they deserve to be respected: '…because they are angry and [to] tell the message. […] They refuse to cook because they're angry and they refuse because they want to show the husband… [that] she is the only sourc[e] of getting…[making] that food in the house'.

Although women cannot always avoid providing meals for their husbands (especially if husbands know what time wives feed their children), when they are able to stand by their refusals to cook, they force their husbands to make difficult decisions. Husbands can choose to apologize or to otherwise attempt to make amends by providing for their wives, they can seek food outside the house, or they can suffer what most men consider the indignity of cooking for themselves (if there is food available). When it came to the question of whether or not husbands could cook in households within which a wife had refused to do so, most men deemed this to be inappropriate. For example, Ezekiel proclaimed: 'You don't expect me to go there and cook when I have a wife who should be doing that?' However, some men, including Boniface, responded that although it would not be ideal, they might consider cooking. Suggesting that by choosing to cook, he might be able to diffuse a tense situation and, at the same time, undercut his wife's attempts to challenge his *mamlaka*, Boniface explained:

> ...I do cook sometimes in our house. So if she refuses to cook, it's now the time that I want food and she refuses to cook, that way is not opposing me because I was doing that before. I can do it even the time that she refuses to do it, I can do it! And it does not mean that that time that I'm cooking, she is now opposing my authority. It's only, what she can do that is against my will is the one that can oppose me. But if she can do something that is on, that I have been doing, I say it that it is not opposing me...

According to Lydia, however, if a husband '...prepares his own meal and eats alone [...] you should not ask; if you dare ask, you get the beating of your life!' Lydia also confirmed Boniface's suggestion that by appropriating the otherwise female-associated domestic activity of cooking, a husband may reverse challenges to his authority as the man and head of the household. In explanation, she expressed how husbands who cook or do other chores, including washing their own clothes, frustrate wives because it suggests that they are not needed and have no purpose in the home.

Food Insecurity, Uncertainty, Infidelity, and Household Instability

The primacy of food within domestic relationships,[10] especially with regard to conflict and negotiations of power, is unsurprising given that food is the most essential material component of family life (Richards 1932: 14). As Appadurai (1981: 494) makes clear, '...unlike houses, pots, masks, or clothing, food is a constant need but a perishable good. The daily pressure to cook food (combined with the never-ending pressure to produce or acquire it) makes it well suited to bear the load of everyday social discourse'. In the impoverished environment of an informal settlement, where the material difficulties associated with sustaining a household are often extraordinary, and where come-we-stay arrangements are often particularly vulnerable to break-up, food takes on an exaggerated significance for conjugal partners. In Bangla, wives cooking for their households, families eating together, and husbands fulfilling their roles as breadwinners are vital acts and displays of marital harmony, commitment, security, and stability. When meals are skipped because a breadwinner has failed to provide, because a wife has refused to cook, or because members are unwilling to sit together and to share a meal due to interpersonal friction, these enactments of conjugal unity go unfulfilled. Either partner's consistent failure to meet respective gendered expectations related to household production tends to be perceived as an egregious betrayal of a central covenant of the conjugal union.[11] As such, these failures introduce or intensify feelings of mistrust and insecurity in the household and engender a sense of uncertainty. As a result, couples may begin to call into question the future viability of their households as productive and reproductive units.

For a husband, a wife's refusal to cook 'well and on time' (or at all), indicates to him that she is dissatisfied with their life together, that she is otherwise unhappy, or that she is simply trying to 'frustrate' him, and in doing so, challenge his *mamlaka*. Either way, such behaviour suggests to a man that his marriage is vulnerable to *kwachana* (divorce). Similarly, a husband's consistent failure to provide food for his family suggests to his wife that he lacks commitment to their relationship or that he is an unworthy breadwinner and partner because he is unreliable or lazy. A wife's sense of insecurity and feelings of uncertainty are further fostered by a husband's failures to provide since for all a wife knows, he could be using what money he does have to buy food for himself, or for another woman, whilst he is away from home each day.

Likewise, husbands who miss meals, particularly evening meals, without an acceptable excuse, or who refuse to eat what their spouses have prepared, cause their wives to suspect them of unfaithfulness. As Elijah explained, 'When you, the husband, misses to eat the food, they [wives] simply think that you've already eaten at another woman's house.[12] So if you're the husband, you have to eat, even if you're full; you have to taste the food'. When I asked Elijah if he had ever seen his father, Boniface, eat his mother's food when he knew that his father was not hungry, he replied, 'Okay...yeah, yeah, he has...but not that he wanted to impress my mum, or that...maybe I can say for, so that we can see that, we the children, can see that he has eaten'. For Diana, one of the first clues she had that Barnabas was cheating on her was his refusal to eat lunch one day when he had been away from home assisting a female neighbour. Recalling her suspicions, especially when she learned that they had eaten together before returning home, she described:

> So I prepare the lunch, I take for them, everybody with a plate. So Jafari [Diana's nephew] [was] the only person [to] take that lunch; Fatuma [the female neighbour] and Barnabas, they refuse. And Fatuma, [she] don't refuse food, is one who is like a hyena, [she] don't refuse anything you give her. I wondered that day, [why did she] refuse, my heart was very, I was feeling a lot of pain. [...] I say why, every day you eat here, why do you refuse and you have come from a long distance, you have to fill a lot of *njaa*, a lot of, why? I start asking a lot of questions in my head. So, I couldn't put it in my heart because I'm full of words of question. I go and ask Barnabas, 'Why?'

Associations between missed meals and infidelity are especially problematic in informal settlements where the unpredictability of employment means men are often unable to come home for lunch and may be additionally unable to foresee what time they will be home in the evening. Furthermore, when men fail to provide, but their wives somehow manage to do so, husbands too may become doubtful. From his own experience, Isaac told me that when he does not have money to give his wife, she sometimes cooks and eats with their children anyway, and then attempts to hide this from him. When this happens, he is left with nothing to eat and only wonders where she got the money she used to buy the food. According to Imara, a single mother, a '...woman can bring food on the table for the husband, and [he] will not give money saying "You *malaya* [prostitute], where did you get money to buy this food?"'

In addition to arousing suspicions of infidelity, members skipping meals at home, or households forgoing them entirely because of a lack of food, mean opportunities are lost to engage in the everyday sorts of communication that are essential to domestic life. Underscoring the importance of mealtimes as practical opportunities to converse, to share thoughts and the day's events, and generally to keep in touch with what is happening in each other's lives, Moses explained:

When there is lack of food in the house, between a husband and a wife, there is no love. First of all, there is no love. They cannot sit and maybe share ideas because they just feel that there is no time to sit together. You know, people do come together round a table when they've got something to share, especially when there is food. Okay, when you…sit round the table, you eat and you share ideas, and when there is no food in the house, you just find that even the husband don't have time to be at home; he will just be walking, malingering outside, he will not have time to be at home because every time [he'll] be asked: 'We need salt, we need this, we need, we don't have water', so you just find the husband malingering outside.

Extending this argument, whilst echoing earlier observations, Diana again links food insecurity and quarrelling, and a resulting lack of communication, to feelings of insecurity and uncertainty between partners: 'There are some things, they come through that lacking of food, like quarrelling…maybe somebody has…[kept] quiet, you don't know if he is angry with you or don't know…many things, it doesn't bring peace if you don't have that food in the house'. Moreover, describing her decision to purchase fish as a special meal for Barnabas after a particularly emotionally draining and extended quarrel, Diana also made clear the importance of food in communicating positive feelings of forgiveness, appreciation, and renewal. She told me: 'I decide[d] [to] go and take food which my heart will also be happy and Barnabas also will be happy with that food. So we'll start a life, a new one again'. For his part, Ezekiel made clear how simply discussing important decisions is absolutely vital to men and women living together happily and to avoiding feelings of uncertainty. He offered: '…because [then] everybody is certain of the future. From where we are now, we can know what is next. Nobody's in darkness'.

Taken together with aforementioned statements linking food insecurity, especially *njaa*, to experiences of interpersonal conflict, the comments offered by Moses, Diana, and Ezekiel strengthen the claim for the disintegrating effects problems with food may have on domestic relationships. Describing the consequences of a lack of food at home, Barnabas likewise offered:

The relationship is getting worsened, Adam. Because there is no happiness in the house. Everybody is annoyed. The only thing […] that they can share is pain. I realize a relationship, what you have is what you share with your partner. So when your partner is sad, you cannot be happy. And you cannot be happy without eating. Like hunger is pain. So the pain which you have you will be sharing. So that household will be having problem already....

Over time, as experiences of chronic food insecurity and interpersonal conflict take their toll on conjugal relationships, spouses may turn against each other, question each other's commitment, challenge each other's motives, and blame each other for circumstances which are frequently beyond the other's control. If conditions do not improve, some wives may seek out new sexual partners as a means of gaining access to needed resources. Referring to relationships outside of marriages as 'prostitution', Moses told me: '...the day-to-day needs, what somebody needs in order to survive, talk of clothings, shelter, and enough food, yeah. So that one has been the major cause of say prostitution, because if somebody lacks the major necessities, and...the basic human needs, then one is easily tempted into going out for an affair'. As marital relationships become adversarial, husbands, too, may look for additional partners, or *mipango wa kando* (side plans; singular: *mpango wa kando*), in attempts to find respite from conflict with their wives at home. According to Moses:

> And some men also go out because they're frustrated. ...okay, I'd say that most of these houses don't have the necessities and there is not enough money... Okay, some women are quarrelsome with their husbands, so husbands go out because they want to get some peace of mind. He may see that if he goes out, he will have somewhere to go and settle without being quarrelled or being asked A, B, C, and D.

For both men and women, *kutembea vibaya* (walking badly), or straying from marital relationships, increases the risk of acquiring an HIV infection and of introducing *Ukimwi* (AIDS) into the household. However, men's infidelity tends to present an additional hazard. Whilst a wife's infidelity may augment available household resources, a husband's pursuit of new partners often means that cash needed desperately at home is diverted to other women's households.

Eventually, the burdens of food insecurity, interpersonal conflict, and/or infidelity may inspire one partner to run away and to abandon her or his relationship and household temporarily or permanently. Citing a time in the past when she briefly ran away from Barnabas, Diana described the experiences which led to her decision to leave: '...life was very difficult and I was very depressed, I was very, I was having many stress, especially in married life. My husband was very harsh and also he was having stress, he [couldn't] manage to feed us...'. In an interview with Diana during a period when she was considering running away from Barnabas again, I asked her about what risks in life caused her the most worry. Alongside eviction from their land and infectious diseases, she included her marriage: 'Okay, it is maybe married life. I'm worried if it is, if it will last long or it will be short and it will finish because of certain things I've even explained yesterday [discovering Barnabas's infidelity]. So I'm very worried because of the children. For me, I will not bother too much because I've grown up, but I worried about the children because they are too young...'.

Offering a further example of how conjugal relationships are susceptible to breakdown over time, Elijah described what happened between his parents in the lead up to his mother running away and how the state of their relationship was reflected in his household's experience of food security. Recalling memories of when his parents were getting along, he told me: '...when they were together, life was just good. Because my mum would provide and then in the evening, if dad has, he provides, and if he has not, he was not able to have money, to get the money, my mum would as well have provide[d] for the supper'. Later, likely referencing a time after his parents' relationship began to unravel, Elijah offered: '...you know, sometimes when my parents quarrel, my mum would leave; and remember that she used to provide the breakfast and the lunch. Whenever she, when she was not there, we had to suffer [because] nobody [would] provide the breakfast and lunch. We'll have to wait for the supper that will be brought by dad'.

Conclusion

In Bangla, food is the principal medium through which commitment and security are enacted and communicated within households. The everyday actions of husbands consistently providing food, wives preparing and serving it, and households consuming these meals together are all not only important to ensuring that everyone has enough to eat, but also to negotiations of power and to the cohesion and long-term stability of family units. In this chapter, I argue that failures, disagreements, and misunderstandings concerning food tend to introduce (or exacerbate) experiences of conflict between spouses (including physical and emotional abuses) and a sense of uncertainty about the future of conjugal relationships. This uncertainty may intensify experiences of worry concerning food, personal safety, and the well-being of children in the household. Additionally, it may signpost the vulnerability of marriages to infidelity and divorce. Following Appadurai (1981) and Nichter (1981), food may be seen in Bangla as an 'idiom' of domestic conflict and power in at least three ways. First, refusals to cook offer wives the means to communicate their dissatisfaction or unhappiness with their husbands, especially with their failures to provide. Second, failures to provide money and/or food suggest to wives that husbands are ineffectual, that they lack commitment, or that they are unfaithful. Third, by providing food independently, women challenge their husbands' *mamlaka* and may inadvertently suggest to husbands that they are *kutembea vibaya*.

Although there is insufficient space to consider fully the issue here, data and findings presented in this chapter suggest that whilst conditions of food insecurity tend to inspire interpersonal conflict, experiences of interpersonal friction and abuse may also contribute to experiences of food insecurity (see Gilbertson 2013). As conjugal relationships become increasingly antagonistic, it becomes more difficult for partners to coordinate the efforts needed to ensure food security. Moreover, food insecurity may worsen if conjugal conflict and conditions at home inspire one spouse to run away. For Elijah, his brothers, and their father, Boniface, Mama Rukiya's permanent departure from their household with another man meant that, on top of the stress and hurt caused by the estrangement of a wife and mother, the income and meals her food kiosk provided were no longer available. In combination with Boniface's continuing difficulties (and outright failures) to provide food (as well as rent and school fees), the result was an increase in long-term household food insecurity. Alongside conflict and abuse, risks for household food insecurity are also, therefore, intimately tied to the status of conjugal relationships.

Discussing the importance of a partner's behaviour, in addition to one's own, with regard to the risk of HIV infection, Whyte (1997: 223) observes how '[d]anger and uncertainty inhere in others; it is not just a question of your individual responsibility but also of theirs'. Drawing parallels between Whyte's work on the Nyole and her own concerning risk, uncertainty, and contingency related to reproduction in Gambia, Bledsoe (2002: 21) notes how '[a] sense of vulnerability applies even to intimate social relations, despite the security these relations appear to offer'. Applying a similar argument to an analysis of household food security in Bangla suggests a dual nature for conjugal relationships with respect to risk. At the same time that these relationships represent a resource through which risks may be mitigated (see Doss 1996), hunger avoided, and household food security achieved, marital relationships also represent a potential source of risk. Therefore, households cannot be conceived of as bastions of safety and security within the greater risk environment of the informal settlement without simultaneously considering their potential contributions to risk in terms of conflict, abuse, and food insecurity.

In the epilogue to *Dealing with Uncertainty in Contemporary African Lives*, Susan Whyte (2009: 214) writes: 'Insecurity itself gives rise to uncertainty, yes. But it is also a state of limited resources for action. Dealing with uncertainty is perhaps not so much about making certain, as it is about trying to make more secure. It is security that people seek to strengthen in their efforts to exert some degree of control, drawing on the social and cultural resources at hand...'. Whilst this statement is intended to speak to experiences of uncertainty and insecurity more generally, it aptly (and specifically) applies to experiences of household food insecurity within informal settlements such as Bangla. Here, achieving food security is a matter of successfully managing insecurity related to employment, income, and interpersonal dynamics within conjugal relationships. In these environments, resources and choices are often heavily constrained by poverty and by one's dependency on a spouse to fulfil gendered expectations of domestic production. When wives challenge existing power structures by refusing to cook, or by appropriating the roles of breadwinners, these efforts aim to manage insecurity and to help to ensure future well-being. Difficulties associated with achieving food security in Bangladesh, Mombasa, are therefore not limited to poverty and an inability to afford sufficient and preferred food. With respect to conjugal households, where many men continue to expect to be the sole authority, further challenges include the negotiation of gender-based power inequalities within a greater economic environment which increasingly forces women to take on the burden of providing for their households.

Notes

1 Whilst the term 'slum' is utilized widely, it may be considered offensive by the residents whose homes, schools, and communities it is used to describe.

2 The first three domains (uncertainty/worry, food quality, and food quantity) are incorporated within the nine-item measure of food insecurity called the Household Food Insecurity Access Scale (Coates et al. 2007). Uncertainty/worry is identified as the least severe indicator within this measure (Coates et al. 2007: 6) and, therefore, is likely the most common experience related to food insecurity.

3 This population estimate was offered through personal communication by one of the men in charge of the 2009 Kenyan census in Bangla.

4　See Whitehead (1981) for a discussion of the 'conjugal contract'.

5　The July 2013 draft of the Kenyan Marriage Bill (Republic of Kenya 2013: 417) provides for the legal recognition of certain come-we-stay unions. It states that couples married under 'customary law' may apply (in person) for a certificate 'within six months of their marriage'.

6　*Chang'aa* is an illicit alcoholic drink made from sugarcane, which is commonly distilled and sold cheaply in informal settlements.

7　*Unga wa mahindi* is maize flour. This is the main ingredient in *ugali* (boiled maize meal), the staple food in Bangla.

8　Ellis (1983) links husbands' disapproval with their wives' cooking to domestic abuse.

9　Mikindani and Magongo are relatively more affluent areas located near Bangla.

10　Prince and Geissler (2010: 127–28) note that among the Luo, cooking and eating are as important to 'the enactment of marriage' as is sexual intercourse and that, '…the state of a marital relation is gauged by the woman's willingness to cook for her husband and his willingness to eat her food'.

11　Ellis (1983) makes a similar argument concerning 'working class' couples in the United Kingdom.

12　Prince and Geissler (2010: 128) also make this observation.

References

African Population and Health Research Centre (APHRC) (2002) Health and Livelihood Needs of Residents of Informal Settlements in Nairobi City. Occasional Study Report (Nairobi: African Population and Health Research Centre).

African Population and Health Research Centre (APHRC) (2002a) Population and Health Dynamics in Nairobi's Informal Settlements. Report of the Nairobi Cross-sectional Slums Survey (NCSS) 2000 (Nairobi: African Population and Health Research Centre).

Amuyunzu-Nyamongo, M., L. Okeng'o, A. Wagura & E. Mwenzwa (2007) 'Putting on a Brave Face: The Experiences of Women Living with HIV and AIDS in Informal Settlements of Nairobi, Kenya', *AIDS Care* 19 (Supplement 1): S25–S34.

Amuyunzu-Nyamongo, M. & N. Taffa (2004) 'The Triad of Poverty, Environment and Child Health in Nairobi Informal Settlements', *Journal of Health & Population in Developing Countries*, http://aphrc.sprintwebhosts.com/wp-content/uploads/2013/11/The-Triad-of-Poverty-Environment-and-Child-Health-in-Nairobi-Informal.pdf.

Appadurai, A. (1981) 'Gastro-Politics in Hindu South Asia', *American Ethnologist* 8 (3): 494–511.

Bledsoe, C. (2002) *Contingent Lives: Fertility, Time, and Aging in West Africa* (Chicago & London: University of Chicago Press).

Boonzaier, F. (2005) 'Woman Abuse in South Africa: A Brief Contextual Analysis', *Feminism Psychology* 15 (1): 99–103.

Charles, N. & M. Kerr (1988) *Women, Food and Families* (Manchester: Manchester University Press).

Coates, J., E. A. Frongillo, B. L. Rogers, P. Webb, P. E. Wilde & R. F. Houser (2006) 'Commonalities in the Experience of Household Food Insecurity across Cultures: What are Measures Missing?', *Journal of Nutrition* 136: S1438–S1448.

Coates, J., A. Swindale & P. Bilinsky (2007) Household Food Insecurity Access Scale (HFIAS) for Measurement of Household Food Access: Indicator Guide (v. 3) (Washington, D.C.: Food and Nutrition Technical Assistance Project, Academy for Educational Development).

Counihan, C. M. & S. L. Kaplan (eds.) (2004 [1998]) *Food and Gender: Identity and Power* (London & New York: Routledge).

DeVault, M. (2008 [1997]) 'Conflict and Deference', in Counihan, C. & P. Van Esterik (eds.) *Food and Culture: A Reader* Second Edition (New York & Abingdon: Routledge), pp. 240–258.

Doss, C. R. (1996) 'Intrahousehold Resource Allocation in an Uncertain Environment', *American Journal of Agricultural Economics* 78 (5): 1335–1339.

Ellis, R. (1983) 'The Way to a Man's Heart: Food in the Violent Home', in Murcott, A. (ed.) *The Sociology of Food and Eating* (Aldershot: Gower Publishing), pp. 164–171.

Food and Agriculture Organization of the United Nations (FAO) (1996) Rome Declaration on World Food Security, World Food Summit, Rome: 13–17 November, [Online] Available from: http://www.fao.org/docrep/003/w3613e/w3613e00.htm [July 2013].

Food and Agriculture Organization of the United Nations (FAO) (2003) Food Security: Concepts and Measurement, Trade Reforms and Food Security: Conceptualizing the Linkages, Commodity Policy and Projections Service, Commodities and Trade Division, FAO Corporate Document Repository. [Online] Available from: http://www.fao.org/docrep/005/y4671e/y4671e06.htm [July 2013].

Frederiksen, B. F. (2000) 'Popular Culture, Gender Relations and the Democratization of Everyday Life in Kenya', *Journal of Southern African Studies* 26 (2): 209–222.

Gilbertson, A. (2013) *The Ecology of Risk in an Informal Settlement: Interpersonal Conflict, Social Networks, and Household Food Security*, D.Phil. (Oxford: University of Oxford).

Gulis, G., J. A. A. Mulumba, O. Juma & B. Kakosova (2004) 'Health Status of People of Slums in Nairobi, Kenya', *Environmental Research* 96: 219–227.

Guyer, J. I. (1981) 'Household and Community in African Studies', *African Studies Review* 24 (2/3): 87–137.

Hartmann, H. I. (1981) 'The Family as the Locus of Gender, Class, and Political Struggle: The Example of Housework', *Signs* 6 (3): 366–394.

Murcott, A. (1986 [1983]) '"It's a Pleasure to Cook for Him": Food, Mealtimes and Gender in Some South Wales Households', in Gamarnikow, E., D. Morgan, J. Purvis & D. Taylorson (eds.) *The Public and the Private* (Aldershot: Gower Publishing), pp. 78–90.

Mweru, M. (2008) 'Women, Migration and HIV/AIDS in Kenya', *International Social Work* 51 (3): 337–347.

Nichter, M. (1981) 'Idioms of Distress: Alternatives in the Expression of Psychosocial Distress: A Case Study from South India', *Culture, Medicine and Psychiatry* 5: 379–408.

Oppong, C. (1970) 'Conjugal Power and Resources: an Urban African Example', *Journal of Marriage and Family* 32 (4): 676–680.

Preston-Whyte, E., C. Varga, H. Oosthuizen, R. Roberts & F. Blose (2000) 'Survival Sex and HIV/AIDS in an African City', in Parker, R., R. M. Barbosa & P. Aggleton (eds.) *Framing the Sexual Subject: The Politics of Gender, Sexuality, and Power* (Berkeley: University of California Press), pp. 165–190.

Prince, R. J. & P. W. Geissler (2010) *The Land Is Dying: Contingency, Creativity and Conflict in Western Kenya* (Oxford: Berghahn Books).

Republic of Kenya (2013) *Kenya Gazette Supplement No. 97 (National Assembly of Bills No. 13)*, pp. 391–438, Nairobi: The Government Printer. [Online] Available from: http://www.klrc.go.ke/images/images/downloads/Marriage-Bill-2013-KLRC.pdf [July 2013].

Richards, A. (1932) *Hunger and Work in a Savage Tribe: A Functional Study of Nutrition among the Southern Bantu* (London: Routledge).

Sen, A. (1981) *Poverty and Famines: An Essay on Entitlement and Deprivation* (Oxford: Oxford University Press).

Silberschmidt, M. (1999) *Women Forget that Men are the Masters: Gender Antagonism and Socioeconomic Change in Kiisi District, Kenya* (Uppsala: Nordiska Afrikainstitutet).

Silberschmidt, M. (2001) 'Disempowerment of Men in Rural and Urban East Africa: Implications for Male Identity and Sexual Behaviour', *World Development* 29 (4): 657–671.

Strebel, A., M. Crawford, T. Shefer, A. Cloete, N. Henda, M. Kaufman, L. Simbayi, K. Magome & S. Kalichman (2006) 'Social Constructions of Gender Roles, Gender-based Violence and HIV/AIDS in Two Communities of the Western Cape, South Africa', *Journal of Social Aspects of HIV/AIDS* 3 (3): 516–528.

United Nations Human Settlements Programme (UN-HABITAT) (2003) The Challenge of Slums: Global Report on Human Settlements 2003, United Nations Human Settlements Programme (London: Earthscan) [Online] Available from: http://www.unhabitat.org/pmss/listItemDetails.aspx?publicationID=1156 [July 2013].

Whitehead, A. (1981) '"I'm Hungry, Mum": The Politics of Domestic Budgeting', in Young, K., C. Wolkowitz & R. McCullagh (eds.) *Of Marriage and the Market: Women's Subordination in International Perspective* (London: CSE Books), pp. 88–111.

Whyte, S. R. (1997) *Questioning Misfortune: The Pragmatics of Uncertainty in Eastern Uganda* (Cambridge: Cambridge University Press).

Whyte, S. R. (2009) 'Epilogue', in Haram, L. & C. Yamba (eds.) *Dealing with Uncertainty in Contemporary African Lives* (Stockholm: Nordiska Afrikainstitutet), pp. 213–216.

Part Two
Future Visions

Social Invisibility and Political Opacity: On Perceptiveness and Apprehension in Bissau

Henrik Vigh

Introduction

This chapter looks at the relationship between apprehension, social invisibility, and political opacity. Building on fieldwork in Bissau, Guinea-Bissau, it illuminates the way people grasp the persistent political instability and uncertainty that characterizes the small country. Politics is, in Bissau, currently described as enigmatic and mysterious. It is seen as embedded in an environment of cloaked and concealed figures and forces that work beyond the control and grasp of ordinary people. The chapter clarifies how perceptiveness, within this context of enduring unpredictability, has come to be seen as a central social and political competence. The ability to see behind and beyond the present and presented has become a necessary power needed to secure one's safety and well-being in a climate of insecurity. The chapter thus illuminates how people struggle to gain clarity and knowledge of the 'invisible' yet dangerously present forces which are understood to influence political life and argues that the prolonged period of conflict and strife in the country has generated a bearing towards the political, an apprehension which is simultaneously characterized by fear, interpretation, and anticipation. In conclusion, the chapter dwells more generally on the issue of social invisibility and argues that our attentiveness towards it is a foundational characteristic of social life.

Ordinary but Intensified

Building on empirical material from ethnographic fieldwork in Bissau, the capital of the small West African country of Guinea-Bissau, this chapter looks at the way people struggle to gain insights and overviews in situations of heightened instability and political turmoil. The empirical material stems from participant observation and interviews with impoverished young men from the inner suburbs and neighbourhoods of the city. The chapter focuses on the orientational intensity that emerges from situations of uncertainty and insecurity. In such circumstances, our views of our social worlds often become exploratory and probing. When things are out of sync or out of place, when our expectations are challenged, routines contested, and our imaginaries unsettled, our attention turns towards the social as a site of emergence and unpredictability, resulting in an increased effort to anticipate the way surfacing relations and realities may touch upon our being and influence our lives.

Focusing on the 'perspectival intensification' that emerges from the combination of low-intensity conflict and heightened insecurity, the chapter dwells analytically on the concept of 'apprehension' as an optic, which may enable us to nuance some of the social effects generated by such critical situations. 'Apprehension' generally defines an experience of disquiet and anticipation of misfortune. More specifically, however, the term directs our attention towards a compound practice as it encompasses the attempt to sense, to understand, and to control the way that our surroundings engage us. This combination of the perceptual, intellectual, and practical may, I argue, provide us with an insight into the way people seek to survive and manage in worlds that are characterized by danger and unpredictability. Building on this trivalent notion of apprehension, the chapter shows how my interlocutors fathom political volatility and precariousness (Vigh 2011). It progresses by moving across levels of political mastery and power, from the occult to the ordinary, and from figures of importance to the man on the street. The point of departure is, however, in what my informants see as an exemplar of apprehension, namely the political prowess of the country's former president, João Bernardho 'Nino' Vieira. Vieira was feared and admired for his ability to stay in power and navigate the turbulent politics of the small country; a capacity which was seen to imply the command of an assemblage of political powers ranging from brute rule to tactical cunning and, not least, the harnessing of occult forces and supernatural potencies.

Apprehension and Perceptiveness

> He has 'eyes', *i tene odju*. He went to a *mouro* [a Muslim sorcerer] and that *mouro* gave him 'eyes'. If anyone wanted to hurt him he would know. If someone did something behind his back he would know. That is why people did not dare [to go against] him.

Tene odju, 'having eyes', signifies perceptiveness. Not the rare, momentary version of insightfulness that can befall us all, but a more profound capacity to see the true state of affairs behind social facades and charades. The above quote is taken from an interview with Kadi in Bissau in 2009, in which he spoke about the power of former president Nino Vieira. Vieira's gift of clear-sightedness granted him, according to Kadi, an uncanny ability to hold on to power in a political environment as volatile as the Guinea-Bissauan. He was, Kadi told me, able to apprehend what was otherwise thought hidden and concealed and thus to pre-empt the myriad of coups and conspiracies against him.

I suma paotero, 'he is like a *paotero*', Kadi explained. 'He could see everything. If people wanted to be invisible, like a *futchero* [a witch], he would see them'. A *paotero* designates, in Bissau, a person who has the ability to perceive evil forces. In a similar manner, Vieira was able to make visible the invisible and see through political smokescreens and cover-ups. 'Having eyes' enabled Vieira to fully sense, and make sense of, his surroundings. It gave him an awareness of underlying dangers and negative potentialities (Vigh 2011), allowed him to detect the deals and treacheries that took place behind his back, and, importantly, enabled him to act before being acted upon. Being like a *paotero* means, thus, to have an intensified capacity to gain *in*sights and *over*views, the capability to enhance one's vision in both a microscopic and panoptic sense, a power to register the hidden movements of political networks and alliances, as well as the motives and intentionalities embedded within them. Vieira's occult ability was a gift of political perceptiveness, making it possible for him to see both the details and the larger picture of the political struggles he was engaged in. Kadi generally spoke of Vieira in a tone of admiration. Yet, like so many people in Bissau, he had mixed emotions about the ex-president. The gift of political perceptiveness was a precondition for becoming and being powerful, and violence the means of staying so. 'He was powerful [*poderoso*]', Kadi said. 'If you did not speak the truth, he would go and tell someone, "This one is no good", and then they would just kill you'. Though Kadi had fought in the war in 1998–99 as part of Vieira's private militia, the Aguentas, he was frank about the ex-president's many misdeeds and shifted between portraying him as a patron, a criminal, and a tyrant. Kadi is not alone in this. Vieira is generally recognized for making the best of opportunities in terms of politics, business, and romance. Yet, his relational insightfulness went hand in hand with brutality, and he is seen as a person who ruled through fear and oppression.

Perceptiveness and Perseverance

Whether Vieira was especially politically percipient is debatable. His capacity for clear-sightedness ended, in any case, demonstratively, as he was killed in a feud over power and profit in 2009, a few months before the above interview was conducted. The president was beaten, shot, and dismembered – the excessiveness of the mutilation communicating his absolute loss of power(s). Despite the brutality of his death, his rule was truly extraordinary. In a country where no other president has ever finished his time in office, due to the many coups and conflicts that haunt the place, Vieira actually managed to stay in power for nineteen years. Yet, he ruled with disregard for other people's lives and well-being, and the welfare of the average citizen did not seem to rank high on his political agenda. Rather than leaving a legacy of political flair and insightfulness, he left, as such, one of autocracy, conflict, and crisis, of economic greed and power mongering. From his early years as military commander in the PAIGC,[1] during the war of liberation, to his time as head of the Guinea-Bissauan army,[2] and his later days as an Afro-Marxist dictator and democratically elected tyrant, Vieira eliminated political opposition to a degree that earned him the nickname of 'the Butcher from Bissau'.

Vieira's death followed a decade of heightened unrest which arose with the start of the civil war in 1998 and the removal of Vieira from office in 1999. The civil war in '98 was the result of a prolonged power struggle within the network of former war veterans from the war of independence, the so-called *antigo combatentes*, over the few resources that circulated through the country. A handful of influential figures within this network had dominated Guinea-Bissauan politics since independence, with Vieira as the prime figure, yet the group was in itself polarized into conflicting factions, making Vieira's stay in power as contested as it was brutal. As the military finally united against him, he was deposed from office in 1999, when soldiers from the *Junta Militar* overran Bissau and defeated the remnants of the army that he had haphazardly mobilized to protect his presidency. The capture of Bissau by the Junta caught Vieira by surprise. As he came to realize his defeat, he sought protection within the French diplomatic delegation who had supported him during the war and hid in the French Cultural Centre, yet after a brief exchange of gunfire, he was captured and removed from the building by Junta soldiers. The pictures circulating of his capture portray a deflated figure. Soiled and shabby, Vieira was dragged from the building by his triumphant capturers. He had apparently wet himself in the process of his arrest, and the former 'big man' looked fragile, with any allure of power or politico-magical abilities gone. Vieira certainly had cause to fear for his life. The leading group behind the Junta consisted of people he had humiliated, tortured, and tormented in the past; yet, instead of being killed, he managed to negotiate his future with the head of the Junta, Brigadier Asumane Mane, and gained refuge in France and Belgium. As the Junta took power, it installed a new government and proclaimed a new era for the small country. Liberated from its long-term despot, Guinea-Bissau was declared free to prosper. However, despite the change in government, and the proclamation of a new dawn for the troubled country, the situation in Guinea-Bissau did not get better after Vieira's exile. In fact, the common opinion on the streets was that things were deteriorating. The country's economy crashed, development aid was being withheld, and the political situation was as repressive and turbulent as ever, with one coup or purge following another within the next five years. The situation turned so bad that people were starting to articulate their longing for stability through a nostalgia for Vieira's repressive regime, a dictatorial order being seen as better than none at all.

At the time their wishes seemed unrealistic. Yet, as another coup had rolled through the country, Bissau was preparing for elections, and six years after having been forced to leave the country, rumours emerged of Vieira's possible return and dates of his imminent homecoming started to circulate in Bissau. A few months after the first rumours started to emerge, he announced his candidature for the presidential elections in 2005, entailing that he come back to the city early the same year. Vieira was flown into the national stadium, in a helicopter from the Guinea Conacrian air force, and driven into town in an armed escort. The same people who had ousted him a few years earlier were now protecting his return to the city. It was an amazing turn of events, testifying both to the political perseverance of Nino Vieira and the exceptional unpredictability of Guinea-Bissauan politics. From being a hated figure after the war, publically spoken about as a thief and tyrant, he was, upon his return, greeted by a crowd of people seemingly ecstatic to see him again. I was standing in the crowd with Braima watching him drive by. Braima shared the excitement and was delighted by his return. 'You will see', he said, 'now Bissau will go forward, now we will go... Only he [Vieira] can build Bissau. You will see'.

Braima had been mobilized and demobilized repeatedly within the last ten years. Moving in and out of military life, he sought to get by by aligning himself with the factions that he judged most likely to be victorious. Braima seemed, in fact, to be relatively at ease in situations of heightened tension and confusion, *confusão*. He was a chaos pilot, waiting for political deadlocks to break so that he could make the best of the ensuing strife or conflict. Yet, though adept and experienced in handling situations of conflict, Braima had a longing for peace and prosperity, and Vieira was, in his point of view, the only one who could contain the multiplicity of political tensions and relations in Bissau. 'This is the one who has eyes', Braima said. 'He knows everything, he will know. Now things will be straight [*derieto*]'. Vieira was able, according to Braima, to see and, hence, control the interests and intentions of diverse political networks and fractions. Being able 'to see' granted him the knowledge needed to create order and bring the country out of the prolonged situation of heightened instability and insecurity.

Braima's faith in Vieira's abilities was echoed in the ex-president's own statements as he addressed the media in Bissau. Though his autocratic behaviours and his lack of economic and political abilities can be seen to have led the country towards the political and economic abyss in which it was so thoroughly entrenched, Vieira spoke of himself as the country's saviour and protector. Upon his return he proclaimed himself to be 'God's gift to the Guinea-Bissau' and re-entered the political scene as the man who would be able to bridge the many different factions and interests competing for positions and power. Vieira was, he said, what was needed to generate stability and economic growth.[3] His capacity to control made him the only one capable of ruling the country. 'He does not sleep', Raul told me, continuing:

> ...even when he goes to bed, his power gets up and goes elsewhere. He looks like he is sleeping. Even the person who lies next to him, even his wife, does not know, but in reality he is not here. His soul will be walking. It goes and looks there and it goes and looks there [he points to one direction and then another]. This is why he knows. If we sit he will see what we are doing, what you are thinking about doing, he will know your future. He knows.

Vieira's powers were, as such, seen to grant him not just insight but omnipresence, fusing the pervasive and perceptive, and enabling him to harness the many different political interests and intentions in Bissau. Despite the belief in his powers, Vieira, however, only managed to keep half of his promise of generating stability and growth. After almost four years in office, the increasing political tension between various political factions and networks in Bissau culminated in a series of political assassinations, including Vieira's on March 2, 2009.

Invisible Powers

Rather than demystifying Vieira's politico-magical abilities, his death was, interestingly, seen as a sign that such capacities were spread out across competing networks and possessed by many of the figures that are seen to constitute the topography of the political environment in Bissau. Having eyes, *tene odju* – the aforementioned politico-magical perceptiveness – is understood as needed in order to provide the necessary clarity to survive in the shifty and turbulent political climate in Bissau. With new political configurations and alliances constantly undermining the existing ones and placing the unobservant at risk, apprehension, in the shape of perceptiveness and sagacity, is understood as a political asset and part of the arena of power struggles themselves. Employing hidden forces is needed in order to compete on a level playing field, and instead of challenging the idea of Vieira 'having eyes', his assassination was seen as a sign that he had equally been defeated in the hidden political realm of the occult. People had, I was told, *junta poder*, joined powers (worldly and occult), and in unison made them work against him. In other words, instead of being seen as exemplifying the fallacy of his postulated magical abilities, Vieira's death was perceived to consolidate their existence.

Vieira's turbulent political history exemplifies the many dimensions that seem to coalesce in the sphere of the political in Bissau, as well as the insecurity and uncertainty that this multiplicity of potencies stem from and generate. Yet, it also tells us something about the way politics, power, and, not least, protection is seen to be found in hidden abilities and capacities. In relation to danger and insecurity, the occult is, as such, both a cause and a cure. Though it may be spoken about in terms of witches and evil, and often used to dramatically exemplify the perils of greed, lust, and envy within social relations, the pragmatics of such practices is very much a defence or guard against the invisible side of social or political life (Evans-Pritchard 1976). Occult literally means 'hidden', yet, it would seem, that in Bissau this dimension of life is directed towards the exact opposite, namely illumination. The movement, when seeking the advice of sorcerers, mediums, or medicine men – *baloberos*, *djabakus*, or *mouros* – is from experiencing uncertainty and insecurity to gaining clarity and, subsequently, acquiring protection. In a place where many people survive on a single meal a day, people spend incredible amounts of resources consulting spirit mediums in order to know who or what is acting upon them and acquiring the necessary safeguard and cures, *protecson* and *medicinho*, to make it stop. In other words, people may talk about the occult in terms of dangerous and aggressive figures, i.e., as witchcraft, but their engagement with it is primarily protective – a question of revelation and evasion. Intentional evil, curses, and spells are areas of deliberation and speculation, yet protection is the common practice.[4]

This tension between the visible and invisible in politics is, of course, not unique to Guinea-Bissau. The focus on invisible figures and forces has been a dominant theme within much research on Africa: from the early missionary encounters with animist beliefs, to the seminal work of Evans-Pritchard (1976), and the more current focus on, for example, occult economies (Comaroff & Comaroff 1999), modernity (Geshiere 1997), and politics (Mbembe 1992). In his work on the Azande, Evans-Pritchard argues that the reason why witchcraft is such a vital explanatory model among the Azande is that it grants people the possibility of addressing and making sense of social structure by figuring it in semi-visible figures and forces, thereby enabling people to engage it via intervention (1976: 73). Similarly, in a more recent piece of work, Comaroff and Comaroff have looked at the occult in relation to economy and politics, arguing that its current prominence in much of contemporary Africa is related to its capacity to provide an explanatory point of departure for the impact of the dynamics of late capitalism. Dealing with the occult can be seen, they say, as attempts at avoiding or controlling the presence and effects of invisible powers (Comaroff & Comaroff 1999: 293).

The Opacity of Politics and the Enhancement of Perspective

In similar ways, 'having eyes' in Guinea-Bissau is both a description of, and explanatory model for, the way to survive in an opaque and relatively impervious environment such as the Guinea-Bissauan, where power is experienced to work behind people's grasp and beyond their reach. The occult provides people with both a means of making sense of uncertainty and insecurity and a way of negotiating them. Cutting across scales and dimensions, from the mundane to the mysterious, and from the ideational to the material, it offers relational insight and over-views and grants people a means to appropriate and illuminate hidden interests, arrangements, and acts.

In a lengthy interview, Orlando tried to explain to me the nuances of having 'eyes' and the kind of apprehension it enables. Orlando was himself no stranger to the world of the occult. Having fought in the

Aguenta militia, he carried an abundance of *protecson* and *medicinho*, magical charms worn around the wrists, arms, neck, and stomach as protective devices designed to shield him from the specific dangers of war, such as knives, bullets, and shrapnel, and to guard him from the more social dangers of conflict, such as the vengeance and hatred that people may hold towards him due to the misdeeds he has committed during times of conflict. Orlando had purchased his protection dearly, as he did not possess powerful occult capabilities of his own. Seeking to explain the difference between those who have 'eyes' and those who do not, he said:

> There are those that have it and those that do not have a lot. Everyone can have [eyes] but [for] those that have a lot it is in the family. If you have a child it will cross to him [*kampal*].
> *If you do not have a lot...?*
> If you have problems and you do not know why [then] you can go [to a medium] to know. So that you will know what put this [in you]. He [the medium] takes a chicken, and he opens it, and he look at the two eggs, the testicles [ovaries?]. If they are white, the medium [*djambakus*] he will help you and if one is black then he cannot.
> *If everyone can have eyes, why do you go to a* djambakus?
> Because he has more than you. He sees everything. He will ask the spirit [*iran*] and it will tell you. He will say, 'This one is doing this because of this'. He will help you.
> *So what happens if you have eyes?*
> You will know, you will see what you have to do. You will know what is doing you harm. If I have eyes and something happens I will know, I will protect my head. If someone sends a curse after you then you will know. Blacks are powerful; you must protect yourself, that is why everyone has *medicinho*, this *djudju* [drags his finger across his stomach to indicate where it is]. Even during the war people who have them...when there was war they would stand and walk, if you fire you will not hit. Those who have eyes, it is like this, If a bullet comes it will not hit, because he will know [...].

The quote directs our attention towards the fact that 'having eyes' is commonly shared but can be individually enhanced. It is a general but differentiated ability, which some people may put to more forceful use than others, allowing them to see further and deeper. Intensifying one's capacity to 'see' grants one an advantage in terms of anticipatory and pre-emptive action. The insights and overviews it bestows enables people to predict, evade, and counteract oncoming forces. This means that politics, in Bissau, is in part seen as centred on a competition for the depths and intensity of perspective, as it bestows knowledge of what is at play and at stake and feeds into concrete political practices. Having eyes allows people to protect themselves from the forces that conspire against them, as well as to obscure the insights of others, all of which are necessary prerequisites for political success.

The prevalence and importance of this kind of vision is, in Bissau, directly related to uncertainty and insecurity. In a situation as volatile as the Guinea-Bissauan, 'having eyes' is related to the need for apprehension, to gain a measure of control of the social environment one's life is set in. However, the conflictual and contested nature of politics in Bissau entails that insights and overviews are needed not just by politicians and soldiers, but by the population at large. As the quote clarifies, the phenomenon of 'having eyes' may differ in intensity from person to person. It may vary in degree and scope of vision but not in substance. As people attempt to figure out which conflictual fault lines are looming in the horizon, what forces are gathering in the penumbra, what obscure allegiances are being shaped and, not least, what outcomes should be expected, they turn towards an enhancement of vision that will enable them to avoid present or prospective hardship and suffering.

In this manner, the focus on apprehension opens up a larger and more general field of study. Though it is currently in vogue to portray occult practises and animist beliefs as examples of radical alterity, ontologically different from 'Euro-American' ways (Viveiros De Castro 1998; Henare et al. 2007), my empirical material seems to direct us towards an understanding of the occult as a socially situated modality approached, in Bissau, when probing opaque and impervious situations and configurations. In other words, rather than being a particular Bissauan, West African, African, or merely non-Western phenomenon, what we are looking at is a way of grasping the world which resonates with the experienced indeterminate and unpredictable nature of it. Instead of being examples of ontologies, and one-to-one exclamations of 'what things are' (Henare et al. 2007: 2), 'having eyes' in Bissau is intricately related to doubt and interpretations of what may be. The problem with the non-representational point of departure, within perspectivism and the ontological turn, is, in relation to the current context, that people do not see themselves as inhabiting a world where what 'is' merely is, but rather a world that is enigmatic, insecure, and highly uncertain, where what 'is' never really is. Furthermore, even when enhanced by occult powers, what one sees in Bissau is always conditional and dependent on what others enable you to see, as perspectives interact and compete, entailing that political life in the city is approached as a site of partial truths, precarious potentiality, and negative becoming. Perspectives are, as such, not ontologies but epistemological technologies. They are a means of knowing, as probing and wandering perspectives set to fathom movement and change within the density of the social relations that people imagine as constituting their social environment (Vigh & Sausdal 2014).

In this manner, the idea of 'having eyes' and the striving for apprehension, insights, and overviews goes beyond Bissau and relates to the very condition of sociality itself. Life is experienced as 'embedded in an intricate network of visible and invisible forces', Hecht and Simone state (1994: 77), as the complexity and simultaneity of relations and associations are simply too dense for full overviews to be gained and clarity achieved. The idea of obscure potencies can, thus, be seen as grounded in what Weber calls *vielseitigkeit* (1958: 194 [note 35]), that is, in many-sidedness. In Bissau, as elsewhere, the multi-dimensionality and multiplicity of any social given entails that what is presented and made visible is often seen as merely the surface figuration of an amount of other possible configurations: the relation enacted is perceived as the epiphenomenon of the social environment it surfaces from, consequently creating an engagement with the world that is attentive to ulterior movements and motives. The very prevalence of ideas and experiences of 'social invisibility' – in other words, that forces act upon us and influence our lives but remain outside our sensory or practical grasp – in cultures and societies around the world, direct our attention not towards particular ontologies but the precarity of the social. 'Having eyes' is, in this manner, a way of perceiving the socially invisible dimensions of visible interaction and figurations, what may be termed the shadow side of the relationality. It is, in Bissau, a 'determined effort for signifying politico-economic changes or even gaining control over them' (Geschiere 1997: 3). As a mode of apprehension, 'having eyes' is *not* a different perspective on the world but a different intensity of insight. It signifies perspectival enhancement, an augmentation of vision, which is seen to empower people to gain clarity, find protection, and instigate proaction. In situations where the impact of social forces is felt but the agent or actant remains unclear, we approach our social environments with apprehension, as a vigilant attempt to grasp the complexity of the situation or condition at hand – a search for knowledge of the influences that touch upon us.

Alert and Attentive

Though focused on invisible figures and forces, the concern with gaining clarity is, thus, related to a concrete worry. It is connected to the fear of being caught off guard if obscure relations and politics should bare themselves in dangerous ways – a concern which is as visible in the lives of 'small men' as of 'big men', in the mundane as in the magical. Everyday life in Bissau is, as such, characterized by an intense effort to sense, decipher, and predict emerging dangers and potential threats. 'If you do not stay attentive [*fica attentive*] you do not know what will hit you [*panjau*],'[5] Raul told me. Being 'hit' means, in this context, to be engaged upon by someone or something you did not see coming, and staying attentive, *fica attentivo*, in similar manner to 'having eyes', provides the key to avoiding being caught by surprise, as a vigilant attempt to safeguard one's present and future well-being (Vigh 2011).

What becomes clear, when doing fieldwork in Bissau, is that the tumultuous nature of the political landscape and social environment entails that people cannot take the state of affairs for granted. *Anos no ka sibi ke ke na bin acontisi*, 'we do not know what is going to occur', people say when referring to the political development and emergent configurations of power, yet lack of knowledge does not result in apathy or passivity, but in an attempt to gain knowledge and to apprehend danger. As many of the young men I talk to in Bissau have formerly been actively engaged in the conflicts that have punctuated the last fifteen years of the city's history, they spend a substantial amount of time trying to decipher signs of trouble within the flow of political life. Though they do not 'have eyes' in a manner comparable to the magically enhanced abilities of Nino Vieira, they talk about themselves as people who have the knowledge and skill needed to apprehend potential risks and possibilities. As Vitór, a former militiaman, told me,

> ...no one knows what will happen – no one. We just sit here and look at the situation, but if the place starts smelling rotten, or if someone wants to hurt me, I will be ready.

Vitór was at times hyper-vigilant. Having lost every war he has entered into, and subsequently left to survive in Bissau without the aid of the patrimonial networks he had fought for, he was penetratingly aware of political changes and tensions. 'No one knows what will happen', *no ka sibi ke ke na bin acontisi*, he says in the above, yet the sentence would most often be followed by the word *mas*, 'but', and a statement of what was most probably happening and how one could react to it.

Similarly, my fieldwork notes and interviews are dotted with another relatively passive-sounding statement, which is actually active, namely, *no ta djubi situason so*, 'we are just looking at the situation'. Instead of being a passive observation, 'just looking' refers to keeping a watchful eye on social processes. What appears idle is, in fact, a state of intense awareness in which the social environment is scrutinized and interpreted for signs of what to expect and how to react. 'Just looking' revolves around sensing, making sense of, and pre-empting what will occur next, and refers, more broadly, to any registering of movement or change. 'If the place starts smelling rotten', *si kau na bin chiera fedi*, Vitor says in the above quote, indicating that the present political situation is examined multi-sensorially for the hidden conflicts and violent potentials embedded in the competition for power by the city's big men.

'Having eyes' and sensing when things start 'smelling rotten' thus term perceptiveness of the way the political world unfolds. They are concepts that are especially evoked in relation to the escalation of social tension, once again as a process that can be registered, but only in hints, glimpses, and allusions, making the need for scanning the socio-political environment for 'early warning signals'[6] ever present. People may, as such, see signs of danger in occurrences that otherwise appear benign. In the early years of the millennium, when Bissau was caught in a prolonged state of tension, a lack of goods at the market would, for example, spur rumours of oncoming conflict as people were imagined to be hoarding supplies, just as a lack of cigarettes in the city was perceived as a sign that smokers were stocking tobacco in order to be able to feed their addiction even in a situation of conflict. The examples may be strange, yet they speak to the fact that people in Bissau use a great deal of time trying to gain knowledge of the dynamics and movements of the social environment, and in imagining how its more critical potentialities may unfold, in order to avoid being caught off guard by unforeseen conflict or strife. As political formations are experienced as brittle, delicate, and full of impending disasters, they are monitored with apprehension: equal measures of anxiety and awareness.

Suspicion and the Underneath of Things

That perceptiveness and apprehension are central areas of signification in Bissau is, as said, not surprising taking the country's turbulent history into consideration. The conflictual dimensions of Nino Vieira's dramatic life story, which started this chapter, exemplifies the insecurity and instability that has come to define post-independence Bissau, as the city has been caught in a prolonged state of feuding and power struggles in which every proclamation of peace and impending progress has been followed by renewed political turmoil and regression. In terms of political awareness, the consequence of this schism between proclamations and practice has been the emergence of a deeply held suspicion of official politics and a persistent attention to the *realpolitik* that is seen to be led in the shadows.

The move from hardship to suffering is, in this manner, experienced as potentially always possible, ingrained into the Guinea-Bissauan society, and the tension between groups and networks within it. The presumed underlying existence of conflict entails that peoples' awareness becomes centred on the shadows from where problems may emerge. I re-met Aliu in December 2010 after a turbulent year that included the assassination of the army chief of staff, the president, and numerous politicians and a purge in the military. Aliu was born into the factional conflict that has troubled political life in the country since independence. His father fought for the liberation movement, PAIGC, during the war of liberation, and served as an officer in the Guinea-Bissauan army after independence. As war broke out in 1998, his father chose to join the side of the former president and convinced Aliu to serve in the militia supporting Vieira, entailing that they both ended up losing not just the war but their livelihoods and social standing. In the aftermath of the conflict, Aliu's family was dispossessed of their house and possessions. Left alive but destitute, they were déclassé and desperately struggling to survive in a city that afforded very little in terms of possibilities and life chances, and where conflict seemed set to re-emerge:

> There are people who say that now there is peace, but I do not think so. There is too much hate. It will never stop. If I kill someone in your family, you will have hate, is it not so. You will have hate! And when you see power, you will try to kill me. Us, we look at the situation...

so that we can know what will happen. Bissau is always on the move [*i ta ainda, ainda sempre*]: it is never stable. We do not know stability. There is a kind of cold war [*guerra fria*]. But how can there be peace when every garrison has its own commander.

Peace, for Aliu, merely means that violence lies dormant. Though Bissau may be calm, he is 'busy' figuring out when politics will turn violent and conflict step out from the shadows. He is constantly on the lookout for signs of trouble as an attempt to gain a forewarning by clarifying hidden movements and arrangements. Aliu was not alone in this. Instead of taking the stability of configurations and representations (verbal or visual) as a given, people in Bissau inspect political life for indications of possible alterations and transformations embedded within it. They do not passively register the flow of people and events but scan and examine them for signs of what to expect in terms of possible mutations and negative potentialities as the very obscurity of political processes in Bissau makes conflict a constant as a potential social state that, even when immaterialized, is seen as always about to be, installing an element of heightened insecurity into everyday life. In other words, even when people in Bissau go about their lives, when the city is calm, they do so with an understanding of peace as a state of suspension, of latency rather than harmony. Equally, suspicion becomes a common sentiment, as it is driven by an indication that there is more to a situation or relation than meets the eye. From my informants' point of view, the bellicose potential in Bissau never seems to be confined to the past but appears as an always already embedded part of the future, spurring an orientation towards precarious and compound prospects (cf. Whyte 1997: 24).

Social Invisibility at Large

Bissau clarifies, as such, how situations of long-term violence and conflict can stimulate a certain bearing towards the social environment. It illuminates how apprehension can become a dominant feature of social life, related to the fear of invisible backstage figures and forces and the attempt to gain a grasp of their quasi-presence. The belief in detrimental yet indiscernible and hidden influences can, however, be found more commonly around the world, just as the idea that politics is ripe with coexisting yet concealed actors is prevalent elsewhere. The obsession with social invisibility and the striving for clarity reveals itself, thus, not just to be confined to my informants, but also to be a more general concern. It is, furthermore, a preoccupation that the scholarly world is as preoccupied with as anyone else. Whether researcher or layman, the idea of invisibility and potentiality figures prominently in our understanding of social life. Etymologically, suspicion means to look underneath, which is, as Rancière states, exactly what 'the social theorists of the modern age elevate [...] to the rank of a theoretical virtue, an appropriate means of *apprehending*, beneath the appearance of commonality, a truth which belies it' (2007: 45, my italics). Science and the occult can, as such, be related in terms of focus. They both stand as ways of enhancing our view and knowledge of the powers affecting us: a focus on that which we cannot clearly sense nor determine, yet which impacts upon our lives (cf. Canetti 1960). The influence of invisibility and potentiality is not just restricted to the ideational dimensions of our lives and often results in very palpable concrete acts of exposure. People not only reflect upon invisible figures or forces, they act upon them, trying to avoid or pre-empt their touch. They may be seen to lie outside the reach of our bodily senses, yet as they are seen as capable of influencing social and physical bodies in very concrete ways, we often strive to bring them into being. The intersection between apprehension and social invisibility thus carves a conceptual space from where we can see the relation between uncertainty, insecurity, interpretation, and action.

Conclusion

The unseen and unknown stirs not just trepidation but equally a search for certainty. Focusing on the way people attempt to apprehend the opacity and unpredictability of the political environment in Bissau, this chapter has illuminated some of the interpretational and perspectival consequences of the prolonged state of insecurity and strife that has characterized the city. Across the political scale, from high to low, a great deal of resources, time, and effort are spent, in Bissau, trying to gain the insights and overviews of the political situation. This focus on the hidden and opaque becomes perhaps most clear in the occult aspects of politics, where visibility and clarity are sought within the mystical dimensions of life. The mystical is used to demystify, so to speak, and the chapter argues that the occult, in this manner, can be seen as a kind of perspectival enhancement, as an augmentation of sight which is seen to allow people to gaze into the cloaked and concealed and see what is coming at them before damage is done. The concept of apprehension may, thus, have more than merely descriptive value and be analytically useful as it captures the interplay between uncertainty and insecurity and our ways of dealing perceptually, practically, and intellectually with these social and experiential states.

Notes

1   The PAIGC (*Partido Africano pela Independencia de Guiné e Cabo Verde*) was the name of the liberation movement for Guinea-Bissau and Cape Verde and is currently an independent political party in Guinea-Bissau.
2   Where he is said to have been responsible for the elimination of thousands of *commandos Africanos*, i.e., the African soldiers that fought for the Portuguese colonial army against the Luso-African liberation movements.
3   http://news.bbc.co.uk/2/hi/africa/7918462.stm
4   Though they may, in other situations, engage in occult practises to make something happen, i.e., to bring about employment, luck, or love, they use the occult politically to make the invisible visible, allowing them to act so as to avoid the unforeseen touch.
5   *Panha* means 'to take' but is also used in the sense 'hit' or 'struck'.
6   Understood as local perceptions of signs of unfolding dangers rather than isolated politico-economic variables.

References

Canetti, E. (1984 [1960]) *Crowds and Power* (New York: Farrar, Straus and Giroux).
Comaroff, J. & J. L. Comaroff (1999) 'Occult Economies and the Violence of Abstraction: Notes from the South African Postcolony', *American ethnologist* 26 (2): 279–303.
Evans-Pritchard, E. E. (1976) *Witchcraft, Oracles, and Magic among the Azande* (Oxford: Clarendon Press).
Geschiere, P. (1997) *The Modernity of Witchcraft: Politics and the Occult in Postcolonial Africa* (Charlottesville: University Press of Virginia).
Hecht, D. & A. M. Simone (1994) *Invisible Governance: The Art of African Micropolitics* (New York: Autonomedia).
Henare, A., M. Holbraad & S. Wastell (2007) *Thinking Through Things – Theorising Artefacts Ethnographically* (New York: Routledge).
Malinowski, B. (1922) *Argonauts of the Western Pacific: An Account of Native Enterprise and Adventure in the Archipelagoes of Melanesian New Guinea* (London: Routledge and Kegan Paul).
Mbembe, A. (1992) 'The Banality of Power and the Aesthetics of Vulgarity in the Postcolony', *Public Culture* 4 (2): 1–30.
Rancière, J. (2001) *On the Shore of Politics* (London: Verso).
Sartre, J.-P. (1958) *Being and Nothingness* (London: Methuen & Co.).
Simmel, G. (1906) 'The Sociology of Secrecy and of Secret Societies', *The American Journal of Sociology* 11 (4), 441–498.
Viveiros De Castro, E. (1998) 'Cosmological Deixis and Amerindian Perspectivism', *The Journal of the Royal Anthropological Institute* 4 (3): 469–488.
Vigh, H. (2006 [2003]) *Navigating Terrains of War: Youth and Soldiering in Guinea-Bissau* (Oxford: Berghahn Books).

Vigh, H. (2006b) 'Social Death and Violent Life Chances', in Christiansen, C., M. Utas & H. Vigh (eds.) *Navigating Youth, Generating Adulthood: Social Becoming in an African Context* (Uppsala: NAI).

Vigh, H. (2011) 'Vigilance: on Conflict, Social Invisibility, and Negative Potentiality', *Social Analysis* 55 (3): 93–114.

Vigh, H. and D. Sausdal (2014) 'From Essence Back to Existence: Anthropology Beyond the Ontological Turn', *Anthropological Theory* 14 (1): 49-73.

Weber, M. (1958) *The Protestant Ethic and the Spirit of Capitalism* (New York: Schreibner's).

Whyte, S. R. (1997) *Questioning Misfortune: the Pragmatics of Uncertainty in Eastern Uganda* (Cambridge: Cambridge University Press).

Rhythms of Uncertainty and the Pleasures of Anticipation

Julie Soleil Archambault

In *Moments of Freedom*, Johannes Fabian (1998) writes,

> If freedom is conceived not just as free will plus the absence of domi-
> nation and constraint, but as the potential to transform thoughts,
> emotions, and experiences into creations that can be communicated
> and shared, and if 'potential', unless it is just another abstract condi-
> tion like absence of constraint, is recognized by its realizations, then it
> follows that there can never be freedom as a state of grace, permanent
> and continuous. As a quality of the process of human self-realization,
> freedom cannot be anything but contestatory and discontinuous or
> precarious. Freedom, in dialectical parlance, comes in moments (21).

Based on ethnographic material from the city of Inhambane in Mozambique,[1] this chapter examines young people's temporal experiences with
material uncertainty. In line with Fabian's understanding of freedom – a
shorthand for a sense of authorship and control over one's life (Jackson
1998) – as discontinuous, I propose to think about uncertainty as an
experience broken up and shaped by moments of respite, by recurrent
interludes set to the tempo of payday, as well as by more ad hoc ones,
such as when one gets a lucky break (*bolada*). Key to my discussion is the
idea that particular rhythms shape and modulate experiences of material
uncertainty in ways that translate into experientially distinct temporalities. These phenomenologically discrete experiences are nicely captured
by the distinction Inhambane residents like to make between living
and merely surviving. A rhythm, with its recurrence and tempo, brings
an element of predictability, if not a degree of certainty, into a social
environment otherwise marked by unpredictability. A rhythm either
interrupts, draws attention to, or muffles whatever is going on in the
background. In Mozambique, like in other countries in Africa, although
only a few may have direct access to wages, most will nonetheless feel

payday through a trickledown effect as recipients of remittances, entrepreneurs, or individuals relying on the generosity of others. As Kwei Armah's (1968) bus conductor puts it in the novel *The Beautyful Ones Are Not Yet Born*, 'Much better the days after pay day, much, much better. Then the fullness of the month touches each old sufferer with a feeling of new power' (2). This chapter examines this feeling of new power, these moments of freedom, which come with payday through the *planos*, or plans, young people make for 'the near future' (Guyer 2007).

Permanently Living in Survival Mode?

When describing how they get by, young Mozambicans use the word *desenrascar*, which literally means to disentangle oneself from a situation (Honwana 2012: xii). Echoing young people the world over (Amit & Dyck 2012; Honwana 2012; Jones 2010; Mains 2012; Vigh 2006), they speak of timely improvisation and highlight their resourcefulness in the face of adversity and uncertainty. The idea of *desenrascar* repeatedly comes up in everyday conversation, thus giving a sense that everyone lives life in survival mode. On a visit to Inhambane in 2012, I told Inocencio, a close friend and key research participant, that, inspired by such experiences of everyday improvisation as well as by an Africanist literature that documents similar tribulations in other locales, I was using the concept of uncertainty to make sense of everyday lived experiences of young people like him. He responded: 'What do you mean "*incerteza*"? I have a permanent job, I get my produce for the month at the shop around the corner, of course I always run out of money before the next payday, but I know that when the month ends I'll get paid again'. When this encounter took place, I had yet to fully appreciate how much the prospects of the cohort of young people that I have been following for nearly a decade had improved. Inocencio, who had recently taken up a teaching position at one of the city's secondary schools, was no exception; in fact, a significant number of the young men and women I knew who, only a few years earlier, commonly described themselves as not doing anything (Archambault 2012), now had jobs – not very well-paying jobs, but jobs that came with a salary and a sense of achievement, nonetheless. If I had overlooked this important change, it was in part because it did not appear to make much difference in these young people's lives, as I still repeatedly heard them talk about how they were having to *desenrascar* in order to make ends meet. These were more than mere commentaries, as I also knew first-hand that such concerns were often very real.

I have come to see Inocencio's qualms about the concept of uncertainty not as a direct challenge to my analytical framework but rather as speaking, first, of his sense of personal achievement;[2] and, second, of a clash of temporal perspectives between my own simultaneous focus on the everyday and on longer-term life trajectories, and Inocencio's views of the (near) future. Inocencio did complain about having to improvise to make ends meet – something I understood as material uncertainty – but his experience was also shaped by the fact that, every month, this everyday uncertainty would be temporarily relieved when he received his salary. I therefore take Inocencio's reaction as a cue to look more closely into different temporalities and more specifically into the different rhythms that modulate lived reality, so as to get a sense of what material uncertainty actually feels like. Simply put, I suggest that uncertainty feels differently at different points in a person's life but also at different times throughout the month. This is an important point because such monthly rhythms do not attract the same sort of local commentary – young people often give the impression that they are always having to *desenrascar* – nor the same level of academic scrutiny as do everyday struggles, on the one hand, and the crisis of social reproduction (Comaroff & Comaroff 2004), on the other. While building on the literature on coping tactics and on the structural and cultural underpinnings of material uncertainty (Haram & Yamba 2009; Honwana 2012; Steffen, Jenkins & Jessen 2005; Whyte 1997), the temporal perspective adopted here challenges the image of individuals permanently living in survival mode, given that, for most, a breather from daily improvisation eventually comes, even if only fleetingly. I suggest, through a look at the allocation of resources in Inhambane, that material uncertainty needs to be understood not as an ontological condition in the *longue durée* but rather as discontinuous and interrupted by intervals and moments of varying duration and intensity. In short, there are rhythms of uncertainty.

Rhythms of Uncertainty, Punctuated Time, and the Near Future

Although Durkheim[3] and Mauss had broached the subject of rhythm, especially in exchange and ritual contexts, it was Evans-Pritchard who introduced the idea of rhythms as shaping experience. In his attempt to uncover the influence of Nuer ecology on Nuer conception of time and space, Evans-Pritchard distinguished ecological time and its cyclical nature from structural time, or socially constructed distance. He showed how the distinctive rhythm of Nuer society was tuned to the diapason of rains and drought that guided the Nuer and their cattle back and forth between village and camp (Evans-Pritchard 1969 [1940]: 95). It followed that predictability and control were closely connected to particular rhythms. In Evans-Pritchard's words, given that 'seasonal and lunar changes repeat themselves year after year, [...] a Nuer standing at any point of time has conceptual knowledge of what lies before him and can *predict* and *organize* his life accordingly' (Evans-Pritchard 1969 [1940]: 95, my emphasis). Of course, even before we started worrying about global warming, seasons were not always as predictable as Evans-Pritchard postulated. In fact, in many cases, an increasingly unpredictable global ecology triggers anxiety more than comfort (Robins & Webster 1999). But, even if seasons, like other rhythms, are sometimes subject to arrhythmia, thinking of uncertainty as shaped by specific rhythms is, as I show below, a lead worth pursuing.

Doing so involves bracketing a Bergsonian understanding of time prevalent in anthropology that privileges a conception of time as fluid and continuous. Indeed, such a perspective ties into a wider paradigm of processual analysis in which continuity prevails. In Hodges's (2008) words, 'as globalization has become indubitably implicated in anthropological analysis, and the notion of bounded cultures increasingly problematic, the sense that social experience is "fluid", and exists in relation to a global capitalist system that is constituted of capital, labor and other "flows", has clearly become the dominant paradigm – propositions which are in turn predicated on implicit notions of temporal flow and historical flux' (401).[4] As a result, and as intimated by Fabian (1998), we sometimes fail to recognize that individuals may experience time as discontinuous and punctuated by events. Picking up on Jane Guyer's (2007) historical analysis of temporal sensibilities, I argue that it is in part owing to the temporal lens we privilege, one which occludes what Guyer calls the near future, that phenomenologically distinct experiences end up conflated.

Guyer (2007) suggests that such an oversight concerning the near future stems, firstly, from anthropology's interest in studying the past in the present, along with memory over hope (despite notable exceptions such as Crapanzano 2004; Miyazaki 2004);[5] and, secondly, from its commitment to the study of everyday life and what she calls the 'dailiness of postmodern spontaneity' (411). This is evident in the Africanist literature on youth where everyday struggles and longer-term ones are commonly conflated and seen as symptomatic of the same underlying forces, with the former understood as morphing into the latter. Indeed, the scholarship on youth, while attentive to everyday struggles, has developed around the core premise of unattainable adulthood (Brison & Dewey 2012; Cole 2010; Durham 2000; Groes-Green 2010; Honwana 2012; Larkin 2008; Peters 2011; Mains 2012; Sommers 2012; Weiss 2009; Vigh 2006). My aim is not to challenge this literature – in fact, I am very much indebted to it – but rather to argue for the need to also focus on the near future.

Guyer (2007) expresses a profound unease with the event-driven, punctuated time, and her lament is worth quoting: '[I]n many literatures and in informal and formal daily life, I perceive a similar rising awareness of a time that is punctuated rather than enduring: of fateful moments and turning points, the dates as events rather than as positions in a sequence or cycle, dates as qualitatively different rather than quantitatively cumulative' (416). What Guyer (2007) finds problematic is that this emphasis on punctuated time imposes a certain discipline on 'people's actions and imaginations' (416). Although I do not share Guyer's (2007) disquiet with punctuated time – and this is perhaps essentially because I look at payday whereas she looks at debt repayment dates – I answer her call to pay closer attention to the near future. To do so, I propose to focus on aspiration as a cultural capacity (cf. Appadurai 2004) and, more specifically, on the role of money in (near) 'future making' (Green et al. 2012). In fact, I find that the way punctuated time disciplines actions and aspirations can be a source of great pleasure. This is evident in the *planos* that individuals draft before getting paid or receiving remittances, and which are guided by a profound desire to have something to show or, in Fabian's (1998) terms, to yield a 'recognizable realization'. Before examining *planos* in more detail, I wish to situate in historical context local imaginaries around the salary and, more specifically, the rationales behind the allocation of scarce resources.

Wage Work in Southern Mozambique: Salaries to Live More than to Survive

Every month, the seemingly endless queues that suddenly start forming at the ATMs across town are a tell-tale sign that salaries have been paid. Daunting as they look, the queues are also deceiving and even slower than they appear, as many in line, equipped with several bank cards and scribbled down pin codes, are also there to withdraw money for colleagues or neighbours. Some of the people waiting patiently in line are wage workers who just got paid, but many are dependents of the latter. Although only a small percentage of the population engages in wage work, households usually have at least one wage earner living either within the household or abroad who contributes financially on a monthly basis.

Ever since it became a labour reserve for the South African mining industry in the late nineteenth century, southern Mozambique has been shaped by 'wage-labour capitalism' (Cooper 2002: 194; Harries 1994; Hull & James 2012). In its heyday, labour migration offered men a modest but nonetheless reliable source of income and became an important career path for many Mozambicans. By the same token, low salaries also consolidated forms of dependency and interdependency between men and women, and more broadly, between migrant workers and those they left behind in the countryside. Agricultural work, which soon became an essentially feminine mode of production, remained the main mode of subsistence for rural households while wages were channelled towards the purchase of modern consumer goods, as well as towards the formalization of marital unions that would further strengthen male authority (Harries 1994). To a large extent, wages earned through migrant labour were transformed into assets, if not spent on alcohol (Penvenne 1995), rather than allocated to day-to-day subsistence.

In urban centres like Inhambane, work in the civil service offered opportunities for advancement that were particularly appealing to an increasingly cosmopolitan and educated population. Like in rural areas, although households also came to depend on money to acquire staples like rice and bread, subsistence continued, in large part, to rest on agriculture, fruit trees (coconuts are a fundamental ingredient of the local diet), and fishing. Even today, residents still depend very much on such sources of food. Most households own coconut trees and grow vegetables for personal consumption, especially different types of green leaves such as cassava and pumpkin leaves used to make sauce. Those who have spent time in Maputo or abroad are confronted with the reality that everything when away needs to be purchased, unlike in Inhambane where one can easily gather foodstuff here and there.

Both economies bore important similarities. First, in both cases, many came to expect and rely on the financial contributions of a few wage workers. Second, income acquired through wage work was, to a large extent, used to purchase life's little extras rather than strictly for subsistence. The population came to depend on salaries to live (*viver*), more than to survive (*sobreviver*), a local distinction discussed in more detail below.

Trouble began after independence in 1975 when wage work opportunities started to dry up. First, the terms of the labour agreements between Mozambique and South Africa were seriously altered, and the number of migrant labourers was drastically cut (Roesch 1992: 465). Second, the labour market was also affected by the armed conflict (1977–92) and, later, by the adoption of structural adjustment programs in the late 1980s, which, together, resulted in major state retrenchment, including a drastic reduction of the civil service and a drop in salaries (Hanlon 1996; Pfeiffer, Sherr-Gimbel & Augusto 2007), a scenario found in many parts of the continent (Mbembe & Roitman 1995). Following the resolution of the civil war in 1992, Mozambique was soon hailed as an African success story owing to the country's earnest post-war reconstruction and its demonstrated commitment to democratization. However, as reports of deepening poverty among large segments of the population started emerging and as the urban poor took to the streets in protest of rising food prices in 2008 and then again in 2010, observers started talking about a more nuanced Mozambique paradox that better captures the growing economic disparity underlying economic progress. With the turn of the century, interest in the country's reconstruction which was manifest by the influx of aid has started waning, as mega projects now channel the better part of foreign aid (Castel-Branco 2009). More recently, the discovery of oil and gas in the north and the country's overall resilience to the global financial crisis has rekindled optimism. As Mozambique enters an era of prosperity – it now boasts one of the world's fastest-growing economies (Smith 2012) – it remains unclear how the country's economic growth will translate in terms of socio-economic security. But for the secondary-school educated young people I work with, things appear to be looking up.

Access to wage work is also shaped by local networks of patronage. Jobs are usually secured through a sponsor (*padrinho*) who is then entitled to the candidate's salary for a predetermined number of months. This is called *pagar a vaga* or paying for the vacancy. If young people see this protocol with cynicism, they have little choice but to play along with it. Such manoeuvers also reveal a lot about how salaries are imagined and used, and this is what I wish to highlight here. For example, after completing a course in meteorology, Jhoker, a young man in his mid-twenties, finally secured a position at the weather station. When I last saw him, he had been working at the weather station for the past six months and had only just started receiving his wages. This is how he made sense of the process:

Jhoker: The first few months were used to pay [my *padrinho*] for the vacancy. Until I got paid last month, I didn't even know how much I'd be making.

Julie: But how did you manage without a salary for nearly half a year?
Jhoker: Ah, you know, one has to *desenrascar*, I've survived all my life before that without a salary.

Indeed, people do not rely on salaries to survive, in part because salaries tend to be lower than the cost of living. According to a recent report on the cost of living,[6] it was technically impossible for someone earning minimum wage to support a dependent, let alone a family.[7] In reality, even individuals on minimum wage manage to support several dependents, thanks to improvisation, wider social networks, and urban agriculture. I argue, however, that if people have recourse to such alternatives, it is not only because salaries are insufficient, but also because salaries are understood to serve other purposes than everyday subsistence. Jhoker's statement should, therefore, also be read more literally: Inhambane residents do not rely on salaries *to survive*, because they rely instead on salaries *to live*. Young people draw a distinction to which the Portuguese language lends itself well between *viver* (to live) and *sobreviver* (to survive), that highlights how, as they struggle to get by, they also seek, in their words, 'to live' and 'feel alive' (Archambault 2013: 89). In short, the allocation of resources is informed by this important distinction between surviving and living.

Technically, the distinction is not entirely accurate, as a proportion of one's salary or remittances is usually set aside to buy a *rancho* – a ration of products that typically includes basic items such as rice, cooking oil, sugar, tea, salt, and soap. Payday is also the day when most repay some of their debts, especially to shop owners, as produce are often paid for in arrears.[8] But a significant proportion is usually allocated to *planos*. *Planos* are specific objectives that people hope to achieve when they receive an expected sum of money. Common plans include the purchase of building material, an electronic appliance such as a television set or a freezer, a blanket, clothing or pair of shoes, as well as the visit to a traditional healer, the performance of a ritual, or monthly payment to a rotating credit scheme. For the remainder of the month, individuals improvise, they *desenrascar*, to find ingredients for sauce and to address other punctual needs. Within this time frame, many suffer considerably, even going to bed hungry, and bodies often bear the signs of malnutrition.

Further insight into the earmarking of wages comes from a young woman who emphasized the importance of having a salary. 'Even if it's not much', she said, 'at least you know it'll come and you'll be able to buy things'. She criticized her sister-in-law who had recently given birth to a fourth child only shortly after her husband had secured a job – his first salaried job – as a garbage collector for the municipality. 'Now that Samo finally has a salary they could have felt a little more secure. They could have *fazer tempo* [waited] between salaries. With a salary, you can divide it: allocate one part to buying a *rancho* and the other to doing something else. But now that they have a baby, and need to buy formula, they can't buy things, they have worry about food, just worry about surviving'. The idea of *fazer tempo* (to wait) explicitly points to the temporal experiences at play. Along a similar line, when I ask people if they are happy with their salary, they usually reply: 'It's worth waiting for' (*da para aguardar*). Recurrence and predictability are part of what makes access to a salary so appealing.

Hungry Divas and the Allocation of Resources

The first time I went to Inhambane was to help manage a small guesthouse owned, at the time, by South African friends of mine. It was only a couple of months after the great floods of 2000 and the few tourists that did venture into the area usually preferred to head straight to the nearby beach resorts. Today, although tourists still tend to bypass the city, the guesthouse survives under new ownership and offers employment to nearly twenty people. I have since returned to Inhambane several times to conduct doctoral and postdoctoral research. Over the years, I have developed close friendships with several guesthouse employees, a number of whom still work there today. In 2012, I spent six weeks conducting research on consumption and household formation with employees. I also resided at the guesthouse for the duration of my stay. The mostly female staff (fourteen of the nineteen employees were women) were aged between eighteen and forty-one. Most already had children – according to the boss, some even planned their pregnancies so that their maternity leave would fall during the busy Christmas period – but all, except two who were married, lived as single women.

When I returned from running errands one afternoon, I found most of the employees sitting around the table in a heated debate. It was the end of the month and the boss had paid only part of his staff as he was waiting for money to come through to pay the rest. Thinking I was taking their side, I suggested that the boss should have given a little to everyone rather than pay some at the expense of others. I assumed that their very survival depended on their salary and that, had they all received a little, they could have managed to get by until they received the full amount. Shocked by my insensitive suggestion, the employees agreed that that would have been even worse. 'With the little he gives you now, you won't be able to do anything', Zenabo explained. 'Same thing with the little that will come later', she added. 'You've made your plans [*teus planos*] but then you don't get paid! That's the problem!' Everyone wanted to have the lump sum to pursue their plans and to do so all at the same time,[9] for fairness, even if this meant waiting a week or two. As I explained, the relationship between salaries and subsistence is not as straightforward as could be expected.

Despite receiving more than the minimum wage, the staff regularly complained among themselves, as well as to their boss and me, that they had no money and that they were hungry. The boss thought this was nonsense. As he put it to me: 'They dress like divas and half of them are overweight yet they say they don't get paid enough!' Underlying his understanding of poverty was the assumption that poor people should address basic needs before tending to what are commonly seen as more frivolous forms of consumption (cf. Douglas & Ney 1998). Whatever the boss thought, hunger was a recurrent topic of conversation. The employees were not guaranteed a staff meal but were allowed to help themselves to leftovers and could usually improvise in order to put together a hot meal for everyone. They were rather cynical about their predicament and liked to say that they enjoyed eating the bones and scraps that tourists would leave behind. Sometimes, when there was really nothing lying about, they would either go without eating or would collect contributions of MZN 5 or 10 towards the purchase of ingredients. Although MZN 5 amounted to less than 0.2% of their monthly wages,[10] most could rarely afford to do so. And this was mainly because they had already allocated most of their wages to *planos*. Instead of using their wages to minimize the need to *desenrascar* throughout most of the month, they preferred to use them to buy stuff.

Planos and the Pleasures of Anticipation

For Henri Lefebvre (2004 [1992]: 8), cyclical time, like the rhythm of the salary, although always interacting with linear time, distinguishes itself from the latter in that it contains a beginning. Building on a similar idea and echoing Evans-Pritchard, You (1994) emphasizes the anticipation that accompanies such expected beginnings. In her formulation, 'the essence of rhythm is not merely the perceived order (or pattern) of repetition (recurrence) of something; it is the demand, preparation and anticipation for something to come' (363). It is this orientation towards the future, a near future, contained in rhythms that *planos* speak to. Part of the salary's appeal lies in the pleasures of anticipation as plans are drawn up that may or may not materialize (cf. Nielsen 2011). 'I have my plans', people say rather secretively, often unwilling to disclose the details so as to hold on to an idea that could potentially never take shape, were a deal to fall through, a more pressing need to arise, or some sort of misfortune to set in. The contrast with borrowed money illustrates the role of anticipation in the pleasures of planning. As Gina, a young unemployed woman who relies on remittances, explained: 'When you ask someone for money, you inevitably have that terrible feeling of shame. You use the money, but because of that feeling you don't really feel the pleasure of the money. Then when the time comes to pay it back, what you did with the money no longer has any weight'. This sort of day-to-day borrowing – not the larger-scale borrowing in the pursuit of entrepreneurial ends – tends to operate in a time frame of urgency and immediacy. *Planos*, in contrast, are prospective in nature.

Although they did not necessarily verbalize their excitement in ways that I could compellingly reproduce here, the pleasures of anticipation accompanying *planos*, the elation prompted by a prospective purchase, was manifest in other ways. The way Inhambane residents handled or simply stroked items that were on their wish list – a comforter, a smart pair of shoes, a new mobile phone – suggested an unspoken yet no less tangible enjoyment. The pleasure of anticipation was also perceptible when individuals shared their plans with me. For example, when I accompanied Benedita, a young woman I know well, to have a look at a glass-door cabinet that she was saving up for, it was evident how waiting to gain ownership was, in itself, a source of delight. Benedita did not say much other than give specific details on how much the cabinet would cost and how long she had been saving up for it, but the way she lit up when she examined the smoothness of the cabinet's hinges and caressed its polished surface was arguably more revealing than words. It was no secret that, at the time, Benedita was finding it particularly challenging to feed her children, but alongside this daily hardship she was proud of her ability to think about the future. This was by no means seen as a case of misguided priorities; instead, it was understood as a manifestation of what Appadurai (2004) calls aspiration as cultural capacity.

The contours of anticipation as a cultural capacity become clearer when contrasted to hope. Hope, as Crapanzano (1985, 2004) so nicely shows, is the 'passive counterpart' of desire, the 'field of desire in waiting' (116). As Inhambane residents like to say: 'Hope is the last thing to die'. Anticipation, on the other hand, operates in a more proximal time frame; one that is also more palpable. And unlike hope, anticipation rests more on human agency – in this case, on careful planning and self-control than on some other form of agency – call it God, luck, or fate (cf. Crapanzano 2004) – though these forces are often understood to also interfere. The capacity to aspire and desire, the potential to transform thoughts into creations, is a source of pleasure, even if *planos* often remain just that: imagined projects. Frustration easily sets in when plans remain out of reach; however, the ability to step aside from the daily grind of improvisation to imagine a more comfortable future is in itself part of the crafting of meaningful and purposeful lives.

Although they struggle with everyday subsistence, and despite the fact that many *planos* never materialize, it is, in part, through such *planos* that young people in Inhambane project themselves into the near future, beyond everyday concerns with subsistence but also, in a sense, in dialogue with longer-term aspirations. *Planos* are the stuff of the near future, but their materiality also speaks of more far-sighted objectives: ones of respectability and membership (cf. Ferguson 2002). After all, the recurrence of payday is also plotted as increments in a more linear, ideally cumulative, progression (cf. Lefebvre 2004 [1992]: 8). One is in a hurry to see the end of the month arrive. In fact, I heard young people in Inhambane wish out loud that salaries be paid weekly. By this they did not mean that they wanted their monthly salary to be divided into weekly instalments, but rather that the monthly rhythm of payday be accelerated to a weekly one. The end of the month never comes soon enough.

Unpredictability and the Dangers of Liquidity

The quest for predictability and security is, by no means, specific to the Inhambane context. For example, in his research on the economics of life on a farm in Zimbabwe, Bolt (2012) shows how his informants similarly 'strive for predictability under unstable conditions', though in the Zimbabwean case this involves combining wage work and trade not only to maximize revenues, but also to secure one's position on the farm and gain access to a room from which to run a business (114–9). The paths imagined and deemed most appropriate to attain such predictability are, however, predicated on local specificities. Like the cyclical ecological rhythms that once framed how the Nuer *predicted* and *organized* their lives, to paraphrase Evans-Pritchard (1969 [1940]: 95), it is to the rhythm of payday that Inhambane residents predict and organize their lives.

As the following example illustrates, the appeal of a salary (or of remittances) lies not only in its monetary value but also in its recurrence and predictability. When I first met Pascual, he was working as an ambulant photographer, which entailed walking around the city with a camera and taking pictures of those willing to strike a pose. The contract was unwritten and easily broken. At the time, Pascual had to make the trip to Maxixe, the city on the mainland side of the bay, to develop his films, expending without any guarantee that his clients would pay for the photographs. Since then, Pascual has acquired a digital camera and, following a considerable increase in profits, was able to secure a piece of land on which he is currently building a house. Although Pascual is doing rather well, he nonetheless wishes that he had a job as a civil servant, confident that receiving a salary rather than ad hoc payments would allow him to better manage his income. In his words: 'Say I get MZN 500 one day, I can easily spend it all in one go, say a desire suddenly appears, as I know that I'll probably get money again the next day. But it's hard to plan, as I never know exactly how much I'll get. And there's no security. If I stop working because I'm ill or something, then the money stops coming in. [...] It's hard to plan', he concludes, 'without a salary'.

Others who, like Pascual, were running small businesses also touched on the challenges of unpredictability and the need for discipline. Much can interfere with the realization of one's plans. As Green et al. (2012) point out, '[T]he liquidity of money renders it a flexible vehicle for personal and collective aspirations while representing risk of leakage to other persons or ventures' (1641). The realization of plans often involves intermediary phases in which cash is first transformed temporarily into objects that have a store value. For example, I encouraged my research assistant to open up a bank account, but he found himself unable to save up money. He decided that the only way he could, in his words, 'have something to show for', was to buy corrugated iron sheets. These he stored carefully with an eye on one day fixing his house or selling them to purchase something else. Transforming his income into building material saved him both from the pressures of redistribution and from his own indulgence.

Likewise, by temporarily transforming cash into mobile phone airtime scratch cards for resale, young people were able to hold on to money until they had amassed a sufficient amount to put towards a larger *plano*. 'It's like a bank', explained a young woman who worked at the university and sold airtime from home on the side, 'so that I don't end up spending all my money'. There is, in fact, an important distinction to make between the fluidity of cash and the security of things. Given that theft is rather common, however, such a distinction should not be overemphasized.

The metaphor of consumption is commonly used to refer to money that 'disappears', that is, money that is not used towards the purchase of something durable. In many cases, it is a rather literal metaphor as money is often simply used to buy food or drink. This folk distinction between investment and consumption departs from the one drawn by economists regarding the productive and consumptive use of money whereby productive use refers to money that is invested into education, housing, or business, whereas consumptive use refers to money spent on consumer goods and food (Green et al. 2012), mainly in its looser understanding of what qualifies as an investment. As Benvinda, a woman in her late twenties with a history of failed business ventures, put it: 'It's hard to run a business. The first day that you start your business, you still have to eat that day so it's easy to eat the money of the business right from the beginning. Already on the first day you're jeopardizing your business'. Moving to the specificities of her recent experience, Benvinda explained how after her husband lost his job, the family started 'feeling hunger' and were forced to use the produce and profit from their market stall to feed themselves. The stock soon ran out, leaving them with little choice but to sell the stall. They found a buyer who gave them half their asking price and agreed to pay the rest in instalments. A few months later, the man decided that he no longer wanted to purchase the stall and asked for his money back. But, as Benvinda explained, they had already 'eaten' the money. The couple later managed to find a second buyer, but one who was only willing to pay considerably less than the original asking price and therefore only partially covering their debt. Unlike the first buyer, the second one only paid little by little and, in Benvinda's words, they 'never saw the money'. 'The money just disappeared', her husband added emphatically. Like with Pascual's experience and that of the guesthouse staff, money that trickles in appears to vanish, as it is consumed on day-to-day expenses rather than on things that will remain, on *planos*.

Bush's rendition of his arm-wrestling days further clarifies how plans emerge and stand in contrast to other forms of resource allocation:

> There was a time when we used to play arm wrestling in the neighbourhood. At first it was MZN 10 winner takes all but then it went up to MZN 20. When one wins and then another, that's fine, as money just circulates among the players. The problem is when one starts winning repeatedly and accumulating money. You would arrive there with MZN 100 and soon end up with nothing… That's when the *planos* appear! When you arrived, you had no *planos* but once the

money's gone, that's when you start thinking about what you could have done with the money.

On another occasion, Bush was angry with China, an electrician he sometimes worked for. 'China has a problem', he told me. 'He makes sure that I don't know how much he's getting paid for the contract. Then when he gets paid, he takes me out drinking with him but he doesn't realize that maybe I have my own plans, that maybe I want to buy cement or something. Everyone needs to buy stuff, at least tooth-paste'. As these examples suggest, *planos* cannot be dissociated from the material context in which they emerge, but their imagined dimension is just as important when it comes to understanding what material uncertainty entails and feels like.

Alongside this monthly cycle, everyday uncertainty is also interrupted by lucky breaks.[11] Every now and then, improvisation yields unexpected returns, such as when one has the opportunity to do a *bolada* (literally, a lucky break) after 'finding' something with a resale value. For example, the last time I was in Inhambane, on my way to Jhoker's house, I saw DB, a young man well known for his shady dealings, who was drinking at the old train station. A few hours later, DB came knocking on Jhoker's door. He showed us the laptop that he was carrying in a messenger bag and explained that if we knew of anyone interested, he wanted MZN 13,000 for it. Off he went in search of a buyer. Later that evening, as I was walking home, I saw DB a third time. He no longer had the bag and instead was sporting a very big smile. Even if he only managed to get half his asking price, as the rumour that circulated the following day suggested, he would have pocketed double the minimum monthly wage in less than a day. While few are professional thieves like DB, a number of young people in Inhambane participate in petty crime every now and then, not as a way of life but as a means to fulfil certain aspirations that may otherwise remain beyond their reach. Like the portion of one's salary allocated to *planos*, the proceeds of a *bolada* are also spent to make one feel alive. In the case of *boladas*, however, this is usually achieved through conspicuous consumption of a more ephemeral nature than through an investment in durable stuff. As a young man put it to me: 'When you steal something, money, the money isn't part of your plans, the money just appears all of a sudden and as a result it will also disappear suddenly'. Being at the right place at the right time to find something or to benefit from the generosity of someone who has is key. Such lucky breaks also punctuate everyday uncertainty, though in less predictable ways, and offer welcomed moments of respite from life in survival mode. Like the realization of *planos*, these more hedonistic forms of consumption are experienced in contrast to survival-mode consumption, as part of what makes one feel alive, however temporarily. Like the small-scale entrepreneurs who dream of the regularity and predictability of a salary, some young women also attempt to secure a reliable source of income through their relationships with men in the form of *mensades* (monthly allowances). In his research on the informal sexual economy in Maputo, Mozambique's capital, Groes-Green (2013) shows how securing such *mensades* involves not only the young women themselves but also their female relatives. Like in Maputo, the intimate economy in Inhambane also offers livelihood opportunities for young women and their families (Archambault 2013). Some of the women I worked with used a market idiom when talking about such relationships. For example, they would refer to a boyfriend as a boss (*meu patrão*) to highlight both the man's authority and their expectations to receive regular monthly financial assistance.

In Inhambane, though young people's narratives tend to emphasize life in survival mode in which material uncertainty is cast as an inescapable feature of everyday life, a closer look at rhythms of uncertainty suggests a more complex picture in which everyday uncertainty is no doubt very real but also punctuated by recurrent intervals of varying duration and intensity that are tuned to the tempo of the salary. And so plans are made, whether one is a wage worker or enjoys the favours of one who is, and although payments are sometimes postponed, such delays do not so much transform the cycle as slow down its rhythm. It is by making plans that individuals feel alive rather than merely surviving.

The Temporality of Spatial Metaphors

Anthropology has made considerable headway in showing how individuals living in social environments marked by material uncertainty participate in different, at times overlapping, fields that command and complement each other, often in unexpected ways. Indeed, the once-rigid dichotomy between the formal and the informal economy was collapsed to leave way for a more dynamic framework (Hart 2010; Hull & James 2012). Concepts such as social navigation (Vigh 2006), tactical agency (Honwana 2005), and zigzag capitalism (Jeffrey & Dyson 2013, building on Jones 2010) are particularly useful in making sense of how people address and engage with material uncertainty. However compelling, such spatial metaphors risk overemphasizing spatial practices at the expense of temporal experiences. By casting economic activities in space, in terms of more or less discrete spheres within which and between which individuals navigate everyday uncertainty, there is a risk of overlooking the underlying rhythms to which individuals move between wage work, sex work, improvisation, urban agriculture, and petty crime. One of the main insights in Lefebvre's essay on rhythmanalysis is precisely into the workings of different layers of rhythms that influence each other but which, instead of morphing into some sort of process, are experienced and imagined as phenomenologically distinct. There are always moments of respite that interrupt uncertainty and during which one can feel alive, perhaps even free, for a moment (cf. Fabian 1998). For these reasons, uncertainty is better understood as an experience broken up and shaped by such moments, as discontinuous though no less momentous.

Notes

1 The paper draws from ongoing ethnographic field research in the city of Inhambane, Mozambique, among young adults in their twenties since 2006 which was funded, in part, by the Economic and Social Research Council UK. A Leverhulme Early Career Fellowship then allowed me to work on revisions. I am very grateful to both funding bodies for their generous support. I had the opportunity to present the chapter at the Anthropology Seminar at the University of St Andrews and at the African Studies Seminar at the University of Edinburgh. I thank the participants for their probing questions and useful comments.

2 Inocencio was not going to let me downplay his success and rightly so.

3 Durkheim's discussion of collective effervescence was built on an understanding of ecstasy as rhythm through ritual (You 1994: 368–9).

4 Ferguson (2006) offers a compelling critique of flows and flux by showing how the circulation of capital on the African continent is better understood as hopping between enclaves, thus bypassing some regions all together, rather than as flowing.

5 A growing body of Africanist literature has since emerged that looks at how individuals project themselves into the future (Cole 2010; de Boeck 2011; Mains 2012; Piot 2010).

6 In 2009, the minimum monthly wage for a state employee was 1,826 Meticais (MZN) while the basic monthly cost of living per person was estimated at MZN 1,221 (O País 2009). The NGO sector, on the other hand, offers more competitive salaries but jobs are scarce.

7 At the time, MZN 20 was worth about USD 1.00. For comparison, the daily wages of unskilled workers were between MZN 50 and 60 per day.

8 Expenses like electricity and telephone bills are on a pay-as-you-go basis, allowing households and individuals to manage their consumption according to what they have at hand whenever they run out and many take the opportunity to top up on payday. Unless they are recent immigrants, few pay rent, though most pay an annual land tax.

9 Rotating credit schemes follow a similar logic.
10 Everyone except the night-watchmen and the manager received MZN 3,000 (about USD 100) per month. The one-dollar-a-day benchmark commonly used in the development industry is of limited relevance in this context.
11 Overlapping these different rhythms is the agricultural cycle that affects the price and availability of fresh produce.

References

Amit, V. & N. Dyck (2012) *Young Men in Uncertain Times* (New York & Oxford: Berghahn Books).

Appadurai, A. (2004) 'The Capacity to Aspire: Culture and the Terms of Recognition', in Rao, V. & M. Walton (eds.) *Culture and Public Action: A Cross-Disciplinary Dialogue* (Washington: World Bank Publications), pp. 59–84.

Archambault, J. S. (2012) '"Travelling While Sitting Down": Mobile Phones, Mobility and the Communication Landscape in Inhambane, Mozambique', *Africa* 82: 392–411.

Archambault, J. S. (2013) 'Cruising through Uncertainty: Cell Phone and the Politics of Display and Disguise in Inhambane, Mozambique', *American Ethnologist* 40: 88–101.

Bolt, M. (2012) 'Waged Entrepreneurs, Policed Informality: Work, the Regulation of Space and the Economy of the Zimbabwean-South African Border', *Africa* 82: 111–130.

Brison, K. & S. Dewey (2012) *Super Girls, Gangstas, Freeters, and Xenomaniacs: Gender and Modernity in Global Youth Cultures* (Syracuse: Syracuse University Press).

Castel-Branco, C. N. (2009) 'Economia Política Da Fiscalidade E a Indústria Extractiva', in Second Conference of the Institute of Social and Economic Studies. Maputo, Mozambique.

Cole, J. (2010) *Sex and Salvation. Imagining the Future in Madagascar* (Chicago: University of Chicago Press).

Comaroff, J. & J. L. Comaroff (2004) 'Notes on Afromodernity and the Neo World Order: An Afterword', in Weiss, B (ed.) *Producing African Futures. Ritual and Reproduction in a Neoliberal Age* (Leiden: Brill), pp. 329–348.

Cooper, F. (2002) *Africa since 1940: The Past of the Present* (Cambridge: Cambridge University Press).

Crapanzano, V. (1985) *Waiting. The Whites of South Africa* (London: Random House).

Crapanzano, V. (2004) *Imaginative Horizons. An Essay in Literary-Philosophical Anthropology* (Chicago: University of Chicago Press).

de Boeck, F. (2011) 'Inhabiting Ocular Ground: Kinshasa's Future in the Light of Congo's Spectral Urban Politics', *Cultural Anthropology* 26: 263–286.

Douglas, M. & S. Ney (1998) *Missing Persons: A Critique of Personhood in the Social Sciences* (Berkeley: University of California Press).

Durham, D. (2000) 'Youth and the Social Imagination in Africa: Introduction to Parts 1 and 2', *Anthropological Quarterly* 73: 113–120.

Evans-Pritchard, E. E. (1969 [1940]) *The Nuer. A Description of the Modes of Livelihood and Political Institutions of a Nilotic People* (Oxford: Oxford University Press).

Fabian, J. (1998) *Moments of Freedom: Anthropology and Popular Culture* (Charlotesville: University Press of Virginia).

Ferguson, J. (2002) 'Of Mimicry and Membership: Africans and the "New World Society"', *Cultural Anthropology* 17: 551–69.

Ferguson, J. (2006) *Global Shadows. Africa in the Neoliberal World Order* (Durham & London: Duke University Press).

Green, M., U. Kothari, C. Mercerand & D. Mitlin (2012) 'Saving, Spending, and Future-Making: Time Discipline, and Money in Development', *Environment and Planning* 44: 1641–1656.

Groes-Green, C. (2010) 'Orgies of the Moment: Bataille's Anthropology of Transgression and the Defiance of Danger in Post-Socialist Mozambique', *Critique of Anthropology* 10: 385–407.

Groes-Green, C. (2013) '"To Put Men in a Bottle": Eroticism, Kinship, Female Power, and Transactional Sex in Maputo, Mozambique', *American Ethnologist* 40: 102–117.

Guyer, J. (2007) 'Prophecy and the Near Future: Thoughts on Macroeconomic, Evangelical, and Punctuated Time', *American Ethnologist* 34: 409–421.

Hanlon, J. (1996) *Peace without Profit. How the IMF Blocks Rebuilding in Mozambique* (Oxford: James Currey).

Haram, L. & B. Yamba (2009) *Dealing with Uncertainty in Contemporary African Lives* (Uppsala: Nordiska Afrikainstitutet).

Harries, P. (1994) *Work, Culture and Identity* (Portsmouth: Heinemann).

Hart, K. (2010) 'Informal Economy', in Hart, K., J. Laville & A. D. Cattani (eds.) *The Human Economy: A Citizen's Guide* (Cambridge: Polity).

Hodges, M. (2008) 'Rethinking Time's Arrow. Bergson, Deleuze and the Anthropology of Time', *Anthropological Theory* 8: 399–429.

Honwana, A. (2005) 'Innocent and Guilty. Child-Soldiers as Interstitial and Tactical Agents', in Honwana, A. & F. De Boeck (eds.) *Makers and Breakers. Children & Youth in Postcolonial Africa* (Oxford: James Currey), pp. 31–52.

Honwana, A. (2012) *The Time of Youth: Work, Social Change, and Politics in Africa* (West Hartford, CT: Kumarian Press).

Hull, E. & D. James (2012) 'Introduction: Popular Economies in South Africa', *Africa* 82: 1–19.

Jackson, M. (1998) *Minima Ethnographica. Intersubjectivity and the Anthropological Project* (Chicago: Chicago University Press).

Jeffrey, C. & J. Dyson (2013) 'Zigzag Capitalism: Youth Entrepreneurship in the Contemporary Global South', *Geoforum*.

Jones, J. L. (2010) '"Nothing Is Straight in Zimbabwe": The Rise of the Kuyika-Kiya Economy 2000–2008', *Journal of Southern African Studies* 36: 285–299.

Kwei Armah, A. (1968) *The Beautyful Ones Are Not Yet Born* (Harlow: Heinemann).

Lefebvre, H. (2004 [1992]) *Rhythmanalysis: Space, Time and Everyday Life* (New York: Continuum).

Mains, D. (2012) *Hope Is Cut: Youth, Unemployment, and the Future in Urban Ethiopia* (Philadelphia: Temple University Press).

Mbembe, A. & J. Roitman (1995) 'Figures of the Subject in Times of Crisis', *Public Culture* 7: 323–352.

Miyazaki, H. (2004) *The Method of Hope. Anthropology, Philosophy, and Fijian Knowledge* (Redwood City: Stanford University Press).

Nielsen, M. (2011) 'Futures Within: Reversible Time and House Building in Maputo, Mozambique', *Anthropological Theory* 11: 397–423.

País, O. (2009) 'Salários Mínimos. Propostas Ainda Aquém Das Necessidades Básicas', in País, O. pp. 16. Maputo.

Penvenne, J. (1995) *African Workers and Colonial Racism* (London: James Currey).

Peters, K. (2011) *War and the Crisis of Youth in Sierra Leone* (Cambridge: Cambridge University Press).

Pfeiffer, J., K. Sherr-Gimbeland, O. J. Augusto (2007) 'The Holy Spirit in the Household: Pentecostalism, Gender, and Neoliberalism in Mozambique', *American Anthropologist* 109: 688–700.

Piot, C. D. (2010) *Nostalgia for the Future* (Chicago: Chicago University Press).

Robins, K. & F. Webster (1999) *Times of the Technoculture* (London: Routledge).

Roesch, O. (1992) 'Renamo and the Peasantry in Southern Mozambique: A View from Gaza Province', *Canadian Journal of African Studies* 26: 462–484.

Smith, D. (2012) 'Boom Time for Mozambique, Once the Basket Case of Africa', *The Guardian*, London.

Sommers, M. (2012) *Stuck. Rwandan Youth and the Struggle for Adulthood* (Athens & London: The University of Georgia Press).

Steffen, V., R. Jenkins & H. Jessen (2005) *Managing Uncertainty: Ethnographic Studies of Illness, Risk and the Struggle for Control* (Copenhagen: Museum Tusculanum Press).

Vigh, H. (2006) *Navigating Terrains of War. Youth and Soldiering in Guinea-Bissau* (New York: Berghahn Books).

Weiss, B. (2009) *Street Dreams and Hip-Hop Barbershops: Global Fantasy in Urban Tanzania* (Bloomington: Indiana University Press).

Whyte, S. R. (1997) *Questioning Misfortune* (Cambridge: Cambridge University Press).

You, H. (1994) 'Defining Rhythm: Aspects of an Anthropology of Rhythm', *Culture, Medicine and Psychiatry* 18: 361–384.

Embracing Uncertainty: Young People on the Move in Addis Ababa's Inner City[1]

Marco Di Nunzio

Multiple Lives

This chapter discusses how young men's understanding of the unpredictable as a ground for action and hope in inner-city Addis Ababa can inform anthropological examinations on the productivity of uncertainty. I start by narrating the biographies of three young men who, more than anybody else, taught me about the promises and the predicaments of living with uncertainty. As Cooper and Pratten have reminded us in their introduction, accounting for the messiness, the contingencies, and the multiplicities of life trajectories is not just a mere exercise of ethnographic writing. Studying biographies provides scholars with interpretative tools to consider how people translate the indeterminacy of existence into a sense of possibility and, ultimately, seek to connect what has been with what could be.

Haile, Ibrahim, and Said[2] were born in inner-city Addis Ababa in the period between the early 1970s and the mid-1980s. As with many of their friends, they belong to the first generation of those born in Addis Ababa in families originally from areas away from the capital. Their parents were among those who migrated from their home regions from the 1960s and through the following two decades, and came to constitute the bulk of the population of the Ethiopian capital in that period (Getahun Benti 2007). The three grew up in a poor neighbourhood in Arada, the old city centre of Addis Ababa. They lived in tin-roofed government houses and their family members were engaged in work which did not allow them to consider themselves well off. When Haile was a child, his mother engaged in commercial sex to support herself and her sons. Despite some attempts to run a small retail shop, Ibrahim's father had worked as a waiter in an established pastry shop for over thirty years.

149

Haile, Ibrahim, and Said lived through a period marked by significant transformations in the history of the country. When Haile was four,
junior army officers deposed Haile Selassie, the emperor who had ruled
Ethiopia continuously since the 1930s, with the exception of the five
years of Italian colonial occupation. In the mid-1980s, when Haile was
thirteen, Ibrahim was six, and Said just a small child, the country had
seen nearly ten years of the rule of the military junta, the *Derg*, the
dramatic days of the Red Terror,[3] and the gradual transformation of the
country into a socialist regime, with the nationalization of private assets
and campaigns of resettlement and 'villagization' in rural areas. When
I started my fieldwork in October 2009, Ethiopia and my informants
had experienced yet more transformations. In 1991, the downfall of the
military junta and the victory of the Tigray People's Liberation Front
(TPLF) were followed by the opening of the free market and a gradual
liberalization of the economy. Since then, the Ethiopian People's Revolutionary Democratic Front (EPRDF), a coalition of political parties led
by the TPLF, had ruled the country through a combination of repressive
measures and extensive developmental politics (Vaughan & Tronvoll
2003).

During this span of time, a succession of reversals, conjunctures, single events, relations, and interactions steered the lives of my informants towards one direction or another. Potential life trajectories opened
up and were closed down as they dealt with the challenges, obstacles,
opportunities, and misfortunes that dotted their existence. When I met
Ibrahim, he was in his early thirties. He had recently found a job as a car
attendant – or, as people say in Addis Ababa, a 'parking guy' – in a cooperative the local government had established for unemployed youth.
The job of 'parking guys' consisted of issuing tickets every half an hour
to cars parked on the streets assigned to them by the local government
and then collecting payments from the drivers. This government initiative was not a localized one. It was part of a broader attempt by the
Ethiopian ruling party to recapture the 'youth' who had supported the
opposition parties in the 2005 election and participated in the subsequent riots and demonstrations.[4] On top of his job, Ibrahim made extra
money by brokering the sale of second-hand mobile phones part time.
In the past, he had had multiple engagements with both wage labour
and the informal street economy. He had been a street fighter, a skilful
hustler and thief, and a manager of video houses, but also a specialized
construction worker, a guard, an assistant carpenter, a stoneworker, and,
for a short time, a successful shoe-seller. The plurality and heterogene-
ity of potential trajectories and possible lives that Ibrahim had engaged

with over the years had made his life, as he himself reckoned, 'long' and intense.

Said and Haile had also had long and intense lives. Said, a young man in his late twenties – after hearing my own personal history, mainly revolving around schooling and, for a period, political activism – told me that I had led a very short life. He himself had been a student until his late teens and, after that, a hawker, a renter of bicycles on the street, a thief stealing car parts and mobile phones, and, latterly, a 'parking guy'. At the time of my fieldwork, Haile was in his early forties. He had been a student until he was fourteen and then, during the socialist regime, a pickpocket, a house robber, and a daily labourer in construction sites. When the *Derg* fell, like many other young people, Haile tried to make his way out of the country. At the age of twenty he spent nine months as a refugee on the Ethiopian-Kenyan border. As soon as he realized that he was not going to be able to leave the continent, he returned to Addis Ababa. A new succession of possible lives followed. He worked as a manager of video houses then enrolled as a soldier on the Ethiopian-Eritrean front.[5] Then, after a few years hustling on the street, he worked as a precast concrete block production worker and a car attendant. His personal life had many ups and downs. He was married to a woman he had met whilst in military training in the Amhara region before going to the front, but things were not going well with her. At the time of my fieldwork they had a four-year-old boy whom Haile cared for greatly. One of his main concerns, I soon understood, was to enable his son to live a life that was radically different from the life Haile himself had lived.

Life Trajectories, Youth, and Uncertainty

Haile, Ibrahim, and Said and their contemporaries and friends were seen as 'young people' by the government that mobilized them in its 'youth programmes', and they described themselves, as we will see soon, as 'being young' or 'still young'. Their stories offer a picture that is significantly different from the common representation of youth as a condition of crisis (Cruise O'Brien 1996), 'being stuck' (Hansen 2005), and social death (Vigh 2006b). From this perspective, scholars have often argued that lives of young people in Africa are framed by a disjuncture between expectations of progress and social advancement and the lack of opportunities to achieve desired and desirable social goals: a stable job, marriage, and parenthood (Abbink & van Kessel 2005; Cruise O'brien 1996; Honwana & de Boeck 2005; Mains 2012). Thus, young people have been described as being both 'stuck' and 'hopeful'. They are stuck because their present experiences are far from the achievement of their goals (Hansen 2005). Yet, they are hopeful because while they wait to achieve these goals, they elaborate new identities, discourses, visions, and ways of getting by (Ralph 2008; Mains 2012). As I got deeper into the life trajectories of my informants, I realized how ineffective these narratives were in making sense of the multiplicities of engagement that constituted their lives, as well as the constraints they encountered in their social navigation. Despite their poverty, my informants played an incredible variety of roles, including parenthood. In spite of the multiplicities of their engagements and experiences, they rarely ever found a way out of poverty and exclusion. It is true that many young people, including those in this chapter, described themselves as being stuck. However, the present is rarely experienced and navigated as a limbo between the lack of social opportunities and visions of a better future. Likewise, although it is true that marriage, parenthood, and a stable job – or better, becoming rich – are highly desired social goals, these should not be taken for granted as the criteria against which young people consistently elaborate and evaluate their life trajectories.

To reorient our knowledge and understanding of the experiences of young people, I propose an open-ended approach to the examination of life trajectories. I do this by learning from the fact that my informants' engagement with a multiplicity of terrains of practice, roles, and careers was grounded in a fundamental appreciation of the limits of not only what they could do, but also of what they could know. In other words, the fact they could not know what was next made them aware that life was uncertain, and thus unpredictable and indeterminate. This was not necessarily a concern. Rather, this uncertainty was perceived as enabling them to think of the state of their lives, and their condition of poverty and exclusion, as neither final nor irreversible. In a way, I argue, Haile, Ibrahim, Said, and many of their contemporaries not only valued uncertainty as a ground for social practice and hope, they embraced it. Understanding why and how young men in Addis Ababa's inner city did so, I believe, will help refresh the anthropological imagination of studies of youth on the continent and provide an ethnographic grounding to the theoretical debate on uncertainties in Africa.

As a first step, we need to consider the fundamental definition of uncertainty. Expanding on the pragmatist philosopher John Dewey, Susan Reynolds Whyte argued that uncertainties are inherent in the way people act and live through existence. Uncertainty pertains to our inability to know or even to 'predict the outcome of events' (Whyte 2009: 213). In other words, uncertainty expresses the unpredictability and indeterminacy of what is going to be next, both immediately and in the long term. Living through uncertainty thus implies living in a state of contingency, that is, being dependent on courses of actions and events we cannot predict or know (Bledsoe 2002; Whyte 2009).

Despite these broader definitions, uncertainty and contingency have become common themes of anthropological and ethnographic examination on the continent fundamentally because they shed light onto broader experiences and conditions of social insecurity, vulnerability, and risk. Similarly to other contributions in this volume, and drawing on material I collected during eighteen months of fieldwork on street life in Addis Ababa's inner city between 2009 and 2013, I propose to see uncertainty from a different perspective: as a terrain of possibilities. This does not mean underestimating the ambiguities of social relations, which Susan Reynolds Whyte (1997) studied in her accounts of misfortune, or overlooking existing conditions of exclusion, social insecurity, and vulnerability and their relations to experiences of uncertainty. The lives of the young men with whom I conducted my research in Addis Ababa's inner city were framed by marginality and subjugation. By shifting the focus away from vulnerability, however, I intend to look at the ways the unforeseeability of existence is translated into a terrain of action and hope.

Philosophers such as Dewey (1930) and Bloch (1976) have pointed out that uncertainty and indeterminacy may be fruitful. To study ethnographically how and why this could be, I believe we need to make an important distinction. The fact that the future is unknown makes it indeterminate and potentially changeable. However, this is often not enough to inspire a sense of possibility, especially in contexts of exclusion and marginality. Studies of marginalized youth on the continent have shown that, despite the enormous potentialities of an indeterminate future, deep anxieties and worries still arise (Weiss 2009). As Miyazaki (2004) argued in his ethnographic study on knowledge in the Fiji islands, this is a matter of reversing philosophers' assumption that the indeterminate and the uncertain intrinsically contain the seeds of possibility. The productivity of indeterminacy is not a given condition. Rather, it is seeing and appreciating the potentialities of indeterminacy that makes uncertainty a productive condition; and this is an existential achievement that people pursue with the means available to them. From this perspective, I argue that my informants were 'embracing uncertainty' as an attempt to achieve indeterminacy. In other words, they were not simply capitalizing on a generic belief that what has not yet been could come to be in an unknown future. Rather, they were tuning their social practice and daily life into a 'mode' of existence that they pursued through an everyday exercise of reflexivity.

The rest of this chapter will examine how and why marginalized young men embraced uncertainty while dealing with different domains of their existence. I begin with arguing that we should try to reorient our analysis towards a more open-ended appreciation of the relations between the present and the future, between desired social goals and actual achievements. These initial methodological remarks set the scene for an ethnographic exploration of how and why my informants embraced uncertainty. The following sections are structured in such a way as to trace how my informants came to embrace uncertainty as a mode of existence and social practice whilst dealing with cultural notions and moral and existential concerns. Finally, I conclude by outlining the contribution my analysis of young men in Addis Ababa's inner city makes to the debate on uncertainty in contexts of marginality and exclusion.

Embracing Uncertainty

Adopting an open-ended analytical approach to the relations between present and future, goals and actual achievements, helps illuminate the relations between uncertainty, action, and hope and go beyond normative narratives of youth. The present and future, I argue, are not disconnected horizons of social practice. As Vigh (2006a) and Pedersen (2012) have pointed out, they are closely interconnected because only by living in the present and navigating the ramifications of the immediate can one be in a condition to shape and anticipate a potential future. In other words, the future is better characterized as emerging from the present, and shaped by the contingency and unpredictability of life, than as a horizon of fulfilled social goals against which the present is evaluated as a fundamental failure. This understanding of the relations between the immediate and the long term does not just echo my informants' appreciation of indeterminacy and uncertainty, it also provides a way to pose the question of whether desired social gains, such as a stable job, parenthood, and marriage, have a normative effect on the ways people make sense of the trajectories of life. This is central to understanding why young people in Addis Ababa's inner city embraced uncertainty as a ground for action and hope. The protagonists of this chapter did not spend much time thinking about what their lives could be. They did dream, but visions of a better future were rarely imagined as actual plans to pursue; they were just dreams. Instead, what were perceived to be achievable goals were negotiated and imagined as lives unfolded and options appeared on the horizon. As we will see later in the chapter, these young men described this existential balancing between opportunities and possibilities in the future by referring to the local notion of *idil*, a 'chance' or better, a 'stroke of luck'. Before you get a chance, they argued, you do not know what the future will look like. When you get one, you start to know where your life could be heading. My informants were not concerned so much with figuring out what the future would look like, but with exposing themselves to the possibility of getting a chance. Embracing uncertainty was the method, the mode of existence, the paradigm of social practice that, they believed, could put them in this position.

In this context, how and why does embracing uncertainty become a mode of existence and social practice? To appreciate this, it is helpful to make a distinction between 'hope' and 'social expectation'. The terms are related, but their precise meanings differ significantly. A social expectation involves a sense of entitlement: we feel we are owed something. For instance, educated young people in urban Ethiopia who prefer to stay unemployed instead of taking jobs in the informal sector do not only desire to be employed in the public sector, they feel entitled to it because of their educational backgrounds (Mains 2012). Hope works differently. Crapanzano (2004) pointed out that hoping consists of recognizing that factors outside our control limit what we can do. Miyazaki (2004) goes further. He argues that hope is a way through which we reorient our knowledge and, potentially, readjust our action while facing our limits vis-à-vis indeterminacy and unpredictability. In other words, hoping is both an expression of our limits and a 'method' to deal with them. In Addis Ababa's inner city, embracing uncertainty was the existential toolkit which enabled my informants to hope, or rather, see the lives through the lens of the possible or, as Whyte (1997, 2002) would argue, the subjunctive. They did so because their condition of marginality did not give them much room to 'expect' anything other than the continuation of their exclusion and subjugation – when you do not have much, my informants taught me, it does not make sense to expect and wait for something to come. 'You have to move, go around', as one young man, Abiy, said, reworking the fringes of the real with a restless sense of possibility.

This is the starting point for my ethnographic investigation of how young men in Addis Ababa's inner city recognized the limits of their action and why they embraced uncertainty as a mode of existence and social practice. I aim to show here that my informants' attempts to achieve indeterminacy are a way of navigating marginality and exclusion. I begin by examining how my informants managed their fundamental worries about the irreversibility of their condition of poverty and exclusion. Next, I focus on the concept of 'having time', key to my informants' ability to embrace uncertainty. Diverging from the broader literature on youth in Africa, I show how being young, or 'still young', was not perceived as a serious concern. Conversely, claiming to be 'still young' allowed my informants to think they still had time to change their lives. I then examine how embracing uncertainty is embedded in a moral terrain. I show how my informants juggled with a crucial notion in their imagination of the unpredictable: *'idil'*, a 'stroke of luck'. *Idil* is a religious concept, meaning a gift of God. The centrality of this notion in the lives of my informants, both Muslim and Orthodox Christian, implied that they understood the indeterminacy of life in cosmological terms, linked to the inscrutable will of God. It also had another implication: *idil* gave a moral dimension to the ways my informants' social navigation of poverty and marginality affected their relations with God and thus the possibility of getting a chance through him. Embracing uncertainty was a means of making sense, in moral terms, of the fact that getting by in Addis Ababa's inner city sometimes involved cheating and stealing – which, as these young men were aware, would not have made God very happy. Dealing with worries about one's inability to improve one's life, claiming to have time, and juggling with moral concerns constituted the major ways through which my informants embraced uncertainty as a mode of existence. Yet, as the last ethnographic section of this chapter shows, embracing uncertainty was also a paradigm of social practice, allowing my informants to expose themselves to the possibility of getting a chance. My informants were aware that being able to deal with existential, cultural, and moral concerns was not enough to get a chance. Only by actively inhabiting the contingency and unpredictability of life, or, as they said, by moving around, could they steer their lives towards a potential future away from marginality and exclusion.

'I like my brain'

Two months before I left Addis Ababa for what became a two-year writing 'break', Mikias, a contemporary of Haile and a good friend of both Haile and Ibrahim, described how he saw his own and his friends' lives, comparing them to mine: 'Yes, you are changing, but look at us. Our life is always the same, we chew [*khat*[6]], we play, we drink, we are prisoners…legal prisoners'. He meant that they were prisoners not because they had broken the law, but because they were unable to have a life that was any different from the past. The experience of living a life without potential for change was often a cause of distress, anxiety, and worry. After a day of chasing tourists, looking for ways of getting by, Medhane, a street tourist guide, complained to me:

> I got depression. All the days are always the same. [...] Marco, you are having a great opportunity. You are doing a research and I know that you will make it. I don't know about me, what I will do in the future. All days are always the same, I wish to get one opportunity, only one....

Stress, worry, concern, distress, pressure, anguish, and disturbance in Amharic is *č'inqet*; and *tečenneqe* means to 'have anxiety, be in difficulty, be under stress, be in great straits, show concern, be solicitous, worry, feel uneasy, take great pains' (Leslau 2005: 239). In his ethnography of educated, unemployed youth in Jimma, a city in southern Ethiopia, Mains (2012) compared his informants' experience of *č'inqet* to what Weiss described as the 'too much thinking' of marginalized young men in Arusha. For these young men, these authors pointed out, stress and anxieties were active forms of thinking. By worrying and experiencing anxiety, they worked through the circumstances of their existence (Weiss 2009: 114). Ibrahim and Haile, like many others in Addis Ababa's inner city, worried. In doing so, they recognized that, despite the multiple engagements that constituted their lives, they had not managed to break the oppressive routine represented by the everyday reproduction of their condition of marginality and exclusion:

> You have *č'inqet* when you always do the same thing and you would do something different. For instance, I wake up, I have my breakfast and, then, I do my work, always the same. I have *č'inqet* for this reason.

At the same time, they were aware that living a life through stress and anxiety was an overwhelming existential experience that might have taken them towards self-destruction: the ultimate denial of their ability to act and hope. As Haile told me:

> 90% of my friends, guys of my age, have died. The reason why they died is because they did not survive the tension, they were not happy. [...] Some of them just started to drink too much and died because of this.

When I was in the field, people interpreted Mesfin's gradual descent into madness as the consequence of *č'inqet*. Mesfin was one of the youngest street tourist guides in my field site. He used to smoke marijuana (*ganjia*), and some of his friends thought this was no help whatsoever to him. 'You have to be keep it real when things are difficult, and *ganjia* is not good because it makes you think', said Fasil, also a street tourist guide and a good friend of Mesfin. Because of his stress and anxiety, Fasil said, Mesfin insulted a policeman on the street. He was taken to prison, where he was beaten for days. When he came out, he was a different person. He would not eat; he just smoked and behaved madly. 'Now everybody thinks he is crazy. Mesfin tries to say and show others that he is not crazy and tries to behave normally. This is the way you get crazier and crazier', Fasil told me. Things got worse day by day, until Fasil and his other friends managed to get him into the Maria Theresa hospital.

Friends who had died or gone mad were the most dramatic reminder of the potential consequences of too much thinking. People created ways of living through anxiety about the irreversibility of their condition of poverty, and each had his own solution. Ibrahim, for instance, appealed to his ability to forget:

> It is nice that you think about what you have to do, but don't do it much. People get crazy for much thinking. I like my brain, it is incredible, I can forget things, this makes things easier.

Haile emphasized the importance of being happy while dealing with hardship:

> You know, when I was in prison, or running away to Kenya or fighting on the Eritrean border, it was hard, but I was happy.

Both relied on their ability to keep the noise of their thoughts low, while tuning into the appreciation of what they could do with the materials that life of here-and-now was offering. Taken from this existential perspective, Ibrahim was ready to admit, worrying could be a good thing 'because it pushes you to do something new'. Or similarly: '[H]aving *č'iggir* [problems] is good if you know how to deal with them'.

Forgetting, being happy, exercising one's capacity to deal with problems, I argue, were components of a form of social reflexivity, or a discipline of the self that was grounded in the recognition that we are thrown into a world without control of the circumstances of our existence, as, echoing Heidegger, Jackson (1989, 2005) reminded us in his anthropological writings. For my informants, the existential question was not 'to be' or 'not to be', but 'to do something' or 'to do nothing', and being-in-the-world or slipping away from it through madness or death was perceived to be dependent on this latter dilemma. However, as we will see, this existential struggle was not played out by choosing whether to do something or not, but by dealing with issues concerning time, morality, and the unpredictability of social life. These were terrains where embracing uncertainty became a viable mode of existence and social practice.

Age Is Just a Number

The problem of 'doing something' was not only concerned with how to approach the repetitiveness of everyday life, but with figuring out how such an experience of the present could open up potential opportunities in the future. This was a problem of time, or rather, of having time, that involved how people conceptualized the unfolding of their life trajectories. As we have seen, my informants were able to find ways of getting by and of engaging with a multiplicity of roles, including, in Haile's case, marriage and parenthood. In this context, the social navigation of these 'young men' was thus not centred on transitioning to adulthood, as the literature on youth in Africa has often assumed. This matches with the analyses of Levine (1965) and Molvaer (1995), who pointed out that many communities in Ethiopia, especially in the northern highlands, have long conceptualized the life of an individual as a continuum of social experiences from childhood to old age, rather than as a linear succession of life stages. Moreover, the relation between age, time, and having time was a matter of existential reflection. Interestingly, Ibrahim and his friends did not see 'being young', or rather, 'being still young' as a problem. What concerned them was the eventuality of becoming 'poor old men'. Becoming old, they felt, would eventually relegate them to a final and irreversible condition of poverty and marginalization.

I was sitting in Mikias's house, talking about the past and trying to reconstruct the history of gangs and gangsters in Addis Ababa's inner city. I wanted my informants to be more precise with chronologies, and needed Mikias, Ibrahim, and Haile to tell me their ages. Since there were other people in the room, I soon realized that telling me their age might cause them embarrassment. To break the silence, I openly declared my own age: twenty-six. Hakimu, a young engineer and Mikias's neighbour who found himself in the discussion, followed: 'Twenty-five!' To avoid doing the same, Ibrahim relied on my anthropological interest in the reasons why people do what they do: 'I don't know why Ethiopians have a problem with saying their age'. He continued: 'There is a proverb in Ethiopia that says "Never ask their age of women and the amount of their salary of the men"'. *But you are not women!* I cried out. Ibrahim had his theory: 'People don't want to retire, don't want their bosses to get rid of them. If they know that they are old, they would kick them out'. Netsanet, the woman living in a room next to Mikias's, had a similar theory: 'If the government knew their age, they would not be able to enter into training or even do the jobs that they do!' Ibrahim replied to Netsanet: 'What is age – it is just a number'. Hakimu joined the conversation, 'Age is not a factor here as it is for the *faranjii* [foreigner]'. So I asked people in the room, *But are you afraid of being old?* 'I don't like to be old, do you?' Mikias asked. Ibrahim retorted:

> I don't want to be old. See, I am hanging out with all those kids, I am working with them. I hang out, I drink, I am still young. Then, look, when you are thirty, you want to have your own house, a good job, you want to marry a woman, have children, and settle down. Then, the other stage is when you are fifty. You begin to worry about your health. Now, we are young, when we have something, we will say, 'I don't care, tomorrow it will go away'. When you are fifty, you want to see the doctor straightaway!

In saying that he did not want to be old, Ibrahim was comparing his potential life as an old man to that of his father and other old men in his neighbourhood. As I interviewed young people in my field site, I discovered that many thought that their fathers' jobs were far from desirable. One young man in government employment programmes, for instance, argued that the typical work of a father was that of a guard in a shop, which paid no more than 300 birr (USD 16) per month. This was considered insufficient to support a family on, implying that other members, sometimes including children, had to contribute to the household income. Others complained that their fathers did not work enough and their lack of *yesera fikir*, dedication to work, was the reason for their poverty. Ibrahim respected his father, but recognized that his old man's job did not advance his family. 'He killed his age working there', Ibrahim said, referring to the pastry shop where his father had worked for more than thirty years. 'Some of his friends left the place and opened their own pastry shop. Now they are rich'.

The comparison between their life trajectories and those of their parents and other older people in the neighbourhood suggested to Ibrahim, his friends, and many other young people that becoming an 'adult' did not correspond to an improvement in their lives. For them, improvement, or even success, did not necessarily mean something specific. It was a generic and relative notion of success, and mainly consisted of achieving a certain form of change, being able to afford a better standard of life: 'If you bought a car or a house' – something that my informants were rarely able to do – 'people will say that you are successful', Haile reckoned. By saying they did not want to be old, my informants were expressing their awareness of the fact that old people were more stuck in their condition of marginality and exclusion than young people were. By hiding their real age, claiming to be 'still young', Ibrahim and Mikias, for instance, were engaging in a particular understanding of 'youth', not only as a stage of life, but as the moment of existence when individuals have time to change their lives and to imagine trajectories different from those of poverty and seniority to which they feel their lives are heading.

Having time and claiming to be 'still young' were ways of living in the immediate while looking towards an unknown future. Things *could* change, my informants felt. While Ibrahim's father did not seize the opportunities to improve his life, the old man's friends somehow had managed to do so. Similarly, as Ibrahim and his friends were struggling with their inability to change their lives, the Ethiopian economy was booming and Addis Ababa was witnessing a dramatic transformation.[7] The difference between these trajectories of change and the ones that they experienced directly revealed the constraints that the condition of exclusion imposed on their action. This was the very essence of their worries. The fact that things did change suggested to them that there were still opportunities out there, despite their inability to grasp them in the immediate term. Claiming to be 'still young' enabled them to think of themselves as potential recipients of one of these opportunities: if one has time, the future may be shaped by how one lives the present. As Pedersen observed in his ethnography of dispossessed young men in Mongolia, focusing on the present is not a denial of time, but 'involves an exalted awareness of the virtual potentials in the present' (2012: 145). In the next sections, I will show that such an awareness was achieved in two ways: how my informants navigated their relations with God, the ultimate dispenser of chances, and how they exposed themselves to the productivity of the unpredictable through their social practice.

The Morality of Chance

For my informants, not knowing what was going to be next, coupled with their belief that they still had time to steer the unpredictability of the future, was a reason to have hope. What they hoped for, as we saw, ieve a change, though how they wanted their lives to change ;eneric and unspecified. To appreciate how this could be, we ᴏ deeper into my informants' imagination of the unpredictable and, in particular, the way the local notion of 'chance' (*idil*) informed their appreciation of uncertainty. In their understanding, a chance, or rather, getting a chance, stood at the junction between the lives they had lived in the past, the contingency of the present, and the indeterminacy of the future. A 'chance' is a 'stroke of fortune', an event, or a series of events, which is unpredictable, but when it happens, will take your life in a direction you would not have expected. Thus, young men in Addis Ababa's inner city turned to the future, not looking for a specific and well-defined form of success but for a chance that might take them away from their condition of poverty and exclusion.

Interestingly, while the idea of success and 'change' is unspecified and vague, the notion of 'chance' is grounded in a deep configuration of meanings, revolving around relations with God and, as we will see, morality. For many Ethiopians, a chance is a gift of God, and as such dependent on his inscrutable will (Messay Kebedde 1999). Hence, it might be argued, the unpredictability of existence is therefore an expression of the inscrutability of God and the fact that of what will happen, 'only God knows', as Ibrahim, Haile, and many others I got to know in Addis Ababa's inner city often repeated. Yet, this does not mean that individuals are powerless to change their lives. My informants believed that what they could do was to cultivate a good relationship with God: by signalling their loyalty to him with prayers and religious acts and by showing with their good conduct to be worthy of God's goodwill. In doing so, as Messay Kebedde (1999) would suggest, young men in Addis Ababa's inner city were not looking for evidence of predestination but to gain God's favour exactly because, they believed, God's will can change. In fact, the place that individuals occupy in his plans is never final, since arrogance (*tigab*) or quest for God's forgiveness could result in a change in God's favour and, hence, one's destiny.

Gaining God's favour, my informants knew, was not an easy thing to do, especially amidst all the challenges of life. Haile, Ibrahim, and many others in their circle of friends and contemporaries had past, and sometimes, present involvement in the illegal street economy. They had stolen, cheated, and hustled and this, they were aware, was not something they could be proud of in front of God. How could they reconcile their bad conduct with their attempts to gain the favour of God, the dispenser of chances? One way was to cultivate a good relation with God through religious acts. Haile and Mikias, both Orthodox Christians, often went to church, early in the morning, to ask for God's favour or just to start their days. Ibrahim was Muslim, or as he defined himself during one of our first meetings, a 'plastic Muslim' who knew more about Orthodox Christianity than his own religion. Over the time I got to know him, Ibrahim had become increasingly committed to learning about Islam, while, however, continuing to be a reader of the Bible. When I returned to Addis Ababa in 2013, Ibrahim had begun going a couple of times a week to a religious school not far from his house to study the Qur'an.

On top of their commitments to religious life, my informants also turned to an exercise of moral reflexivity to situate their acts in a more broadly based judgment on their conduct. The conversations I had with them about how they evaluated their deeds echoed what philosophers have debated about moral luck – whether or not what people do in situations outside their control can be an object of moral judgment (Williams 1993; Nagel 1993; Riescher 1993). For my informants, their bad acts were a result of the contingencies of their lives, and as such not subject to clear moral judgement. They did not choose to be poor, and, they believed, when you are poor, you need to do what you need to do in order to get by.

Gabriel, a parking guy and a friend of Ibrahim, helped me to understand why, for example, stealing could be morally acceptable. *What did you feel, when you did something bad, like stealing?* I naively asked.

People don't usually always think about God, it comes when you do something wrong. When you do something wrong, you feel something. It is called *šäšät*.

šäšät is 'repentance, regret, remorse, qualm, sorrow' (Leslau 2005: 243) and, as Gabriel explained to me, it is different from a sin, *hatiat*.

It is different. If you do *šäšät*, you would say sorry to God and he will forgive you. *Hatiat* is when you don't feel any *šäšät*. Then, it is *hatiat*.
What about if you, after the šäšät, keep on doing čebu [literally 'hitting on the neck', that is robbery] *and stealing, would God accept your šäšät again?*
Yes, God is not merciless. He would understand and forgive you. It is life, if you don't have money and a job, what else can you do?

Stealing, Gabriel admitted, was wrong, but not necessarily morally condemnable because of the circumstances in which it was usually committed. In this context, if you are regretful, God may forgive you since, my informants reckoned, this kind of bad deed was driven by the contingencies of their lives. 'I was stealing, doing things, but he [Allah] knew that it was not in my heart and he forgave me...' Ibrahim said.

Belief in God's forgiveness of stealing, however, was complemented by the way my informants judged acts they considered more serious sins, such as killing someone or getting rich through the help of a *tanqway* (fortune teller or spirit medium) or a *debtera* (expert of magic and spirits). Differently from stealing, murder was perceived to be very difficult to forgive on the basis of the circumstances in which the act was committed. Ibrahim argued: 'Stealing small things to eat is not a big deal, where killing someone is a big one and God cares about this'. Becoming rich through magic was considered to be even worse than killing because, Ibrahim reckoned, '...going to the *tanqway* means going away from God'. Relying on magic to get a chance is 'big cheating', as Ibrahim put it – a fundamental betrayal of God's will, an arrogant offence to God. Being poor was not a choice, but becoming rich through magic, Ibrahim felt, certainly was:

> God does not care if you are rich or poor [...] Did God create the money? God does not care about these things of man, it is something among men, and God does not care about this. He gave us some law that we have to respect, but there is big cheating and small cheating....

Hence, he concluded, '[T]he most important thing is to be afraid of God'.

The distinction between big sins and small sins opens a glimpse into the way my informants' embrace of uncertainty and indeterminacy was an issue of both knowledge (cf. Miyazaki 2004; Whyte 1997) and morality – of trying to make sense of what they could do and what they should not do. This was a central matter that concerned the possibility of gaining God's favour and, importantly, as Mikias pointed out to me, the very fact of staying alive, the ultimate requirement of being able to enjoy a chance at some point in the future:

> There is something wrong with the rich people. Look, we are poor, but we are healthy and we don't have health problems. Rich are always

sick! [...] You know, we Ethiopians we can do everything, we all know about magic and how to get money. But we don't do it! Because we believe in God, we eat, we are healthy because of him.

By recognizing the limits of their action, or rather, by arguing that they did not have control of the circumstances of their lives, my informants thought of themselves as moral subjects who could rightfully claim a chance from God. At the same time, these young men were aware that they still had work to do. On the religious side, as I mentioned, feelings of regret and a certain level of commitment to religious life were considered to be central to cultivating a good relationship with God. On the level of their experience, thinking of themselves as good people in front of God opened up to them a sense of the possible; but, as we will see in the following section, being able to get that chance was fundamentally a matter of inhabiting the contingency of their lives.

'Everybody is moving out there'

People in my field site who were considered to have improved their lives expressed awareness of this disconnect between being a good person and finding a chance. For instance, when I asked Mimi, a young hotel manager living in my field site, about social opportunities and chance, she replied that young people should work and move around if they wanted to find opportunities. They should not fool themselves that the *idil* will knock at their door and wake them up, she said.

Haile, Said, and Ibrahim and many amongst his friends had already had a life of moving around, in Amharic, *inqisiqase*. However, despite the multiple terrains they had navigated, Haile and Said did not feel they had been given a chance to radically change their lives. Ibrahim, on the other hand, felt that he had received one but had failed to take advantage of it – receiving a chance did not ensure success. In the early 2000s, Ibrahim's mother and her contacts in the local government office helped him obtain a small street shop through the development programmes the city government had launched to boost income generation through small businesses. Ibrahim started running a small shoe shop. As he recalled, Ibrahim was not just selling shoes, he was looking for new ideas and new products that only he might have sold in the area where his shop was located. Things went well for a while, but he squandered the money he earned and ended up bankrupt. 'I was behaving stupid, I did not think it was my future', Ibrahim told me, trying to make sense of the reason why he did not recognize at the time that the street shop might have been his chance.

In spite of failure or not having had a chance, my informants kept moving. They did not do so because they had a clear vision of their future; indeed, their past and present experiences would suggest to them that they could not expect much from the future. Rather, their moving around was embedded in an understanding of the future through the lens of the possible. By moving around, my informants were not necessarily going somewhere. They were exposing themselves to the possibility that a chance might come. Moving around, or *inqisiqase*, was not just a practice, it was also a method: a way of relating what is here with what is not here yet.

On a hot afternoon in September 2010, Kebe (literally 'butter') came to visit his old friend Mikias. He was just back from Dubai where he had been working as a guard. Like many guys back from Dubai, he wanted to show how successful he was. His sharp dress – a black shirt, a white jacket, and a pair of bright yellow shoes – surely made the point. He sat for a few minutes telling his old friends what his new home looked like. 'Dubai is a very nice city', Kebe kicked off, describing how modern it was and how you could find everything there. Then, he ended:

> You guys, better you move around, you shouldn't stay here chewing *khat* all day. Everybody is moving out there.

As soon as he left, those in the room engaged in intense conversation. Brahanu, an old friend of Ibrahim's, cried out: 'I don't want people to say what I am and what I have to be!' Abiy – in his mid-twenties and a graduate in physics from Addis Ababa University who was then a 'parking guy' with Ibrahim and later an attendant at a petrol station doing twenty-four-hour shifts – retorted:

> I don't know how this guy was before, but he has changed his life. You don't think you will get your chance by just sitting around here do you? Where do you think your chance will come from if you don't work? How could you say this?

Ibrahim looked crestfallen. Abiy turned to me:

> Marco, everybody believes in *idil*. There are these guys having children, they just think that because of the *idil* God will feed them. It does not work like this. You have to work, taking any kind of job and little by little you can move up. You have to get experience of things, you learn how to do things. You have to keep on working, then you

will get your *idil*. Maybe, after one year, two years, five years, when I will be around thirty, I know it will come, but you have to keep on working. You can't understand this by talking to them, Marco, they are done, they are already thirty or even forty, their time has passed...

Ibrahim took the stage and said,

I had my opportunity to be rich, but I failed. But what else could I do? I don't have to be hopeless. I have try to go on thinking that I have a chance (*idil*).

Abiy replied:

...You have to work in this life, you don't have to be hopeless. God is important if you are healthy and alive, but whether you are rich or poor does not depend on him. It is about you, every second is running out, you have to move, go around. It is about your motivation! It is about your feelings inside you. If you don't have it, you don't move.

This discussion about the unpredictable nature of chance and the importance of moving around touched on many of the issues I have discussed in this chapter. With his performance of style, Kebe embodied the man who had achieved a certain form of success because, as Abiy said, '[H]e has changed his life' – even though Kebe's success working as a guard in Dubai was most definitely relative. Brahanu's angry statements voiced the anxieties of everybody else in the room: being unable to change one's life. Abiy played the role of the young man. His university degree did not open up any particular social opportunities. He did not choose his degree: it was assigned to him by a centralized system. Abiy was unlucky and ended up in the physics department – what he said students at Addis Ababa University called the *yemot department,* 'the department of death', because its graduates never found jobs. The fact that he was young, however, let him think he would be able to change his life. He believed in God, and this made him think he would stay healthy and alive. The rest was in his hands, in his ability to move around and expose himself to the possibility of a chance. As we have seen, Ibrahim took a different position: he had had his chance. Unlike Abiy, he had less grounds to say that he had 'time' – this was the very heart of Ibrahim and Abiy's cut and thrust – but still he knew he should not be hopeless.

Despite their differences, the two men agreed on the importance of moving around. In fact, even from their different positions, Abiy and Ibrahim grounded their action and hope by embracing uncertainty. Ibrahim hoped because hoping, as I argued, echoing Miyazaki (2004), is not only a desire for something better. It is a way of readjusting one's action and social navigation in the present to open up for oneself the possibility of the unknown. Ibrahim and Abiy embraced uncertainty by articulating notions of present and future; by situating the idea of getting a chance at the junction between their past, the present, and the indeterminacy of the future; and by referring to an unspecified notion of success. Finally, both Ibrahim and Abiy were convinced they could not be hopeless or indulge their worries. In so doing, they would have denied themselves what really made their lives livable, the fact of being on the move, the fact of looking for a chance.

Epilogue

I returned to Ethiopia in April 2013. As Haile said to me when we met, '[Y]ou found us as you left us'. Most of my informants were still going to spend their afternoons at Mikias's house. I have not met Kebe since the afternoon he showed up at Mikias's with his fancy clothes. Meanwhile, Brahanu had let himself be swallowed by his worries. He was living on the street, walking around by himself, saying nothing to his old friends but '*indet naw?*' (How is it going?). Haile, Ibrahim, and Said continued to work at the cooperative of car attendants, and Abiy also showed up when he had a day off after his twenty-four-hour shift at the petrol station.

As I conclude this chapter, I do not want to give the final word on my informants' social experience. As my informants believe, life is unpredictable. Moreover, as Miyazaki (2004) pointed out, an open-ended approach is methodologically and theoretically valuable to understanding the making of social processes and the unfolding of life trajectories. From this perspective, I examined how and why young men in Addis Ababa's inner city embraced uncertainty as a way of living through their condition of poverty and exclusion. I showed that embracing uncertainty does not eradicate the logic of exclusion that frames the existence of my informants, but has provided a way of grounding their action and hope in a sense of the possible. More than anything else, this has made their lives livable, despite the odds and all the challenges that they encountered.

To capture this tension, I went beyond narratives that see youth as one stage in a linear trajectory. I also avoided giving any interpretation of uncertainty as a sort of trademark and *zeitgeist* of the present – 'neo-liberal' – times; as Whyte reminded us, the past was not necessarily less uncertain than the present (2002: 187). I examined uncertainty as an existential issue and embracing uncertainty as an existential achievement pursued by juggling with cultural and moral concerns. We need to examine people's engagement with the productive side of uncertainty by considering how individuals deal with limits to their actions and elaborate a sense of what they can do in appreciation of these limits.

Judith Butler (1997) reminded us that the subject is both 'the condition for and instrument of agency' and 'at the same time the effect of subordination, understood as the deprivation of agency' (10). Embracing uncertainty is thus embracing one's condition of marginality as the frame of one's existence. By doing so, limits and constraints, my informants hoped, might be overcome, or rather, reconfigured and redrawn. This is possible, they were aware, only by being in the world, by trying to act upon the reality we live in, by living in the contingency of life. As Butler puts it, the formulation of this predicament is 'I would rather exist in subordination than not exist' (7). As Ibrahim said while making sense of his own limits, 'I don't have to be hopeless, I have try to go on thinking that I have a chance'.

Notes

1 I wish to thank the Wenner Gren Foundation, the British Institute in Eastern Africa, the Institute of Social and Cultural Anthropology, Wolfson College, and All Souls' College at the University of Oxford for their support during my doctorate. I appreciate the support of the Fondation Wiener Anspach in Brussels for enabling me to conduct further research and write this paper. I thank the staff at the Institute of Ethiopian Studies in Addis Ababa for facilitating my research in Ethiopia. I am grateful to Liz Cooper, David Pratten, Jonny Steinberg, Henrik Vigh, Laura Camfield, Diego Malara, and Emma Lochery for their insightful comments. This paper is dedicated to Solomon, whom I hope found his own peace.

2 The real names of the people that appear in the text have been changed in order to protect their privacy.

3 After the deposition of Haile Selassie in 1974, fractures within student groups involved in the revolution and a power struggle within the *Derg* resulted in one of the most dramatic and violent periods of recent Ethiopian history. Many young people and students, as well as cadres of the regime, were killed within the context of widespread everyday violence that ended only in 1978 (Tronvoll, Schaefer & Girmachew Alemu Aneme 2009).

4   In 2005, for the first time, the opposition parties registered a significant electoral success, particularly in the Ethiopian capital. When the ruling party declared victory, demonstrations and riots took place, protesting against an election many believed has been rigged (Abbink 2006). The ruling party labelled the protesters 'unemployed youth' and 'dangerous vagrants' and responded with heavy-handed repression: more than 200 people were killed and 30,000 were detained in Addis Ababa alone.

5   Between 1998 and 2002, Ethiopia and Eritrea fought a war that killed tens of thousands of people on both sides. Triggered by border issues, the war was related to the longer history of the relations between the Tigrayan population on both sides and two movements that led the struggle against the socialist regime before Eritrean independence: the Tigray People Liberation Front on the Ethiopian side and the Eritrean People Liberation Front on the Eritrean side (see Tekeste Negash & Tronvoll 2000).

6   *Khat* is a mild stimulant chewed across East Africa and Yemen.

7   In the last twenty years, the Ethiopian economy has expanded, with annual GDP growth averaging 7%. The landscape of Addis Ababa has been reconfigured, with new transport infrastructure, government housing projects, and Dubai-style steel-and-glass buildings in the centre of the city. However, access to the benefits of this economic growth has been unequal. Real incomes in urban areas have increased, but while the wealthiest households have seen significant increases in their income, the income of poorer households has declined (Bigsten, Kronlid & Negatu Mekonnen 1997). As a result, while poor households have been experiencing an increased availability of goods and services in an expanded market, their ability to access these has decreased (Solomon Mulugeta 2006).

References

Abbink, J. (2006) 'Discomfiture or Democracy? The 2005 Election Crisis in Ethiopia and Its Aftermath', *African Affairs* 105 (419): 173–199.

Abbink, J. & I. van Kessel (2005) *Vanguard or Vandals. Youth, Politics and Conflict in Africa* (Leiden & Boston: Brill).

Bigsten, A., K. Kronlid & Negatu Makonnen (1997) 'Dynamics of Income Distribution in Urban Ethiopia 1994–1997', in Bigsten, A., A. Shimeles & B. Kbede (eds.) *Poverty and Income Distribution and Labour Markets in Ethiopia* (Uppsala: Nordiska Afrikainstitutet), pp. 100–132.

Bledsoe, C. H. (2002) *Contingent Lives. Fertility, Time and Aging in West Africa* (Chicago & London: University of Chicago Press).

Bloch, E. (1976) 'Dialectics and Hope', *New German Critique* 9: 3–10.

Butler, J. (1997) *The Psychic Life of Power: Theories in Subjection* (Stanford: Stanford University Press).

Crapanzano, V. (2004) *Imaginative Horizons: An Essay in Literary-Philosophical Anthropology* (Chicago & London: University of Chicago Press).

Cruise O'Brien, D. B. (1996) 'A Lost Generation? Youth Identity and State Decay in West Africa', in Werbner, R. (ed.) *Postcolonial Identities in Africa* (London & New Jersey: Zed Books), pp. 55–74.

Dewey, J. (1930) *The Quest for Certainty: A Study of the Relation of Knowledge and Action* (London: Allen & Unwin).

Getahun, B. (2007) *Addis Ababa. Migration and the Making of a Multi-ethnic Metropolis, 1941–1974* (Trenton, NJ, Asmara: The Red Sea Press).

Hansen, K. T. (2005) 'Getting Stuck in the Compound: Some Odds against Social Adulthood in Lusaka, Zambia', *Africa Today* 51 (4): 3–16.

Honwana, A. & F. De Boeck (eds.) (2005) *Makers & Breakers. Children & Youth in Postcolonial Africa* (Oxford: James Currey; Trenton: Africa World Press; Dakar: Codesria).

Jackson, M. (1989) *Paths toward a Clearing. Radical Empiricism and Ethnographic Inquiry* (Bloomington & Indianapolis: Indiana University Press).

Jackson, M. (2005) *Existential Anthropology: Events, Exigencies and Effects* (New York & Oxford: Berghahn Books).

Leslau, W. (2005) *Concise Amharic Dictionary* (Addis Ababa: Shama Books).

Levine, D. (1965) *Wax and Gold: Tradition and Innovation in Ethiopia* (Chicago: University of Chicago Press).

Mains, D. (2012) *Hope is Cut: Youth, Unemployment, and the Future in Urban Ethiopia* (Philadelphia: Temple University Press).

Messay, K. (1999) *Survival and Modernization. Ethiopia's Enigmatic Present: A Philosophical Discourse* (Lawrenceville, NJ: The Red Sea Press).

Miyazaki, H. (2004) *The Method of Hope: Anthropology, Philosophy, and Fijan Knowledge* (Stanford: Stanford University Press).

Molvaer, R. K. (1995) *Socialization and Social Control in Ethiopia* (Wiesbaden: Harrassowitz Verlag).

Nagel, T. (1993). 'Moral Luck', in Statman, D. (ed.) *Moral Luck* (Albany: State University of New York Press), pp. 57–72.

Pedersen, M. A. (2012) 'A Day in the Cadillac. The Work of Hope in Urban Mongolia', *Social Analysis* 56 (2): 136–151.

Ralph, M. (2008) 'Killing Time', *Social Text* 97 (4): 1–29.

Rescher, N. (1993) 'Moral Luck', in Statman, D. (ed.) *Moral Luck* (Albany: State University of New York Press), pp. 141–166.

Solomon, M. (2006) 'Market-Oriented Reforms and Changes in Urban Household Income: A Study in Selected Small Towns of Ethiopia', *Eastern Africa Social Science Research Review* 22 (2): 1–30.

Tekeste N. & K. Tronvoll (2000) *Brothers at War. Making Sense of the Eritrean-Ethiopian War* (Oxford: James Currey).

Tronvoll K., C. Schaefer & G. Alemu Aneme (eds.) (2009) *The Ethiopian Red Terror Trials* (Oxford: James Currey).

Vaughan, S. & K. Tronvoll (2003) *The Culture of Power in Contemporary Ethiopian Political Life* (Stockholm: Sida Studies No.10).

Vigh, H. E. (2006a) *Navigating Terrains of War. Youth and Soldiering in Guinea Bissau* (New York & Oxford: Berghahn Books).

Vigh, H. E. (2006b) 'Social Death and Violent Life Chances', in Christiansen, C., M. Utas & H. E. Vigh (eds.) *Navigating Youth, Generating Adulthood. Social Becoming in an African Context* (Uppsala: Nordiska Afrikainstitutet), pp. 31–60.

Weiss, B. (2009) *Street Dreams and Hip-Hop Barbershops. Global Fantasy in Urban Tanzania* (Bloomington: Indiana University Press).

Williams, B. (1993) 'Moral Luck', in Statman, D. (ed.) *Moral Luck* (Albany: State University of New York Press), pp. 35–56.

Whyte, S. (1997) *Questioning Misfortune. The Pragmatic of Uncertainty in Eastern Uganda* (Cambridge: Cambridge University Press).

Whyte, S. (2002) 'Subjectivity and Subjunctivity. Hoping for Health in Eastern Uganda', in Werbner, R. (ed.) *Postcolonial Subjectivities in Africa* (London: Zed Books), pp. 171–188.

Whyte, S. (2009) 'Epilogue', in Haram, L. & B. Yamba (eds.) *Dealing with Uncertainty in Contemporary African Lives* (Uppsala: Nordiska Afrikainstitutet), pp. 213–216.

'We Wait for Miracles': Ideas of Hope and Future among Clandestine Burundian Refugees in Nairobi

Simon Turner

Introduction

Turning off Ngong Road opposite the racecourse, I make my way along dirt tracks filled with mud and debris, past worn-down brick buildings that have expanded with lean-tos and shacks around the properties. These shacks are made of corrugated iron and contain a number of small 'flats', as can be seen from the characteristic rows of doors and small windows along one side. The tenants share common pit latrines and a separate outdoor area for cleaning. These are not the densely populated urban slums of elsewhere in Nairobi, and there is something distinctly rural and pioneering to the area. We pass a small open space of grassland with a few grazing goats. Today a charismatic church has built a temporary stage, flanked by massive loudspeakers and a pastor in a worn suit is preaching to the crowd of curious onlookers. I am on my way to visit Jean, a Burundian in his early twenties, who lives together with four other young Burundians in two rooms. None of these men have refugee papers and constantly risk being stopped by the police and asked for a bribe. Neither do they have a regular income.

In the following I explore how these young men and many other men and women like them manage these precarious and uncertain living conditions, and argue that they navigate the present towards an unknown future through hope and faith. I argue that the precarious and unpredictable life in the outskirts of Nairobi offers them hope for a brighter future that they could not get in the relatively safe and predictable refugee camps that they chose to leave. In Nairobi and in the camp, Burundian refugees are neither here nor there; they are in between a past in Burundi and an unknown future. Both places are like parentheses in time – like seclusion sites in rites of passage (Turner 1967). Despite these similarities, however, there are also differences between the camp and the city – just as there are good reasons for these young Burundians to choose to make their way from the security and relative comfort of the camps and take their chances in the city. Even though neither place is lived in for the present or with an eye to permanency, these young Burundian men and women strategically use them to position themselves for the future. In the case of the camp, they inhabit the space allocated to them by the UNHCR through organizing politically and collectively with the objective of reclaiming a position as political citizens in a future Burundi (Turner 2005). The city, on the other hand, does not offer the relative security and protection that the UNHCR provides in the camp. Neither are they offered the predictability of food rations. It is, however, exactly this uncertainty and unpredictability that the clandestine refugees seek in the city because it fosters hope for a better future and hence a means to navigate the present.

As mentioned in the introduction to this volume, uncertainty may be productive, and in the case of these young men and women the uncertainty of the present produces opportunities in the future. In other words, we need to explore their perceptions of future opportunities if we are to understand their life choices in the uncertain present. The question for them is to make choices in the present that optimize their positions in the future. Making such choices depends on the impossible art of predicting an unknown future and projecting this future back into the present in order to be able to affect the future in the best possible way (Vigh 2009, 2006; Kingsolver 2010). This precarious task of moving back and forth between the future and the present is an essential part of agency and of what De Certeau (1984) describes in relation to strategies and tactics.

Refugee youth in the camps and youth living clandestinely in the city have been subject to dramatic changes, fleeing their homes and their country due to war and insecurity. Furthermore, in the case of Hutu fleeing Burundi, they left a country and a political system that did not give them space to realize their dreams and take a place in society as citizens. Once in the camps or in the city, they are forced into a kind of liminal space. However, as opposed to the controlled liminal space of initiands in rites of passage, they do not know when or whether this liminality will have an end. Will this bracket in time – this state of exception – become permanent? In this situation, they have to apply strategies to overcome the present by exploring possibilities of a future that is different – both to their present situation and to the past that they left behind as well as being different to the future that may have once been anticipated. In this process, hope is essential. Hope becomes a means by which to navigate, although this is not navigating along a straight route. In other words, it is their hope for a future that is different from the past and the present that helps them in their everyday strategies in the present. The temporary, indeterminate, and unpredictable nature of life in Nairobi creates room for this hope.

Hoping and Waiting

Hopefulness, Ghassan Hage argues, is 'a disposition to be confident in the face of the future, to be open to it and welcoming to what it will bring, even if one does not know for sure what it will bring' (Hage 2003: 24). This kind of hope resides in the individual and is the capacity to believe in the future despite uncertainties. Hage is here referring to what Darren Webb would term 'open-ended' hope, where one hopes that the future will bring good fortune without defining what it is one is hoping for. Hope in this understanding 'is the human attribute which simultaneously reconciles us to our ontological status as traveller and propels us along the path to ourselves' (Webb 2007: 69). Open-ended hope, or what Hage calls 'hopefulness' implies, in other words, an ontology of becoming rather than being (Vigh 2009). It differs from 'goal-directed' hope, which has a concrete objective, which the hoper believes is obtainable at some point in the future. Open-ended hope has no concrete objective and is concerned with the voyage towards the future.

In Christian theories of hope, the objective is not only unknown; it must remain unknown for hope to be 'real'. Vincent Crapanzano shows how American evangelicals frequently refer to Paul's letter to the Romans, which claims that 'hope that is seen is not hope' (Crapanzano 2003: 8). Good Christians, they claim, must hope for salvation and meanwhile be patient because only God can decide on salvation and define what it is. Hope is, in other words, placed in God. In his 'Theology of Hope' Jürgen Moltmann similarly argues against defining hope concretely and is critical towards any claims to fulfil promises that only God can fulfil. He argues against despair and presumption, the latter being when we prematurely assume the fulfilment of hope. 'Both forms of hopelessness [...] cancel the wayfaring character of hope' (Moltmann 1967: 23). For Moltmann, it is a sin not to hope and a sin to hope prematurely because in both cases it is to take the future into one's own hands. Bernard Dauenhauer has given a secular interpretation of this patient, open-ended hope where one must accept one's life en route and place one's trust not in God but in an other's agency.

> To hope is thus to ascribe intrinsic value to one's enroutedness, to place one's trust in the efficacy of human agents while accepting its contingent indeterminacy, and to possess the conviction that whatever journey we are taken on by ourselves, via others, will be of positive worth (Webb 2007: 70).

Waiting and being patient are central to this kind of hope. I observed what appeared to be patient, hopeful waiting for the future among the young men in Nairobi who could do nothing – they said – but to 'wait for miracles'. Meanwhile, they could not or would not tell me what kind of miracles they were waiting and hoping for. It was, in other words, the open-ended hope as defined by Moltmann. But rather than feeling 'positive resignation' (Crapanzano 2003: 27) or 'patient hope' (Webb 2007: 69–71), they emphasized again and again the hardships of present life in Nairobi. They expressed what Moltmann has, in relation to Christian eschatology as hope, termed 'passionate suffering and passionate longing' (Moltmann 1967: 16) or what Maurice Bloch describes as a restless, future-oriented longing (Webb 2007: 71; Crapanzano 2003: 15). What these young men hope for in the future may not be 'goal directed' but is defined more as the opposite of their present life: a life without suffering. I would argue that their hope feeds on and is dependent on such suffering, and that it is, therefore, essential for them to keep the suffering alive, to the degree that passionate suffering and waiting has become an important discursive presentation of the self for the clandestine refugees in Nairobi. Even though they do engage in the present through everyday survival strategies, they emphasize their present suffering and their position as waiting. To simply wait is to turn your back on the present and to look instead towards the future. This is, I would argue, necessary in order for them to keep hoping. And hope is certainly an important commodity in Nairobi.

In much theorizing on hope, it is implicitly perceived to be individual, perhaps because it is perceived to be an emotion. Hope may, however, also be collective, as in the case of utopian or revolutionary hope. Richard Rorty has discussed the possibilities of a shared, utopian hope – of a future that can be made different from the past (Rorty 1999). This is the kind of hope that is cultivated in the refugee camp; a concrete, goal-oriented hope with the aim of radically reordering the future of Burundi; a hope that demands action in the present. However, Rorty does not touch upon the fact that other forms of hope must also be understood beyond the individual, even when they are not expressions of collective will or concerned with changing the status quo. Valerie Braithwaite distinguishes between collective hope – 'hope that is genuinely and critically shared by the group' – and what she perceives as a less sustainable public hope – 'at its worst a contagious but superficial form of hope peddled by spin doctors and uncritically accepted by expectant beneficiaries' (Braithwaite 2004: 7). While her assessment is normative, she does agree, however, that both forms may coexist and overlap. Hage touches on what Braithwaite calls public hope when he argues that states distribute hope (Hage 2003). Distributing hope is a central component of statecraft, binding citizens to the state as the provider of hope. By distributing hope, the state manages to provide its citizens with a future towards which they can direct their hopes and aspirations. This may not be a common future, equal to all citizens, but it is a future that all citizens can identify with, more perhaps than they can with the present.

I will argue that other institutions than the state may equally distribute hope, from the political parties distributing utopian hope in the refugee camps to the evangelic churches distributing hope for salvation in Nairobi. Hope becomes, in other words, an important commodity in the precarious and liminal situation of the refugees: a commodity over which different institutions may fight. More than a commodity, however, hope may be seen as a mode of governing, shaping the desires and aspirations of subjects through hope.

Hope exists in many different modes and can be a lens through which we may explore and understand how different actors relate to the future and act accordingly in the present. It is through hope that the refugees make the double movement into the future and back in their attempt to find their way in their uncertain present. Hope may be goal-oriented or open-ended; it may be patient, critical, or utopian – in each case propelling the actors forward towards the future. Hope is important in times of uncertainty, and I will argue that uncertainty is, in fact, productive in fostering hope and hence individuals' ability to imagine alternative futures.

From the Hopelessness of the Camp to the Uncertainty of the City

Jean was in his early twenties. He shared two rooms with four other young men from Burundi. The rooms were simple with walls made of corrugated iron on a wooden frame. Their few possessions – mainly clothes and books – were neatly ordered, hanging from nails in the wooden beams or stacked on the small table. The rooms were in a compound consisting of relatively new sheds, all with rooms like his. Most of the inhabitants were immigrants either from abroad or from up country. Many of the Burundians whom I encountered lived in this area – commonly known as Kawangware – in the western outskirts of Nairobi. The place names, such as Dagoretti Corner and Satellite, seem to denote a place that is neither here nor there. It is a satellite added onto the real city, a junction between two roads, housing the rural immigrants who have not quite made it to the city proper. It is a stepping-stone – a waiting room – between other places, for people on their way from one place to another, hoping for a better future somewhere else.

The Burundians whom I met here were mostly refugees without official documents from UNHCR. There are, for obvious reasons, no figures on the number of clandestine Burundians staying in Nairobi. They may be in the thousands. Those who stayed in Kawangware belonged neither to the elite nor to the most marginal and uneducated sections of the population. They were Hutu who had feared the reprisals of the Tutsi-dominated army in the aftermath of the ethnic violence of October 1993. Often their fathers had held some kind of position in the administration prior to leaving the country, and often they had some kind of education and were doing their best in Nairobi to improve their skills and obtain 'certificates'.

Some had made their way directly from Burundi during the war that broke out in 1993. Others had decided to leave the refugee camps in northern Kenya. UNHCR and the Kenyan authorities had a policy of housing all but a small number of refugees in vast refugee camps in Dadaab and Kakuma. The Burundians whom I interviewed all claimed that their physique was not suited for the hot and dry climate there. 'That is for the Sudanese and the Somalis' they would claim. They also claimed that they would become 'living dead' in the camps because the camps promised no future. Finally, a large number of the Burundians in this part of Nairobi had arrived from the refugee camps in Tanzania. Jean and his friends belonged to this group, and it is this group in particular that I follow in this chapter.

Those who had arrived from the camps in Northern Kenya would often mention that despite the security of the camp and the certainty of receiving food every week, they could not have a future there. In the words of one man in Dagoretti Corner: 'But in a camp you cannot be free in mind, psychologically. To be given one kilo of food, of wood...of what? And to stay there...you can become...I don't know, you can become a devil'. Those who left the camps in Tanzania had similar stories. However, there was a slight difference because these camps that housed only Hutu from Burundi actually did offer hope for a future. In Tanzania two political parties dominated camp life and competed to monopolize their version of what Rorty (1999) calls 'utopian hopes'. They gave the refugees hope for a future Burundi that was radically different to the Burundi they had left. It was due to the incompatibility between individual hopes and this collective hope that Jean and his friends made the journey to Nairobi and traded the relative certainty of the camp and its political hopes with the uncertainty of Nairobi.

In the refugee camp, Jean had attended post-primary school. The elite in the camp had established the post-primary school to ensure that their children did not waste their time in exile and fall behind their age group peers who remained in Burundi. There was a well-founded fear among the elite in the camp that life in the camp was equal to putting life on standby; they would be standing still while the world moved on, leaving them behind. So in order to counter this trend, they had established this private school where their children could 'keep up' and prepare for the day they would return to Burundi, enabling them to take up the place in society that they deserved. The school was, in other words, a means for the refugee elite to manage hope and prepare for a future that was detached from their present condition. The refugees in Lukole refugee camp were, however, also preparing for the future – and hence administrating hope – in other ways as well. As Jean explains:

> In secondary school I did well – except in form three and form four it was a bit of a problem because of…this kinds of…what. The…these trainings… this train… Okay, I can say… I think it is known. These trainings for those who want to go to…to war. Yes. Almost every younger man has to participate – by being forced by others – or by your choice. And I liked to go. But then I was thinking why do I have to go to the war and miss the school. Because mixing the training and the school was not possible.

Jean, like all his schoolmates, spent his afternoons training with one of the rebel groups operating inside Burundi at the time. He stutters and cannot find the right words and is hesitant to tell me this news because political activities in general and military training in particular were strictly banned in the camp. Political mobilization and recruitment for the two competing rebel movements were, however, pervasive and can be seen as a means by which the refugees in the camp could create hopes for a better future and manoeuvre according to these hopes. Military training for young men (or rather boys, as they were only fourteen or fifteen years old at the time) was a very tangible way of working towards this future and thereby of expressing hope. Hope may be a waypoint by which to navigate in the present in order to increase one's odds for a better future, in the vein of what Webb has termed 'estimative hope' (2007: 73–74) and similar to Vigh's concept of social navigation (2006, 2009), as when parents send their children to school. Hope may also, however, inspire the kind of action that actually wants to change the future (Rorty 1999), as when the same schoolchildren do military exercises after school. These two forms of hope and positioning oneself vis-à-vis the future clashed in the camp, when the training intensified and the rebel movements in 1998–99 began sending the boys to Burundi to fight. Although many of the parents were active in the political struggle and believed in the cause at a general level, they had other plans for their own sons, whom they did not want to become cannon fodder. Their hope for their own sons' futures was as future leaders of the home country once the rebels had won the war. In other words, they played a two-tier strategy for the future: one was to change the future through armed resistance, while the other was to prepare their sons for the day this had been achieved. Hence Jean's father decided to send him to Nairobi.

He arrived in Nairobi with five other boys and Jean de Dieu, who had already lived here and who could help him crossing the border and settling down in Kawangware. Jean's father – who was a wealthy businessman in the camp, dealing with food rations, and who had been appointed representative of the parents of all five boys in the group – accompanied the boys to Nairobi in order to check whether they had a decent place to stay. He and the other parents continued to assist the young men by sending beans, *unga* (maize meal), and money from Lukole to Nairobi. Despite the support of their parents, many of the young men returned to the camp after a year. For them Nairobi had proven to be too hostile and too far from their dreams of a better future. Those who remained in Nairobi did so against all odds.

Passionate Suffering in the City

I found that Jean and the other young men almost cherished the hardships that they endured, claiming that it strengthened their morale.

Their suffering was stressed in order to strengthen their hope. They illustrated this to me by giving the following account: Once, when the five of them had visited the camp, they brought a whole lot of *unga* back to Nairobi. The problem was that it was too much and it rotted before they could manage to eat it. Jean explains that they did not want to sell it before it rotted because then people in Nairobi would think, 'You are very rich. You are children of presidents. Living a very good life'. It was important for these young men to portray themselves as poor young men, struggling for an education. This kept them in the category of what Moltmann calls 'passionate suffering' (Moltmann 1967), allowing them to keep hope alive and, I would add, providing them with an identity in the present – an identity as persevering sufferers.

Jean received a meagre sponsorship from a woman called Monica. Most of the young men with whom I spoke in Kawangware mentioned Monica, although nobody was able to explain who she was and which organization she worked for. Many students received grants from her, and rumours flourished as to who was getting grants, whether she preferred Rwandans to Burundians, and so on. As far as I could gather, the five young men sharing the house used to receive 2,000 shillings (roughly USD 35) per month: 1,000 to cover the rent and the remaining 1,000 for food. After two years, Monica apparently had reduced the amount by 50%. She also paid almost half of their school fees at Hope International School, a school that was founded by a Burundian bishop from the Methodist Church, teaching refugees and migrants from Rwanda, Burundi, and Congo in French.

They perceived the money that they received as personal gifts, given by an individual, Monica, maintaining that the money they received had the nature of personal and random gifts rather than systematic donations from an organization. It seemed important for them to present themselves as 'living off nothing' and 'waiting for miracles' rather than explaining the various means of income that they had, however small, and the ingenious tactics that they employed to make ends meet. For them, income was bound up with luck or good fortune, rather than being something that you earn from selling goods or labour. Neither did they perceive income as a 'right' in the way that they did in the camp, where the refugees expressed that they had the right to food, health care, schools, and shelter due to being legally recognized refugees under the Refugee Convention. Contrary to this, the clandestine refugees would emphasize the randomness of their present survival. They could remain individuals 'passionately suffering', expecting nothing from the present and hoping for salvation, as opposed to the refugees in the camp who became recipients of aid and clients of the system (Turner 2005). While hope is about being patient and biding time, they also needed to present themselves as suffering in the present. Furthermore, 'critical hope' does not accept any claims to defining the objective of hope or its fulfilment (Webb 2007: 71–72; Moltmann 1967; Crapanzano 2003). Therefore, the young men in Kawangware cannot be seen to be actively hoping for stipends but must just hope that one falls in their lap while they keep their eyes determinedly on the horizon.

The young men lived together in order to make ends meet, but they emphasized that living close together was also about finding moral support and having a fixed point in an uncertain world. The meagre funds that they received from Monica could not even pay the rent, so they shared whatever intermittent funds that came their way – in terms of remittances from relatives in Europe and North America, food from families in the camp, and odd jobs as private tutors for wealthier francophone families in Nairobi. The churches also provided them with material help, although this was far from a constant source of income. Jonas, who was living in a set-up similar to Jean's, explained how he felt less vulnerable now that he was living with three other Burundians. Before, when he was living alone, 'it was not good. It was like losing balance – living in a bad place'. Jonas came to Nairobi with twenty-five other students from Lukole when he was sixteen years old. However, he found life too tough and returned to the camp. The second time he came to Nairobi, he had two friends move in with him. 'There is no rule in this house. The one who has [money] is the one who gives. If I find 500 I might use 100 for a T-shirt and share the rest for tomatoes and so on. If I find 2,000, I might pay 1,300 for the rent. And then all of us, we say amen [laughs]'. Jonas went on to explain that they lived like brothers of the same mother and the same father: they even shared clothes. 'I might wake up and want to wear his clothes [they all laugh]'.

Often these households of young men would have a leader who felt responsible for the other 'boys'. Gerard was one of these leaders, and he explained how he had to make sure not only that they had enough money for the end of the month, but also that the young men remained focused on their main purpose for being in Nairobi, namely to acquire as much knowledge as possible while there. Although they did not have papers, they attempted in various ways to study, either at one of the competing secondary schools for refugees from the Great Lakes or at various computer courses or courses in community development, basically anything they could get their hands on. Gerard was dead serious about learning and pressured the other young men to take part in reading groups, just as he had been teaching himself German. While hope for them was about passionate suffering and waiting for a miracle to happen without hoping for anything in particular, thus leaving it to fate or God to decide what the future may bring, they did have means by which to position themselves in the best possible way in case the future should bring them good fortune. They did so by learning as much as possible. Gerard did not have a concrete goal in mind when beginning to learn German; he simply felt that learning as many languages as possible would increase his chances in the future. So far, learning English and Swahili in the camp had proven very useful later on in his life. Navigating towards a future was not about following a straight line towards a specific end, but about keeping their options open. And while this is an individualistic endeavour towards the future, they seek support in the present in groups of likeminded young, clandestine refugees.

Waiting Actively

Brighton, a young man who lived with Jean, explained that Nairobi is 'un peu développé' as opposed to Tanzania and Burundi, implying that the levels of development of the location will also benefit those who choose to live there, if only they have the will to exploit its opportunities. This idea of Nairobi being more developed than both Burundi and Tanzania was widely shared by the Burundians whom I interviewed. While the young men in Kawangware agreed that the camp provided food, security, and a sense of certainty, they emphasized that hope did not thrive on predictability but on opportunities, even if the opportunities were rare and the odds were low, which means that the camp resulted in hopelessness while Nairobi gave them hope, despite the insecurity and unpredictability of life as clandestine refugees. They perceived opportunities to be created by development, connectedness, and knowledge, and in the city these combined to give hope that one may succeed one day to develop and 'become someone' whatever the odds. The question, then, was how to act in order to make the best of these opportunities, as it was obviously not everyone who managed to exploit the opportunities that the city provided. Obviously, luck was central, but there were also ways in which they believed that they could increase the odds. One such way was to 'wait actively' (Waterworth in Webb 2007: 71) by having faith.

Almost all the young men and women whom I met in Kawangware were born-again Christians, most belonging to a Pentecostal church while some were Baptist or Methodist. While some had belonged to these churches in Burundi, others had converted after arriving in Nairobi, but they all agreed that their faith had become much stronger in the city. When asked why they were 'saved' or born again, a group of young men in Kawangware answered that it was due to the strong presence of preachers in the area, pointing out the door where someone had put up an interim stage and a sound system on one of the empty plots and was preaching energetically and loudly to passers-by. Other refugees said that they had become convinced by the testimonies of other refugees who had been saved when they arrived in Nairobi. They claimed that in the refugee camp people would attend church on Sunday but would fight or get drunk on the way back from service.

According to Crapanzano (2003: 8), Christian evangelics distinguish between hope for salvation and petty hopes for everyday life. There is no doubt that Jean, Gerard, and the other men in Nairobi were also negotiating towards a more immediate future – what Crapanzano calls the petty hopes of everyday life. However, the idea that salvation lies only in the hands of God, and that only God can determine what to hope for, may explain their very vague answers to my enquiries about their present strategies and their concrete plans for the future. 'True hope' to the evangelics 'is not a speculative hope but a "believing" one, secured by God's promises as they are made manifest through the correct reading of his Word' (Crapanzano 2003: 8).

The majority of the clandestine refugees received material help from the churches – usually in the form of food and clothes – which would lead to mutual accusations of nepotism and of others having an instrumental approach to faith. However, for most of these young men, the church meant much more than material gains, as it provided a community and a sense of belonging but also guidance and hope in their precarious lives. As mentioned in the introduction, these people were in a situation where their social skills, their means of navigating, were of little use because they were moving into unknown terrain. Prior to the war in Burundi, life was to a large degree intelligible, and the outcome of their actions therefore highly predictable. In other words, they knew what their options were and knew vaguely what would be the outcome of certain choices. In Nairobi none of the refugees knew what the future would bring for the simple reason that their situation was exceptional and had no precedence. Therefore, everyone had to make his or her life from scratch – guessing what the outcomes of particular actions might lead to. In such a situation of uncertainty and unpredictability, hope for the future relies on a Kierkegaardean 'leap of faith' (Kierkegaard 1963 [1847]). For the young men who did not know how they would pay next month's rent and who were desperately attending dubious courses at equally dodgy 'colleges', this leap of faith was an absolute necessity in order not to lose their bearings and lose their hope for the future and for life itself.

At a Sunday sermon that I attended at the Calvary Centre in Kilimani (an affluent suburb close to Kawangware) which was well attended by refugees from Burundi and Rwanda, the pastor emphasized the need for patience as he explained that some refugees received money from relatives in Europe while others did not. 'But do not lose hope', he told the congregation. 'Be patient. Don't worry. Jesus knows your situation. He knows what you are suffering. Even if you do not eat every day, don't lose hope! You may think "I'm a refugee. I'm illiterate. Who knows me?" But Jesus knows you [...]. The money you get is poisonous – but what you get from Jesus is blessed!' The pastor was preaching for the refugees to stop looking at their present hopeless situation and focus on the future. This requires hope and faith: faith in Jesus who sees you as a human – however little money you possess. He took the step further and claimed that money is actually poisonous because it leads to temptations and shifts focus away from what is important in life.

Gerard, the unproclaimed leader of the young men from Lukole camp living in Kawangware, explained to me in great detail how to ration their meagre incomes to cover all the needs for three persons for one month. This, he explained, required a lot of self-discipline and sacrifice, such as eating only once or twice a day and never buying meat, let alone alcohol. As we discussed life in Nairobi, he talked constantly about perseverance, sacrifice, and discipline, how 'we must sacrifice and meet the challenge in order to succeed'. Apart from being in charge of budgeting, Gerard felt obliged to boost the morale of the young men and keep them on the narrow path of virtue, avoiding the temptations of money and other worldly pleasure. No doubt Gerard's insistence on self-discipline and sacrifice was a practical means to surviving and making ends meet in an otherwise uncertain situation, but it also became an end in itself, to the degree that he claimed that he despised money: 'Money is nothing! You can lose money again, but you cannot lose knowledge'. Not only did he value knowledge above material wealth, he also believed that the harsh conditions of life in Nairobi actually strengthened the character. Gerard echoed the pastor's words in claiming that money actually is poisonous. Money would tempt the young refugees to concentrate on the present rather than the future, spending their time looking for money rather than preparing for their future through sacrifice and discipline. Nairobi offered the opportunity to hope actively for a better future through sacrifice and perseverance. But it required that one resisted the temptations of money and hence of privileging the present over the future.

Not only earning money but also consuming was condemned because consumption makes people focus on the present. It is common for migrants who have a strong desire to return not to consume too much in the place of residence but rather save money for the day of return or symbolically invest in the home village, demonstrating their belonging through consumption. To invest in the place of residence is conceding defeat and accepting a fate in exile rather than maintaining the hope of return. To earn and spend money means entering social relations of exchange in the place of residence, so that earning and using money are a means of living in the present, while abstaining from consumption is the same as abstaining from living life, which was exactly the objective of the young refugees in Kawangware. In order to prepare for the future, they had to remain liminal. The church helped them maintain this approach to life, as it focused on keeping up hope – despite the apparent hopelessness of their present situation. As long as they had faith in the future, they were able to cope with the failures of the present. This is not an optimistic or resigned waiting for the future but 'passionate longing', hoping despite the odds. Gerard and his friends did nothing to change their present misery, but they passionately longed for something else – something that only God can define.

Living in the Present

Not all Burundians in Nairobi lived like Jean and his friends, however. Apart from the Burundians who worked with international organizations and who lived in affluent areas of town mixing with other professional expatriates, I was also fortunate to meet Burundians who had no legal documents just as those living in Kawangware, but who had no connections with them whatsoever. This came about because I had two different research assistants and two different access points during my fieldwork. On the one hand, I was in touch with a young man whom I had met while he was still a teenager in Lukole refugee camp six years previously, and who had moved to Kawangware in the meantime. He became my research assistant and guided me to the Burundians in that area as well as to the different churches, schools, and NGOs of relevance. On the other hand, I had been recommended to get in touch with a couple of young Kenyan men who lived in another part of the city where a lot of immigrants from all of East Africa allegedly had settled.

They lived in the area near Majengo and Pumwani and California Estate bordering Eastleigh. Their hopes for the future were very different from those of the Burundians living in Kawangware. In the following I will introduce them, their background, and their means of navigating the present and the future in order that they may stand as a contrast to Jean and his friends. This is not to make a comparative analysis but rather to frame the context of Jean and his friends and show the limits of the concept of hope.

Whereas Kawangware is semi-rural, this area is decidedly more urban and cosmopolitan and is dominated by a lively informal sector with street traders, hairdressers, 'kioski', bars, tea rooms, and the market dominating the open spaces between the rows of flats and the informal settlements. On the side of the street, people are making furniture, repairing cars and bicycles, and creating charcoal stoves out of old scrap iron. There seems to be a mixture of Swahili culture – itself a hybrid culture – and immigrants from all over East Africa – all with a decidedly 'urban rhythm'. Here I found young Burundian men and women who had settled down and started businesses, buying food in the market and reselling it to people who were afraid to go to the market themselves. I found others who had managed to get an apprenticeship with one of the many Congolese hairdressers while others had taught themselves tailoring and started their own business. They told me how they had arrived recently – often getting a lift with one of the trucks that drive from Bujumbura to Kampala and then to Nairobi. They came from similar urban, Swahili backgrounds in Burundi – often from the Swahili/Muslim and multicultural neighbourhoods of Buyenzi and Bwiza in Bujumbura – and they blended in to the environment of Majengo and California Estate with some ease. Buyenzi is famous in Burundi because apparently it is the only place where people did not get involved in ethnic violence but rather identified as Muslim rather than as Hutu or Tutsi. My impression from fieldwork in Bujumbura (in 2003 and 2008) was also of a cosmopolitanism from below – an identity that draws on being Swahili and hence East African traders rather than autochthon Hutu or Tutsi nobility. This identity also draws on being urban and streetwise – and hence too smart to be manipulated by cunning politicians and their game of ethnic strife. The youth in Buyenzi and Bwiza show their adherence to this identity by wearing a mixture of Muslim attire and American hip-hop clothes and symbols. It was very much this youth that I saw in California Estate, Pumwani, and Majengo, where they were able to continue their urban, multicultural, Swahili lifestyle.

They claimed that they left Burundi due to insecurity, but most left after the worst ethnic violence had calmed down and many arrived after the peace agreement in 2000. They had never believed in politics, in part because the Swahili population in Burundi had always been marginalized and in part because they had seen all the violence that politics had created, in their view. For similar reasons they did not have much faith in the formal education system. The conflict in Burundi, in their point of view, had been a conflict between elites, which meant that any Hutu who managed to get an education risked being killed by the Tutsi who zealously guarded their privileges. They had no hopes for great changes in the political landscape in Burundi due to their marginal political position and lack of education. Instead they saw their future doing business in the informal sector, and for them Nairobi offered the opportunity to follow this strategy.

The young men in Majengo and California Estate were, in other words, not in limbo in the same sense as refugees in camps or the other clandestine refugees in Nairobi. They were pursuing a life strategy that was a continuum of their past in Bujumbura and which was directed towards a more or less foreseeable future. This is not to say that their future was easy or granted, and there were plenty of obstacles to be dealt with along the way. But first and foremost, they were living in the present, trying to make ends meet and to improve their chances little by little, day by day. Their past, present, and future were interwoven. Their hope is neither the 'utopian hope' (Rorty 1999) of the politicians in the camps nor the 'open-ended hope' (Webb 2007) of the Burundians living in Kawangware. Rather, they act according to certain specific goals. When they learn skills, it is not simply to increase their odds for something unknown to happen to them in the future, as when Gerard learns computer skills or German, it is to be able to work as tailors, hairdressers, or mechanics. This may not even qualify as hope but rather what Marcel (1967) in the quote below calls 'work'. Work, Marcel claims, is opposed to hope: '[W]ork implies a thought which is obstinately fixed on an end, but which is by the same token a calculating thought, which knows the slender means and manages them accordingly' (Marcel 1967: 278).

Although the Burundians in Kawangware and Majengo shared similar uncertainties – they had no papers or income upon arrival – they related very differently to uncertainty. In Majengo they attempted to reduce uncertainty and control their futures by blending in and navigating towards fixed futures. In Kawangware, uncertainty was left uncertain for as long as possible because uncertainty fosters hope.

Conclusion

Hope is a means to navigate towards an unknown future in a precarious present. It is through hope that the refugees can make the movement into the future and back in order to act in the present. Hope may be goal-oriented and have a specific objective in mind, but usually it is open-ended and is concerned more with a vague idea of wanting a better future. At first glance, the lives of clandestine refugees in the outskirts of Nairobi seem hopeless, given their lack of income and their lack of legal protection. Apart from being incredibly poor and subject to police harassment, their lives are first and foremost characterized by uncertainty. They do not know when it will be safe for them to return to Burundi, they do not know where their next source of income will come from, and they do not know when they will meet a corrupt police officer. However, hope does not seem to disappear with this uncertainty but rather paradoxically to flourish. In the refugee camps they were also poor, and their futures were also uncertain, but their present everyday lives were secured; they enjoyed the legal protection of the UNHCR and were provided with basic means to survive. However, this security made their lives predictable and removed their possibilities to hope for a future. They became 'living dead'. Nairobi, on the other hand, was unpredictable but left room to hope for a better future.

In Nairobi the young Burundian refugees wait for the day they may return – or go to Europe. The present uncertain conditions in Nairobi are not merely unfortunate circumstances that they have to deal with; in their Pentecostal reading of it, the hard life in Nairobi actually has a purpose in as much as it strengthens the soul and challenges the will and determination of these young men who must not give up, however tough the present may be and however uncertain the future may appear. In other words, the suffering of the present and the uncertainties that they meet every day in Nairobi help them remain pure in their hopes for the future. These hopes, in turn, provide a refuge for them in the present, as it is these hopes that keep them going despite all odds. Although the young men in Nairobi suffer passionately (Moltmann 1967), rejecting any worldly pleasures in the present in pursuit of a future, they also engage in petty everyday hopes and tactics in order to make ends meet. It is also through these everyday hopes that they can look forward and plan for a future. In other words, they do not give in to 'positive resignation' (Crapanzano 2003) but rather strategize in the present in order to strengthen their odds for the coming of unknown futures. While they wait for miracles, they position themselves so that these miracles might happen to them.

While hope and suffering are perceived as individual challenges, hope in the camp and in the city is also distributed collectively, enabling institutions to govern through hope. In the camp, the rebel movements provided a way out of the deadlock of UNHCR's infantilizing embrace. They provided the refugees with an alternative, utopian future (Rorty 1999) and provided the guidelines for what action was to be taken in the present. This goal-oriented and controlled hope left little room for alternatives and little room for manoeuvre, being a main motive for refugees to leave the camps and seek their fortune in the city. In the city, hope was more open-ended and individualized as individual refugees savoured the refuge of hope and the prospect of a miracle happening to them. Meanwhile, hope was also governed here, albeit more subtly than in the camp. The Pentecostal, Methodist, and Baptist pastors all preached how to persevere in the present and how to hope patiently. Similarly, household heads, like Gerard, disciplined his roommates by pushing them to study hard and abstain from worldly pleasure, keeping their eyes determinedly on the horizon while waiting for miracles. Governing through different kinds of hope creates different selves – from the revolutionary rebels in the camp to the passionately suffering and self-disciplined young men in Nairobi. In other words, selves are shaped not simply through disciplining their present, but through their aspirations and hopes for the future.

The fact that another group of Burundians who also lived in Nairobi without papers had chosen a very different way to deal with their uncertain and precarious positions shows that open-ended hope (Webb 2007) and 'passionate longing' (Moltmann 1967) are not the only ways to deal with uncertainty. In Majengo, the clandestine Burundians attempted to reduce uncertainty by taking concrete actions in the present directed to particular, near futures. In Kawangware, uncertainty was not reduced because it was this uncertainty that made Nairobi 'open' as they would often say. It widened their possible futures and provided them with hope.

Much recent literature has explored how groups deal with situations of precarity (Butler 2009), uncertainty, insecurity, and undecidebility. This chapter has shown how the concept of hope may further elaborate our understandings of how people cope in situations of uncertainty. However, I have also shown that uncertainty is not always something to simply 'cope with', something that has to be overcome. In the case of Burundians in Kawangware, uncertainty was a resource that permitted them to hope in ways that they could not in less uncertain situations. For them, uncertainty was an asset.

References

Braithwaite, V. (2004) 'Collective hope – Preface', *Annals of the American Academy of Political and Social Science* 592: 6–15.

Butler, J. (2009) 'Performativity, Precarity and Sexual Politics' *Revista de Antropología Iberoamericana* 4 (3), pp. i–xiii.

Certeau, M. D. (1984) *The Practice of Everyday Life* (Berkeley: University of California Press).

Crapanzano, V. (2003) 'Reflections on Hope as a Category of Social and Psychological Analysis', *Cultural Anthropology* 18 (1), pp. 3–32.

Hage, G. (2003) *Against Paranoid Nationalism: Searching for Hope in a Shrinking Society* (Annandale, NSW: Pluto Press).

Kierkegaard, S. (1963 [1847]) *Kjerlighedens Gjerninger* (København: Gyldendal).

Kingsolver, A. E. (2010) '"Like a Frog in a Well": Young People's Views of the Future Expressed in Two Collaborative Research Projects in Sri Lanka', *Human Organization* 69 (1), pp. 1–9.

Marcel, G. (1967) 'Desire and Hope', in Lawrence, N. & D. O'Connor (eds.) *Readings in Existential Phenomenology* (Englewood Cliffs & New Jersey: Prentice Hall), pp. 277–285.

Moltmann, J. (1967) *Theology of Hope: On the Ground and the Implications of a Christian Eschatology* (London: SCM Press).

Rorty, R. (1999) *Philosophy and Social Hope* (London: Penguin).

Turner, S. (2005) 'Suspended Spaces – Contesting Sovereignties in a Refugee Camp', in Hansen, T. & F. Stepputat (eds.) *Sovereign Bodies: Citizens, Migrants and States in the Postcolonial World* (Princeton: Princeton University Press), pp. 312–332.

Turner, V. (1967) *The Forest of Symbols: Aspects of Ndembu Ritual* (New York: Cornell University Press).

Vigh, H. (2009) 'Wayward Migration: On Imagined Futures and Technological Voids', *Ethnos* 74 (1), pp. 91–109.

Vigh, H. (2006) *Navigating Terrains of War: Youth and Soldiering in Guinea-Bissau* (New York & Oxford: Berghahn Books).

Webb, D. (2007) 'Modes of Hoping', *History of the Human Sciences* 20 (3), pp. 65–83.

Index

Printed and bound by CPI Group (UK) Ltd, Croydon, CR0 4YY